The Development of an Icon

The Development of an Icon

Solomon before and after King David

John W. Herbst

☙PICKWICK *Publications* · Eugene, Oregon

THE DEVELOPMENT OF AN ICON
Solomon before and after King David

Copyright © 2016 John W. Herbst. All rights reserved. Except for brief quotations in critical publications or reviews, no part of this book may be reproduced in any manner without prior written permission from the publisher. Write: Permissions, Wipf and Stock Publishers, 199 W. 8th Ave., Suite 3, Eugene, OR 97401.

Pickwick Publications
An Imprint of Wipf and Stock Publishers
199 W. 8th Ave., Suite 3
Eugene, OR 97401

www.wipfandstock.com

PAPERBACK ISBN: 978-1-4982-8247-5
HARDCOVER ISBN: 978-4982-8249-9
EBOOK ISBN: 978-1-4982-8248-2

Cataloguing-in-Publication data:

Names: Herbst, John W.

Title: The development of an icon : Solomon before and after king David / John W. Herbst.

Description: Eugene, OR: Pickwick Publications | Includes bibliographical references and index | Revised PhD dissertation from Union Presbyterian Seminary.

Identifiers: ISBN: 978-1-4982-8247-5 (paperback) | 978-1-4982-8249-9 (hardcover) | 978-1-4982-8248-2 (ebook).

Subjects: LCSH: Bible. Samuel—Criticism, interpretation, etc. | Bible. Kings—Criticism, interpretation, etc. | David, King of Israel. | Solomon, King of Israel.

Classification: BS1205.2 H47 2016 (print) | BS1205.2 (ebook)

Manufactured in the U.S.A.   OCTOBER 13, 2016

*This book is dedicated to the loving memory of my parents,
John Edward Herbst and Evelyn Frances Gold Herbst,
and my first wife, Rosa Lopez Osorio Herbst.
May they share my joy at the fruition of this project.*

Contents

Acknowledgments | ix
Abbreviations | xi

1. First Kings 1–11 and the Succession Narrative | 1
2. Thirty Years of Solomon Scholarship | 10
3. The Diachronic History of 1 Kings 1–11 | 47
4. Dtr1's Solomon Story | 87
5. Themes of the Revolt Narrative | 115
6. From David to Solomon | 149
7. Solomon in Light of the Succession Narrative | 177
8. Conclusions | 204

Bibliography | 215
Scripture Index | 237

Acknowledgments

THIS BOOK IS A revision of my doctoral dissertation. As with so many dissertations, mine was a team effort. I have stood on the shoulders of giants, and I am grateful for the chance to increase our understanding of the Old Testament just a bit more. A number of people have guided and helped me along the way, and I am delighted to have this opportunity to say, "Thank You!"

My advisor Samuel E. Balentine supportted me throughout my time at Union Presbyterian Seminary. His guidance and feedback have been invaluable, and he has been more encouraging than perhaps he knows. Thanks also to the other members of my committee, Richard D. Nelson and Samuel A. Adams, for their direction and work on this project.

I have also been privileged to take part in annual meetings of the Mid-Atlantic Regional Society of Biblical Literature, where I have been able to test many of my ideas. PhD students cheat themselves when they do not take these opportunities to present their work for serious examination. Those who have warmly provided input and moral support include Jeremy Schipper, Mark Leuchter, Tod Linafelt, and Matthew Gordley.

During my time in Richmond I was a member of Northminster Church, where I always found warmth and unmerited generosity. I also was very blessed with opportunities to serve Browns Presbyterian Church (Farmville, VA); Rosewood Presbyterian Church (Prince George, VA); Lawrenceville Presbyterian Church (Lawrenceville, VA); and Ogden Presbyterian Church (Brodnax, VA). I am certain that the benefits I received from working with the wonderful people at these churches are worth much more than anything I said or did. Thanks to all for your kindness and support.

I also benefitted from a wonderful network of friends during my time in Richmond. I would like to thank especially Patty Wolff, Barry Huff, Aubrey Watkins, Danny Mathews, Raj Nadella, Donald Denton, Mary Downing, Susan Buniva, Marvin Lindsay, Maggie Low, and Hung-Chuan and Daphne Lai. Most of our time together was spent on things besides dissertation matters, but this time has been essential for my well-being, and therefore for my work. I will always treasure the moments we have shared.

Many of us doctoral students find that there is simply no replacement for the support of family. My parents and siblings, with their spouses, have not once uttered any discouraging word (at least in my presence!), so I am honored to share my successful moments with them.

Finally, while it is customary for an author to thank his spouse, I am in the unusual position of being obliged to credit two wonderful, unique women. Rosa Osorio Herbst was great in her own right, even beyond the strong, unwavering support she gave me prior to her sudden death in 2008. I have no idea whether she is still following my work, but I am eternally grateful for the love and care she gave through eighteen fantastic years of marriage.

Hard as it may be to imagine, I have since met another fantastic lady, the Reverend Anne Ruth Kirchmier (also way out of my league), who inconceivably agreed to become my wife in 2013. Did she suspect then that she would spend many hours proofing my work? If this was not enough, throughout our relationship, Anne has provided inestimable loving support and encouragement. I am truly blessed!

Abbreviations

*	parts of verses
AB	Anchor Bible
Ag. Ap.	Josephus, *Against Apion*
AIL	Ancient Israel and Its Literature
Ant.	Josephus, *Jewish Antiquities*
ASTI	Annual of the Swedish Theological Institute
AsTJ	Asbury Theological Journal
AV	King James Version (Authorized Version)
BASOR	Bulletin of the American Schools of Oriental Research
BDB	Francis Brown, S. R. Driver, and Charles A. Briggs, *A Hebrew and English Lexicon of the Old Testament*. 1907. Reprinted, Peabody: Hendrickson, 2004
BethM	Beth Mikra
BHS	Biblia Hebraica Stuttgartensia
Bib	Biblica
BibInt	Biblical Interpretation
BibSem	Biblical Seminar
BIOSCS	Bulletin of the International Organization of Septuagint and Cognate Studies
BMW	The Bible in the Modern World
BN	Biblische Notizen

BZAW	Beihefte zur Zeitschrift für die alttestamentliche Wissenschaft
CBQ	*Catholic Biblical Quarterly*
ch(s).	chapter(s)
DblR	Double Redaction theory of the Deuteronomistic History (aka "Harvard School" or "Cross Model")
DH	Deuteronomistic History
Dtr	Deuteronomistic (History; writer); Deuteronomist
EJL	Early Judaism and Its Literature
EstBib	*Estudios biblicos*
ESV	English Standard Version
HDR	History of David's Rise (1 Samuel 16—2 Samuel 5)
HFL	House of the Forest of Lebanon
HTR	*Harvard Theological Review*
HUCA	*Hebrew Union College Annual*
IndAnt	*The Indian Antiquary*
Int	*Interpretation*
ISBL	Indiana Studies in Biblical Literature
JAOS	*Journal of the American Oriental Society*
JBL	*Journal of Biblical Literature*
JBQ	*Jewish Bible Quarterly*
JNES	*Journal of Near Eastern Studies*
JPS	Tanakh, The Holy Scriptures: The New JPS Translation
JRT	*Journal of Religious Thought*
JSOT	*Journal for the Study of the Old Testament*
JSOTSup	Journal for the Study of the Old Testament Supplement Series
JSS	*Journal of Semitic Studies*
LASBF	*Liber annuus Studii biblici francisci*

LHBOT	Library of Hebrew Bible/Old Testament Studies
LXX	Septuagint
MT	Masoretic Text
NASB	New American Standard Bible
NIB	*The New Interpreter's Bible*
NIV	New International Version
NRSV	New Revised Standard Version
OBO	Orbis biblicus et orientalis
OBT	Overtures to Biblical Theology
OTL	Old Testament Library
PRSt	*Perspectives in Religious Studies*
RBL	*Review of Biblical Literature*
RHPR	*Revue D'Histoire et de Philosophie Religieuses*
RN	Revolt Narrative (2 Samuel 13–20)
SBLDS	Society of Biblical Literature Dissertation Series
SBLSymSer	Society of Biblical Literature Symposium Series
Semeia	*Semeia*
SHCANE	Studies in the History and Culture of the Ancient Near East
SHOFAR	*SHOFAR: An Interdisciplinary Journal of Jewish Studies*
SN	Succession Narrative (2 Samuel 9–20 and 1 Kings 1–2)
TLOT	*Theological Lexicon of the Old Testament*
TynBul	*Tyndale Bulletin*
USQR	Union Seminary Quarterly Review
VT	*Vetus Testamentum*
VTSup	Vetus Testamentum Supplements
WTJ	*Westminster Theological Journal*
ZAW	*Zeitschrift für die alttestamentliche Wissenschaft*

1

First Kings 1–11 and the Succession Narrative

Interpreting 1 Kings 1–11

Solomon reigned in an age of peace, because God made all his borders tranquil, so that he might build a house in his name and provide a sanctuary to stand forever.

How wise you were when you were young! You overflowed like the Nile with understanding.

Your influence spread throughout the earth, and you filled it with proverbs having deep meaning.

Your fame reached to far-off islands, and you were loved for your peaceful reign.

Your songs, proverbs, and parables, and the answers you gave astounded the nations.

In the name of the Lord God, who is called the God of Israel, you gathered gold like tin and amassed silver like lead.

But you brought in women to lie at your side, and through your body you were brought into subjection.

You stained your honor, and defiled your family line, so that you brought wrath upon your children, and they were grieved at your folly,

because the sovereignty was divided and a rebel kingdom arose out of Ephraim. (Sir 47:13–21)

So goes our earliest extant evaluation of the Old Testament's depiction of Solomon, from the second century BCE book of Sirach. Just prior to its concluding hymn of praise, Sirach offers a summary and evaluation of a number of Old Testament figures, including King Solomon. Sirach clearly is enamored with Solomon's wisdom—not surprising, since scholars regard most of Sirach as "wisdom" literature, following the tradition of Proverbs, Job, and Ecclesiastes. Sirach furthermore reads Solomon as a king who was righteous and successful at the start of his reign, only to succumb to the wiles of foreign women later on, leading Israel to ruin in the process.

Sirach's interpretation of Solomon has endured through the ages. Following his account, Solomon's story even today is often taught something like this: Solomon was a good king, specially selected by Yahweh to succeed his father David. As a young ruler, Solomon humbly asks for wisdom to lead Israel. This request so pleases Yahweh that he grants Solomon not only incomparable wisdom, but incomparable wealth and fame as well. Under Solomon's leadership, Israel reaches the height of its prosperity and influence, achieving international acclaim, and Solomon constructs Israel's greatest monument, the temple. But in the midst of his acclaim and accomplishments, Solomon marries foreign wives who turn his heart to foreign gods, away from Yahweh. Solomon's reign ends in ruin, presaging Israel's long trajectory toward exile.[1]

The problem with this reading, however, is the presence of a number of statements within 1 Kgs 1–10 that appear to be critical of the king. While scholars have typically held that, on the whole, these chapters represent a favorable description of Solomon's accomplishments (a few scholars argue that the positive section ends with 1 Kgs 8),[2] more and more acknowledge that certain statements throughout the Solomon narrative were deliberately placed in order to cast a negative light on the king.[3] First Kings nevertheless presents Solomon's chief accomplishment, the construction of the temple in Jerusalem, in seemingly glowing terms.

---

1. Smith, *Brick Bible*, is a fun, modern "interpetation" which takes this view. While a graphic novel composed of Lego® illustrations might be considered "post-modern," Smith's interpretation of the Solomon story follows traditional lines, with 1 Kgs 1–10 favorable toward Solomon.

2. Brettler, "Structure," 87–97, offers an excellent summary, while suggesting that the portrayal of Solomon turns from positive to negative after 9:25. See the excursus in chapter 7 for a fuller discussion of the placement and purpose of 1 Kgs 9–10.

3. Hays, "Narrator," presents a comprehensive "laundry list" of Solomon's failings in 1 Kgs 1–10.

The temple dedication appears not simply as a highlight of Solomon's reign, but as a pinnacle of the Deuteronomistic History (henceforth "DH") as a whole. This leads to the question: Why might 1 Kgs 1–10 portray Solomon in both positive and negative terms?

A few studies appearing over the past several decades try to answer this question synchronically, that is, by trying to make sense of the MT as a whole in its current form.[4] In chapter 2 I briefly discuss works by Kim Parker, Jung Ju Kang, and Eric Seibert that purport to show that passages that appear critical of Solomon in 1 Kgs 1–10 either should not be taken to be critical within their historic, literary contexts, or else work to provide the reader a rich portrayal of the Solomon story. First Kings commentaries which use a synchronic approach often reach similar conclusions.

This book takes a different path. Yes, Israelite scribes certainly composed works containing a great deal of literary complexity. But a diachronic reading will allow us to attribute texts featuring disparate ideologies to different writers, allowing us to trace the development of a text. For the Solomon story in particular, a diachronic approach greatly helps us to interpret 1 Kgs 1–11. Most importantly, we best understand 1 Kgs 1–11 when we consider that its final major revision was made only after 2 Sam 11–20 had been inserted into the broader narrative. The pre-exilic Solomon story, comprised of much of 1 Kgs 3–11, portrayed King Solomon as a king of great bureaucratic power, who suffered disaster when he became involved with foreign women. Signs of danger were prevalent throughout this early edition of the Solomon story; its author was not quite describing the Solomon of Sirach! The Solomon story was then revised during the exile, making Solomon into a darker figure throughout, even more interested in power at the expense of righteous behavior. And the key to this "revisionist" Solomon is 1 Kgs 1–2, which connects the story of David's reign to the story of the reign of his son.

The Approach of This Work

This book works within the framework of the "Double Redaction" theory ("DblR") of the composition of the Deuteronomistic History ("DH"). The

---

4. See the excursus at the end of chapter 2 for a discussion of recent work on the LXX 3 Kgdms 1–11 (= MT 1 Kgs 1–11). As explained there, I hold that the textual development of the Hebrew *Vorlage* of the LXX was distinct from that of the MT.

DH encompasses the books of Deuteronomy, Joshua, Judges, 1–2 Samuel, and 1–2 Kings. The DblR, generally credited to Frank Moore Cross,[5] holds that the DH was initially put together in the late seventh century BCE during the reign of King Josiah, then underwent a significant revision during the exile. The scribe responsible for the Josianic edition, often referred to as "Dtr1" ("Dtr" being the commonly accepted abbreviation for both "Deuteronomistic Historian" and "Deuteronomistic History"), arranged older written materials into a narrative covering the history of Israel from the wilderness period to the Josianic era, adding his own connecting passages and speeches to proclaim his ideology. His theology strongly reflects the theology of Deuteronomy; hence the designation "Deuteronomistic." Dtr1's exilic successor "Dtr2" updated Dtr1's work, bringing the history into the exilic period, and making certain other revisions along the way to reflect concerns of his exilic setting.

Supporters of the DblR often debate over which specific passages belong to which Dtr. Furthermore, some DblR advocates propose multiple Dtr2's, while others posit that the Josianic version of the DH itself represented a revision of some earlier work composed during the reign of Hezekiah or Jehoshaphat. Most agree, however, that Yahweh's covenant with David in 2 Sam 7:4–16 constitutes one of the central passages of the Josianic DH. David eventually becomes the "model king" in 1–2 Kgs, and Josiah is the king most like David, perhaps even exceeding his ancestor's devotion to Yahweh (2 Kgs 22:2; 23:25). The DblR, featuring at least one Josianic Dtr and one exilic or post-exilic Dtr, is the most popular understanding of the DH among scholars today.

In a 2005 article, Richard Nelson specifically promotes an idea that DblR advocates from Cross onward have implicitly accepted all along, that the DblR works best when we attribute as much material as possible to Dtr1.[6] Scholars who adopt the DblR thus try to show how different parts of the DH support Dtr1's agenda. The usual reasoning is that Dtr1 (along with successive Dtrs) was loathe to change the documents from which he copied, and so could and did sometimes include source material which might disagree with his own theology.

Most DblR advocates use this argument when they consider the so-called "Succession Narrative" ("SN," traditionally 2 Sam 9–20 and

---

5. Cross, *Canaanite Myth*, 274–89.

6. Nelson, "Still Compelling," 333. McKenzie, *Trouble*, 135–44, applies this principle even more rigorously, although he has since revised his views away from a double redaction model.

1 Kgs 1–2). The SN represents a problem for the DblR, since it portrays a king David who looks very different from the exemplary David of 1–2 Kings. The David of the SN commits adultery and murder, mismanages his household and his army, and makes a series of poor decisions which create problems for Israel. The SN material is also almost entirely absent from 1–2 Chronicles. And within the Solomon story, there is another problem passage: the account of Solomon and the Two Prostitutes in 1 Kgs 3:16–28. As with the SN, most DblR advocates accept this passage as part of Dtr1, yet this passage does not appear in the 2 Chronicles Solomon narrative (which most scholars agree was based on an early version of 1 Kgs 1–11). This is noteworthy because the only other large blocks of Solomon material not repeated in 2 Chronicles are the SN narrative of 1 Kgs 1–2 and the account of Solomon's fall in 1 Kgs 11:1–40. The omissions of the SN and 1 Kgs 11 seem consistent with Chronicles' tendency to "whitewash" David and Solomon, but why leave out the famous account of Solomon and the Two Prostitutes, which seems laudatory to the king?

I propose that the SN and 1 Kgs 3:16–28 became part of the DH only after Dtr1 had completed his work. Furthermore, I believe that 1 Kgs 3:16–28 is based in part on the SN, drawing significantly upon the account of David and the wise woman of Tekoa in 2 Sam 14:1–20. The DblR therefore holds, but it becomes more useful for interpretation of 1 Kgs 1–11 if we theorize a reduced version of Nelson's Dtr1. Positing the insertion of the SN into the DH subsequent to the work of Dtr1 makes clearer the purpose of the work of Dtr2.

The SN is particularly interesting in relation to the Solomon story it precedes for two reasons. First, these two kings look very different from each other. Contrary to his later reputation, the David of the SN often appears weak and confused, while Solomon consistently projects strength and confidence. David nevertheless operates mostly in the military realm, while Solomon builds and organizes. The immediate juxtaposition of these two invites our comparison, something that Dtr2 surely intended. Second, within the DH, these are the only two passages that clearly take an interest in wisdom. The noun חָכְמָה (wisdom) and its variants appear repeatedly in the SN and in 1 Kgs 3–11, yet only show up in one other (inconsequential) verse from Joshua through 2 Kings (Judg 5:29). These observations give us reason to consider interplay between the SN and the Solomon story.

The DH focuses on Israel's leaders, particularly its royal leaders. The most developed accounts of royal reigns are those of David and Solomon.

Therefore, by comparing the DH description of the reigns of these two kings we can hope to gain a sense of the attitude of the DH toward the monarchy, especially if we can show that the Dtr2's account of Solomon is based in part on ideas presented in the SN.

It should come as no surprise that 1 Kgs 1–2 helps us to navigate the relationship between 2 Sam 9–20 and 1 Kgs 3–11. These two chapters present the beginning of Solomon's reign while drawing upon prominent characters of 2 Samuel, including David, Bathsheba, Nathan, Joab, and Sheba son of Bicri. In his classic *Prolegomena to the History of Israel*, Julius Wellhausen identified 1 Kgs 1–2 as a component of the SN; this identification is still the majority position among scholars today. More and more scholars, however, argue that since 1 Kgs 1–2 principally addresses the beginning of Solomon's reign, these chapters should be properly understood as the start of the Solomon story and thus as the initial component of 1 Kgs 1–11. I will review arguments for both positions in chapters 3 and 5 before ultimately showing that 1 Kings was composed separately from both in order to join 2 Sam 10–20 to the original Solomon story of 1 Kgs 3–11. First Kings 1–2 thus sews together the accounts of two flawed kings: the charismatic David, and the bureaucratic Solomon.

History vs. Historiography

One further point needs to be made in this introduction. A number of recent books read the DH critically in order to glean historical information about Kings David and Solomon. I do not engage in that exercise here. Instead, this book deals with the Solomon story theology promoted by the authors of 1 Kings. What actually happened in the 10th century BCE (scholars' usual conclusion of the date of Solomon's reign) has no particular bearing on my work. What is important is the *Sitz im Leben* of Dtr1 and Dtr2. These author/ editors were presumably doing their best to explain "what happened," but our task here is not to assess historical accuracy. I concentrate instead on unpacking the lessons of their work. We do not have to ask questions about the historical King Solomon; instead, we consider the various elements which went into the work of the Deuteronomistic Historians.

Yet while my examination of 1 Kgs 1–11 does not address the historical Solomon, 1 Kgs 1–11 must still be read as a work of history. Robert Alter has identified the accounts of David (and, by extension,

Solomon) as "historicized fiction . . . not, strictly speaking, historiography, but rather the imaginative reenactment of history by a gifted writer who organizes his materials along certain thematic biases and according to his own remarkable intuition of the psychology of the characters."[7] But Alter's idea of "historiography" is clearly a modern one; the "imaginative reenactment of history" is, according to the tradition of Herodotus and Thucydides, what an historian does in order to communicate what actually happened, and why. Second Samuel and First Kings may not fit our idea of "history," but they served as "history" for the communities of their day.

The Plan of this Book

Chapter 2 consists of a review of scholarly literature on 1 Kgs 1–11 over the past 30 years. Much of this addresses "negative" comments about Solomon in 1 Kgs 3–10. I've organized this review into four parts: 1 Kgs 1–11 as part of the DH; 1 Kgs 1–11 on its own; books and articles on specific sections of 1 Kgs 1–11; and commentaries on 1 Kings. One noticeable trend here is scholars' regular attempts to explicate critiques of Solomon on a synchronic level. My review nevertheless points the way toward the diachronic scheme identified above. Beyond the plan of this book, however, I hope that this chapter will be useful for those who engage in future work on Solomon.

Chapter 3 delineates the "literary layers" of 1 Kgs 1–11, following the DblR. DblR advocates identify (at minimum) four identifiable layers: Dtr1's source material, Dtr1's edits and additions, Dtr2's edits and additions, and post-Dtr2 additions. Most important here is the distinction between Dtr1 and Dtr2, which represents the primary move from Noth. As with most scholars who take diachronic approaches, I expect Dtr1 and Dtr2 to maintain ideological consistency within their contributions, but I also freely look to grammatical, linguistic, and historical-critical evidence to identify the layers. The results of this work allow us to posit some general ideas about the materials utilized by Dtr1 and Dtr2. One of the most striking conclusions here is that the wisdom tradition associated with Solomon almost certainly belongs to Dtr1's source materials. Dtr1 recognizes and duly transmits accounts of Solomon's wisdom, but he is not enamored by it, focusing instead on Solomon's quest for and use

---

7. Robert Alter, *The Art of Biblical Narrative* (New York, Basic 1981), 35.

of power. I also present evidence to explain why almost all of 1 Kgs 1–2 was likely added after Dtr1 had completed his work.

Chapter 4 introduces Dtr1, beginning with his social location. It then moves on to the main ideas of Dtr1's version of 1 Kgs 3–11. Again, while the Old Testament as a whole lauds Solomon's wisdom, Dtr1 is interested first and foremost in Solomon's power. Virtually everything that Dtr1 presents about Solomon stresses his capacity to impact Israel and to match and exceed the power of contemporaneous rulers. Solomon's wisdom is a factor in Dtr1's work, but Dtr1 pushes this aspect of Solomon's identity into the background, so that the real story is about how Solomon's loss of fidelity to Yahweh leads to his loss of power and influence.

Chapter 5 discusses the SN, focusing mostly on a subsection, the "Revolt Narrative" (RN) of 2 Sam 13–20. I show here that the sections 2 Sam 11–12, 13–20, and 1 Kgs 1–2 were all separate compositions. The chapter then goes on to discuss four major themes of the RN: David's inability to manage women under his authority, wisdom as persuasion, the king as ineffective judge, and the folly of the people. All of these impact the MT Solomon story of 1 Kgs 1–11.

Chapter 6 focuses on the crucial transition section 1 Kgs 1–2. As with the RN, I identify only minor editing for this section. I use literary criticism to show how 1 Kgs 1–2 connects the RN and 2 Sam 11–12 to the Solomon story. The main purpose of 1 Kgs 1–2 is to highlight the differences between Kings David and Solomon. As in the RN, David is portrayed as a weak ruler, while Solomon takes solid control from the start. The narrator's main tool is his use of characters who interact with the kings. Bathsheba plays similar roles with respect to David and Solomon, but receives quite different reactions, revealing something of the character of the two monarchs. And we learn more as we see that Solomon's relationship with his general, Benaiah, is quite different from the relationship between David and his general, Joab.

Chapter 7 discusses the work of Dtr2. I give a significant portion of this chapter to an interpretation of the story of Solomon and the Two Prostitutes in 1 Kgs 3:16–28. Most notably, the testimony of the first woman bears careful scrutiny, as her words highlight issues that Solomon will face during his reign. Beyond my discussion of this story, I explain how Dtr2's revisions affect the depiction of Solomon throughout 1 Kgs 1–11, and I further show how the RN and 1 Kgs 1–2 impact the Solomon story.

Finally, chapter 8 explains what has been accomplished. I suggest here that part of Dtr2's overall strategy is to deprecate both David and Solomon, so as to make them characters who better represent Israel. As has often been noted, Dtr2's portrayal of Jehoiachin at the end of the DH (2 Kgs 25:27–30) turns Jehoiachin into a symbol of the nation Israel. Like Dtr2's exilic Israel, Jehoiachin waits, not despairing of the possibility of full restoration. Each in his own way, Kings David and Solomon also represent Israel: flawed characters, ever hopeful for a better future.

Conclusion

In his explanation of historiography, John Fea writes, "Historians realize that the past is *complex*. It often resists our efforts to simplify it or to cut it up into easily digestible pieces . . . While often necessary for overviews and syntheses of the past, textbooks often fail to reveal that the past can be messy, complicated, and not easily summarized in a neatly constructed paragraph or two . . . Historians would argue that those who draw (neatly summarized) conclusions lack an appreciation for the complexity of the past."[8]

Neat summaries have served the purposes of Sirach and his successors. But the authors of the Solomon story were *historians*, fully aware of the complexity of their subject. May this book show an appreciation of their willingness to embrace that complexity.

---

8. John Fea, *America*, xxiv–xxv.

2

Thirty Years of Solomon Scholarship

Literature Review: Prospectus

THE FOLLOWING REVIEW OF scholarly work on the literary history and interpretation of 1 Kgs 1–11 pays particular attention to works published within the last 30 years (1985–2015). While King Solomon is the main character of 1 Kgs 1–11, the subject of this chapter is not research *per se* of the historical Solomon, or of Israel's united monarchy. This chapter instead seeks to explain and evaluate the major work regarding the transmission history and interpretation of 1 Kgs 1–11. After a brief discussion of Martin Noth's positions as reflected in his seminal *Überlieferungsgeschichtliche Studien*, ("*ÜS*," or *The Deuteronomistic History*) and its interpretation of 1 Kgs 1–11, this review breaks down contemporary Solomon scholarship into four parts. The first part deals with works which discuss the transmission history of 1 Kgs 1–11 as an element of the DH. Part Two focuses on works dedicated to issues related to 1 Kgs 1–11 only. These works typically take the Solomon story as a discernable unit within 1-2 Kings, and therefore within the entire DH. Part Three groups together works that discuss specific chapters within 1 Kgs 1–11. Part Four constitutes a brief review of recent full-length commentaries on 1 Kings. The concluding part of this chapter then outlines an approach to address the problem of both positive and negative portrayals of King Solomon within 1 Kgs 1–11.

Martin Noth and the Deuteronomistic History

A "deuteronomistic" influence on the historical books Joshua, Judges, Samuel, and Kings has been recognized since before Julius Wellhausen's *Prolegomena to the Old Testament*. Noth's key contribution in *ÜS* was to marry the concept of deuteronomistic influence to the idea of a fundamental continuity between these books. The progeny of this happy union was the Deuteronomist ("Dtr"), an exilic scribe who assembled older documents into a single work, the "deuteronomistic history" (hereafter: DH), consisting of the above-mentioned historical books, plus Deuteronomy. Besides writing connecting sections and editorial comments, at key points Dtr inserted speeches, including Solomon's prayer in 1 Kgs 8:22–63, to interpret past and future events, and to prescribe a course of action for his readers.[1] Dtr evaluates events and people using as a yardstick ideas presented in the first part of the united work, the book of Deuteronomy (hence the "Deuteronomist/ Deuteronomistic" nomenclature). Per Noth, Dtr's source documents included narrative traditions regarding David, which form the basis of 1 and 2 Samuel and 1 Kgs 1–2, and the "Book of the Acts of Solomon" (1 Kgs 11:41), along with "diverse, disparate, and hitherto scattered material" in 1 Kgs 3–11.[2] The focal point of Noth's entire Deuteronomistic History is the temple's construction and dedication, as stressed by Dtr's careful chronological work backing up the claim in 1 Kgs 6:1 that temple construction began precisely 480 years after the Exodus.[3] Solomon's prayer in 1 Kgs 8:14–53 punctuates this achievement. First Kings 3–8 presents Solomon in his glory, chapters 9–11 relate his decline, and the unpleasantries of 1 Kgs 1–2 belong to the preceding narrative (with some "deuteronomistic" editing all the way through).

ÜS remains an important work for research today. Almost all of Noth's conclusions, however, have been seriously questioned by succeeding scholars. One key issue for the current project lies in the placement within 1 Kgs 1–11 of the division between Solomon's rise and fall. Today, the very presence of such a division is debated, as many scholars read 1 Kgs 1–11 as a seamless narrative. This structural issue is one of a number of factors concerning the relationship and importance of the temple construction and dedication to the rest of the Deuteronomistic History.

1. Noth, *Deuteronomistic*, 5–6.
2. Ibid., 57.
3. Ibid., 18–25.

Numerous "history of composition" proposals have been put forward, so that for many the Deuteronomistic History is the end product of an initial "author" (whose precise role as author or editor is also questioned), followed by one or more redactors ("Deuteronomistic" or otherwise), with somewhat differing insights and agendas. Many scholars further question the nature of the relationship of Kings to the rest of the Deuteronomistic History, and to Deuteronomy itself.

Part I—The Deuteronomistic History since ÜS

The Göttingen School

Beginning in the early 1970's, Rudolph Smend and his students Walter Dietrich and Timo Veijola theorized that individual passages in the DH were systematically expanded subsequent to its original early exilic composition. This theory is often referred to as the *Schichtenmodell*, the "strata" model of DH expansion; proponents are said to be members of the "Göttingen School." The Göttingen School theorizes an "original" DH written by DtrG (for *Geschichte*, "history"), with succeeding editors taking the labels DtrP (*Prophecie*, "prophetic") and DtrN ("nomistic"). Veijola in particular applied the understanding of these three layers to 1 and 2 Samuel, further developing their ideology, with particular attention to the monarchy. He concluded that DtrG was favorable to the Davidic dynasty, DtrP was hostile, and DtrN, while critical, tended to paint David and Solomon in a positive light (as in, for example, 1 Kgs 1:35–37 and 2:3–4a).

Pekka Särkiö's full-length work applies Göttingen methodology to parts of the Solomon narrative having to do with wisdom. Särkiö analyzes 1 Kgs 3–5 and 9:1–11:13 (and Deut 17:14–20 as well) section by section, sifting out original source documents and the deuteronomistic layers. The number and specificity of his layers tends to render his results problematic, as with, for example, his attribution of 1 Kgs 11:2–10 to various nomists alongside DtrP.[4]

Juha Pakkala uses data derived from the Göttingen school hypothesis to show that exilic and post-exilic nomists (including DtrN) were responsible for the movement toward Yahwistic monolatry. He contends that passages in 1 Kgs 1–11 which express an intolerance of other gods

---

4. Särkiö, *Salomos*, 219–24.

(8:60; 9:4–9; 11:2–10, 33) are based on exilic portions of Deuteronomy, and so are relatively late constructions.⁵ His overall argument suffers, however, from his thesis that monolatry is a post-exilic issue; Pakkala himself admits that even DtrG at times prefers Yahweh to other gods, as in 1 Kgs 16:31–33, 2 Kgs 1:1–8, 2 Kgs 3:2.⁶

One key supposition of the Göttingen School is its retention of Noth's position that the initial edition of the DH (more or less equivalent to the Göttingen School's DtrG) was completed shortly after the exile.⁷ (DtrP is usually dated shortly after DtrG, while the range of proposed dates for DtrN runs from 560 to 350 BCE).⁸ Thomas Römer and Albert de Pury question Göttingen school advocates' "axiomatic" dating of DtrG after 586 BCE.⁹ Dietrich responds by pointing out that each of the Göttingen school's Dtrs are at odds with the supposed majority position on the monarchy: they are pro-monarchy immediately after the fall of Jerusalem, becoming anti-monarchy only when restoration becomes a real possibility. For Dietrich, this "anti-majority" theology seems more biblically sound.[10]

Göttingen school critics often express discomfort with the use of *Schichtenmodell*, by which redactional layers are discerned within individual chapters and verses. Göttingen school proponents often have difficulty establishing form-critical controls (what would a pre-exilic or DtrG pericope have looked like?) and dating redactional layers, and may not have much meaningful text with which to work after subtracting the various redactional layers. They also must struggle to account for the apparent importance of Josiah's reforms to DtrG, if DtrG intended to explain the disaster of the exile. The double redaction theory (DblR) particularly addresses this last point.

---

5. Pakkala, *Intolerant*, 153–55.

6. Pakkala, 214–15.

7. Römer and de Pury, "Historiography," 72.

8. Ibid., 69–72.

9. Ibid., 72.

10. Dietrich, "Future," 156–57. In his subsequent "History and Law," 337–41, Dietrich explains how DtrN revised a predecessor Dtr's idea that associated Solomon's forced labor policies and his accumulation of women and horses with practices of the Egyptian pharaohs. DtrN inserted 1 Kgs 9:15–24 to show that Solomon compelled only the Canaanites to work at forced labor. This shifts the comparison of Solomon from Pharaoh to Joshua, and emphasizes DtrN's desire for the Israelites/ Jews to separate themselves from everything non-Jewish.

The Double Redaction Theory

Frank Moore Cross' 1968 article, republished in 1973, recycled a nineteenth-century idea that the DH was composed in two stages: the first during the reign of King Josiah of Judah, and the second during the Babylonian exile. As I mentioned in chapter 1, Cross is usually credited with introducing the modern double redaction theory of the Deuteronomistic History (DblR). Cross developed Gerhard von Rad's contention that Nathan's oracle in 2 Sam 7:11b–16 and David's prayer in 2 Sam 7:18–29 have substantial deuteronomistic features, and thus likely were included by Dtr in order to support a theme of grace rooted in God's eternal promise to David.[11] Cross further highlighted the importance to Kings of the sins of Jeroboam, which culminated in the fall of Israel (2 Kgs 17:1, 17). These two ideas find their fulfillment in the reign of Josiah: Josiah destroys the altar at Bethel (2 Kgs 23:15), and becomes the exemplary Davidic descendant (2 Kgs 22:2; 23:25). That both of these themes come to a head with Josiah suggests that the original Dtr, "Dtr1," did his writing and redaction activity during this time. Later, in the exilic period, "Dtr2" updated the work, adding 2 Kgs 23:26–25:30, revising the role of Manasseh to make him more like Jeroboam, and generally retouching the DH to make it relevant for the exiles.[12] So in the Solomon narrative, 1 Kgs 2:4; 6:11–13; 8:25b, 46–53; and 9:4–9 were inserted by Dtr2.[13]

Richard D. Nelson employs a number of approaches to support Cross' thesis. He uses distinguishing themes and language to sort out the main edition supplements, which he attributes to Cross' Dtr2. Nelson argues that the motif of eternal and unconditional covenant with David was an essential conviction of the first historian, clearly belonging to an author writing prior to the demise of the Judean kingdom. Passages such as 1 Kgs 2:4; 8:25; and 9:4–5, which indicate the conditionality of the Davidic covenant (presented as unconditional in 2 Sam 7) actually refer to Davidic control of the Northern Kingdom: by contrast, Yahweh granted Judah to the Davidic kings unconditionally.[14] The covenant's conditionality therefore does not require the DH to have been composed during the exile; conditionality can be explained in Josianic times by the destruction

---

11. Von Rad, *Theology*, 1:334–37; Cross, *Myth*, 251–60.

12. Gray, *Kings*, 6–9; Lemaire, "Salomon," 28. Gray actually proposed Josianic and Exilic Dtrs for Kings before this, in the first edition (1964) of his commentary.

13. Cross, 274–89.

14. Nelson, *Double*, 99–118, esp. 104.

of northern Israel in 722 BCE. The work of Dtr1 is royal propaganda, celebrating and legitimating Josianic policies in an age of nationalistic fervor. Exilic Dtr2 then transformed the original history into a "doxology of judgment," while contributing only 1 Kgs 8:44–51; 9:6–9 to the Solomonic portion of the DH.[15]

Gerald E. Gerbrandt accepts the DblR, but suggests that Dtr2's theology of kingship is not so different from that of Dtr1. Both Dtrs concentrate on the role of the king. Solomon ranks among the greatest of Israel's monarchs because he built the temple, thus centralizing the cult in Yahweh's chosen city. Even more, Solomon's accession sets the proper standard for the DH: the reigning king (David) picks from among his sons the best man to rule with him.[16] Most scholars, however, continue to hold that the presence of clearly positive and negative assessments of the monarchy points to Dtrs with different views on this issue.

Antony Campbell suggests that a pre-deuteronomistic "prophetic narrative" underlies 1 Sam 1–2 Kgs 10. He proposes that northern scribes associated with Elisha wished to demonstrate the superiority of a charismatic monarchy over the southern dynasty and so incorporated re-worked Saul and David traditions into a history of the monarchy to that time.[17] Aspects of Solomon's reign which would have been included are those which focus on Solomon's accession, elements of his downfall, and information about Jeroboam. Campbell excludes 2 Sam 9–20 from his "prophetic narrative," determining that the prophetic redactors would not have included so much material ancillary to their main concerns. Campbell nevertheless finds 1 Kgs 1–2 to be essential to the narrative.[18] The "prophetic narrative" of Solomon thus consisted of 1 Kgs 1:1a, 5–15a, 16–48; 2:1a, 10, 12; 3:1; 9:15, 17, 24; and

---

15. Ibid., 121–23. With respect to the Solomon narrative, Nelson's disagreements with Cross regarding Dtr2 editing are minor. In his 2005 article, Nelson, "Compelling," re-affirms his affinity for the double redaction, citing signs of a change of authorship toward the end of 2 Kgs and presumed pre-exilic interests culminating in Josiah's reforms.

16. Gerbrandt, *Kingship*, esp. 174–77. Gerbrandt argues that David's instructions in 1 Kgs 2:1–4 then become a charge appropriate for all succeeding kings.

17. Campbell, *Prophets*, 113–14. Campbell holds that a key feature of this document is the application of the term *nagid*, which had an original secular meaning of "chief," to one who had been designated by a prophet to become king (Saul, David, Jeroboam, and Jehu).

18. Ibid., 81–84.

11:7, 26–31, 37, 38b, 40.[19] Campbell does not dispute that some of this material perhaps duplicates information from the "Book of the Acts of Solomon" used by Dtr (1 Kgs 11:41).[20]

Baruch Halpern also accepts the basic DblR, but argues that the Solomonic texts attributed by Cross to an exilic Dtr actually belong to the Josianic Dtr. Following Nelson, Halpern holds that texts which appear to place conditions on the Davidic dynasty promise actually speak to his line's possible loss of control over northern Israel, rather than the "fief" of Judah which in any case belonged to David forever.[21] The conditional covenant does not relate to the exile (as per Noth and Cross), but to the division between Israel and Judah.[22]

Iain Provan uses form-critical and source-critical analyses of the theme of *bamot* (high places), judgment formulae, and the David theme in Kings to argue that the only pre-exilic edition of the DH was completed during the time of Hezekiah, rather than Josiah.[23] Since the result of Jeroboam's sins is the fall of Israel, and the Davidic covenant is unconditional, the reign which best demonstrates these themes is not that of Josiah, which stresses obedience, but that of Hezekiah, during whose reign the northern kingdom fell.[24] The pre-Hezekianic view held that *bamot* were Yahwistic shrines (as in 1 Kgs 3:3 and 1 Kgs 15–2 Kgs 15); the exilic view saw them as idolatrous places.[25] With respect to Solomon, the differing implications of *bamah/ot* in 1 Kgs 3:3 (Yahwistic) and 11:7, 8 (idolatrous) points to the conclusion that the two passages were completed by different redactors.[26]

André Lemaire also finds no fewer than seven editions of the DH, including four "pre-deuteronomistic" editions dating to c. 970 (Abiathar account at ascension of Solomon), 960 (Zadok/ Nathan account), 920

---

19. Ibid., 102.

20. Ibid., 85.

21. Baruch Halpern, *Historians*, 156–57.

22. Ibid., 172–73. The dream sequence in 9:1–9 then becomes the fulfillment of the promise to David in 2 Sam 7: Yahweh fulfills his vow to secure David's dynasty. Halpern thus supports the traditional view that 1 Kgs 3–10 is positive toward Solomon, while ch. 11 is negative.

23 See Weippert, "Redaktion." Provan bases much of his work on earlier observations made by Weippert regarding the regnal formulae.

24. Provan, *Hezekiah*, 131–32.

25. Ibid., 57–89.

26. Ibid., 68–69.

(end of Rehoboam's reign), and 850 BCE (reign of Jehoshaphat). Lemaire's "DH" was thus regularly updated over a span of centuries. With respect to Solomon, Lemaire takes up an older idea, particularly fleshed out by John Gray, that the Rehoboam redaction could be described as "wisdom" or "sapiential."[27] Lemaire's thesis suffers on two counts: identifying seven redactional layers in the DH is problematic, and it is hard to prove that there was extensive scribal activity in Solomon's kingdom.[28]

Steven McKenzie argues against the idea of a systematic exilic deuteronomistic redaction of Kings. McKenzie accepts a Josianic Dtr, but concludes that the exilic author of 2 Kgs 23:26–25:30 made only one other insertion into the text: 2 Kgs 21:8–15.[29] Other exilic and post-exilic insertions were made by other scribes in a non-systematic manner. So, for example, while McKenzie agrees with most scholars that 1 Kgs 6:11–14 and 9:6–9 were inserted after 586 BCE, he argues that their respective viewpoints differ from that of the last two and one-half chapters of Kings: 1 Kgs 6:11–14 concerns the Davidic promise, absent from 2 Kgs 23:26—25:30, and 1 Kgs 9:6–9 addresses the people (plural pronouns), whereas the end of 2 Kings blames Manasseh for the final disaster.[30] Most scholars, however, regard the negative tone of many of McKenzie's additions as evidence that they were inserted by Cross' exilic Dtr.[31]

Mark O'Brien uses Campbell's ninth-century prophetic narrative as the starting point for his reconstruction of the DH's composition history. He synthesizes the Cross and Smend schools by arguing for Cross' Josianic Dtr1, followed by a series of exilic redactors: a historian who completed the work soon after the fall of Jerusalem; a Dtr who created a new theology in light of Josiah's death, a nomistic Dtr (essentially Smend's DtrN), who shifted the focus from Israel's leaders to her people, and certain additions which took place after this.[32] Thus, with respect to

---

27. Lemaire, "Redactional History"; Gray, 46–48, 133–34, 174–75, 208.

28. Lemaire, "Salomon," further describes his layers of 1 Kgs 1–11.

29. McKenzie, *Kings*, 143.

30. Ibid., 138, 140.

31. As noted in chapter 1. McKenzie has since revised his position. See McKenzie, "Kingship."

32. O'Brien, *Hypothesis*, 272–87. See also the earlier work of A.D.H. Mayes, *Story of Israel*, which posits four main layers: a book of Kings written during the time of Hezekiah, a Josianic DH, an exilic redaction of the DH, and a post-deuteronomistic revision and supplement. Mayes essentially follows Noth's division of the reign of Solomon: 1 Kgs 3–8 positive; chs. 9–11, negative.

Solomon, O'Brien posits that the Dtr responsible for the second stage of exilic redaction inserted 1 Kgs 11:5, 8 and possibly 9:6–9 and 11:9–13, 33 (if these were not added by DtrN). DtrN then added 1 Kgs 2:3, 4a; 3:14; 6:11–12, 14; 8:23, 57–58, 61. Since O'Brien regards 8:59–60 as an insertion, this leads him to conclude that these verses, along with 8:29b–54, were added after DtrN had completed his work.[33]

Thomas Römer also utilizes both the Cross and Göttingen models, while arriving at a simpler conclusion. Römer posits three redactions: a Josianic compilation with "deuteronomistic" features; an exilic "DtrH" (akin to the Göttingen DtrG), and a Persian-era DtrN.[34] An especially notable contribution is his idea that an exilic Dtr from the "mandarin" class (bureaucratic officials) would have been comfortable positing both positive and negative images of kingship in the same work.[35] The Solomon story of the Josianic era consisted of a broken-up version of 1 Kgs 3–11, including most of the temple construction narrative and the first part of his prayer in chapter 8. Römer's notable exclusions include 1 Kgs 1–2, parts of the SN (as the tales of David's weaknesses would not have served Josiah's interests[36]), and Solomon's downfall in 11:1–13. The exilic Dtr presented a preliminary story of Solomon's accession to the throne as part of the "first draft" of the SN, including 1 Kgs 2:1–4, which depicts David as the exemplary king who speaks like Moses and refers to his law.[37]

While Gary Knoppers agrees that more than one editor worked on the DH after the fall of Jerusalem, Knoppers concentrates on Cross' Josianic edition.[38] He argues that the Josianic Dtr made Solomon and Josiah into bookends around the anomaly of Jeroboam's northern kingdom.[39] Knoppers includes 1 Kgs 1–2 as part of the presentation of Solomon in 1 Kgs 1–10 as an ideal king: but, contra Noth, 1 Kgs 1–10 idealizes *Solomon*, rather than the temple.[40] Where Noth had held that Dtr taught that the split between Israel and Judah was due to Solomon's infidelity, Knop-

---

33. Ibid., 279–83. The remainder of the Solomonic narrative thus belongs to Campbell's prophetic narrative and the Josianic Dtr's author/ redaction work.

34. Römer, *So-Called*, 41–57.

35. Ibid., 108–57.

36. Ibid., 100.

37. Ibid., 147–48.

38. Knoppers, *Two Nations*, 51.

39. Ibid., 54–56.

40. Ibid., 57–134.

pers contends that Dtr *makes* Solomon's sins the reason for the schism. Dtr subordinates reasons for the split suggested by his sources (Jeroboam's rebellion, Rehoboam's lack of political skill, economic oppression) in order to support his larger argument for cultic centralization.[41] A difficulty with Knoppers' thesis, however, is that he does not explain why Josiah would find foils in Kings of Israel, which had been eliminated 100 years prior, rather than in the more recent kings Manasseh and Amon.

Marvin A. Sweeney also connects Solomon to Josiah, but he argues that Josiah's purpose is to correct the errors of Solomon, rather than those of Jeroboam. Sweeney stresses the importance of 2 Sam 7:14–15, where Yahweh promises to punish David's wayward son (Solomon), while maintaining his steadfast love for David's line (fulfilled in Josiah). Sweeney cites several instances in 1 Kgs 1–10 in which the Josianic Dtr shows Solomon exhibiting poor behavior, including (but not limited to) his subjection of Israel to forced labor (1 Kgs 5:27–32), his placing Israelites under the authority of a foreign ruler (9:10–14) and his accumulation of wealth through foreign trade.[42] Sweeney nevertheless concludes in his subsequent book that 3:3–10:29 is largely positive toward Solomon, despite the fact that his economic policies caused the secession of the northern kingdom. First Kings 1–2 and 11 were added in Josiah's day to a pre-existing core consisting of chapters 3–10.[43] Sweeney determines that "it is important to consider the role that the account in 1 Kgs 1–2 of Solomon's accession to the throne plays in relation to the critique of Solomon that frames the regnal evaluation of his reign in 1 Kgs 3–11…."[44]

Following Cross' double redaction, Thomas W. Mann holds that Dtr2 stresses theological fidelity above ethics, allowing him to ignore David's sins and Solomon's successes in light of Solomon's infidelity and David's loyalty to Yahweh.[45] Israel Finkelstein and Neil Asher Silberman try to identify literary layers based on archaeological and historical data. They stress that, while David and Solomon were probably historical figures, nothing could have been written about them until the eighth

41. Ibid., 158.

42. Sweeney, "Critique."

43. Sweeney, *Josiah*, 93–109.

44. Ibid., 103. Sweeney, "Considerations," furnishes more details of Solomon's failings in relation to the broader section 1 Kgs 1–14. I agree that the addition of 1 Kgs 1–2 impacts one's reading of chs. 3–11, even though I attribute chs. 1–2 to the exilic period.

45. Mann, *Former Prophets*.

century, when we first have evidence of widespread literary activity in the area around Jerusalem.[46]

In summary, while some scholars still locate all deuteronomistic edition(s) of the DH sometime after 586 BCE, the majority hold to some variation of the DblR, with at least one pre-exilic Dtr. Knoppers and Sweeney in particular emphasize the relationship between Solomon's mistakes and Josiah's reforms as they pertain to a Josianic Dtr. Some scholars question whether the level of pessimism throughout the DH allows for the possibility of an optimistic edition dating from Josiah's time (although scholars such as O'Brien and Römer ameliorate this concern by positing much more exilic deuteronomistic editing than do Cross or Nelson). The apparent stress on Josiah and his reforms, along with the universally acknowledged "thematic shift" that takes place in Kings from the reign of Josiah,[47] seem difficult to account for if the DH was composed after Israel went into exile, thus arguing for a Josianic edition of the DH.

Single-Author Theories

Since the advent of the Cross double-redaction approach to the DH, most scholars have shied away from Noth's view of a single deuteronomistic editor/ redactor. Updating Noth, J. Gordon McConville posits a single exilic author for Kings (and for the DH), yet judges as inadequate Noth's idea that the DH was written merely to explain why the kingdom had fallen. The theology of grace, allowing a renewal of Yahweh's relationship with his people, is too strong in the book. Kings deals with the question, "Who is Israel?" Her loss of identity inevitably leads to loss of land.[48] Solomon represents Israel's peak of achievement and thus the beginning of Israel's descent to exile.[49] In a later article, McConville further argues that one of the special contributions of the DH is the concept of a king who himself is under authority. Solomon, the very "apogee" of Israelite kingship, is expressly over to keep the Torah.[50]

---

46. Finkelstein and Silberman, *David and Solomon*.
47. Halpern and Lemaire, "Composition," 140.
48. McConville, "Narrative and Meaning," 31–49.
49. Ibid., 35–38. Among authors who find difficulties through Solomon's reign, McConville is unusual in that he begins with 1 Kgs 3, instead of 1 Kgs 1–2 (chapters which he does not discuss at all!)
50. McConville, "King and Messiah."

Other Works on 1–2 Kings

Richard Nelson observes that one of the main literary functions of the priesthood in the DH is to demonstrate the prophecy-fulfillment schema: for example, this is its sole purpose in 1 Kgs 1–2. The priesthood is also used by Dtr as a redactional tool to drive home ideological truths, as in 1 Kgs 8:3–6.[51]

Roger S. Nam applies the categories of reciprocity, redistribution, and market exchange developed by the Hungarian economic historian Karl Polanyi to 1 and 2 Kings. The redistribution stemming from Solomon's centralization is seen as positive in 1 Kgs 5–8, but negative in chapter 9.[52] Accounts of reciprocity between Solomon and Hiram portray the two as equals, but Solomon is clearly the superior party in his dealings with the Queen of Sheba.[53]

Part II—1 Kings 1–11

First Kings 1–11 and 3 Kingdoms 1–11

Noth confined his work in *ÜS* to a consideration of the Masoretic Text. A number of scholars since Noth have done extensive study of the comparisons between MT 1 Kgs 1–11 and LXX 3 Kgdms 1–11. While this study is interesting and helpful in its own right, there has been a growing consensus that the text traditions of the MT and LXX, particularly with respect to these passages, grew in different directions. Julio Treble Barrera stresses that MT and different versions of the LXX very likely experienced different diachronic histories.[54] T.M. Law further offers that since the Hebrew *Vorlage* of the Old Greek of 3 Kingdoms is not a direct literary ancestor of MT, we generally should not use the LXX to correct MT Kings.[55] As the current project focuses on issues relating to the diachronic history of the MT, there is little opportunity to interact

---

51. Nelson, "Priesthood."
52. Nam, *Economic*, 134–39.
53. Ibid., 76–87.
54. Trebolle, *Salomon y Jereboan*, 22–23.
55. Law, "Plea," 294. Law's conclusion is at odds with Knoppers, *Two Nations*, 1:62, for example, who cites evidence from the Old Greek to argue for the original continuity of 1 Kgs 1–10. Law is likely correct, but the LXX should nevertheless be consulted regularly with respect to text critical issues.

with this recent work. Nevertheless, see the excursus at the end of this chapter for a review of literature on the relationship between 1 Kgs 1–11 and 3 Kgdms 1–11.

Narrative ("New") Criticism: "Literary" Methods of Reading Biblical Narrative

Proponents of modern narrative criticism, sometimes called "new literary criticism" (or simply "new criticism"), usually affirm Noth's DH formulation and terminology. However, they tend to argue that the issue of sources is not all that important for the interpretative task. They therefore avoid locating the DH in any particular *Sitz im Leben*. Instead, in the words of one advocate, narrative criticism "approaches the text as *story*, irrespective of its referential function as historical record or interpretation."[56] A number of major studies which apply narrative criticism to the Hebrew Bible have appeared over the past 25 years, including full-length volumes by Robert Alter, Shimon Bar-Ephrat, Adele Berlin, Herbert Chanan Brichto, R. W. Funk, David M. Gunn and Dana Nolan Fewell, George Savran, Meir Sternberg, and Jerome T. Walsh.[57] These works concentrate on the Masoretic text, while paying little or no attention to the text's composition history[58].

Yet when commentary writers pursue synchronic readings in practice, they usually feel compelled to address issues of text history and *Sitz im Leben*. The problematic nature of a purely literary reading becomes exposed when one must address the entirety of a biblical book, instead of being permitted to select texts on which to work.[59] Alter, for example, accepts the DblR and notes deuteronomistic insertions (although he

---

56. Walsh, *1 Kings*, xiii.

57. Alter, *Narrative*; Bar-Efrat, *Narrative*; Berlin, *Poetics*; Brichto, *Grammar*; Funk, *Poetics*; Gunn and Fewell, *Narrative*; Savran, *Telling*; Sternberg, *Poetics*; Walsh, *Narrative*.

58. Sternberg advocates the consideration of text history and social setting in order to discern meaning from the text (15–16), but never goes beyond synchronistic narrative criticism in his book. See further comments on Sternberg's approach in Long, "Alter and Sternberg."

59. The same of course is true for purely historical-critical readings, or for that matter, any exegetical method.

suggests that these are likely fewer in number than more historical scholars would have us believe).[60]

Eric Seibert has written the most complete work on Solomon in this vein to date, positing that scribes commissioned to compose a narrative favorable to Solomon inscribed a critique of Solomon within the narrative. Seibert essentially sees various "mixed messages" as evidence of a "subversive" hand.[61] Yet he runs into the difficulty of trying to explain how a scribe might write a history which exalts Solomon while simultaneously inserting subversive elements. What prompted the composition of these positive portrayals created, and for whom were the subversive elements inserted? How could the authors be sure that their signals would be read as intended? Furthermore, ambiguities, "strategic omissions," and the like usually have multiple possible explanations, even if a "subversive" hand was at work, so that using textual clues to demonstrate implicit subversion often seems forced.[62]

Among shorter studies, George Savran describes the Solomon narrative in terms of the determination and consolidation of the kingdom, evidencing fulfillment of Yahweh's promise to David in 2 Sam 7:11b–12. First Kings 9:4–7 represents a crucial "rereading" of this promise, converting a source of hope to a foreshadowing of destruction.[63] Pauline Viviano argues that, per the theory of retribution, Dtr judges Solomon's idolatry to be worse than the sins of Saul and David.[64] Amos Frisch shows

---

60. Alter, *David*, xii-xiii. Walsh's commentary on 1 Kings is an exception to this general observation: in case after case, Walsh finds a literary purpose behind what other commentators observe to be Deuteronomistic insertions or refinements. This perhaps adds value to his commentary: while he may not persuade everyone of the full literary coherence of a non-composite book of 1 Kings, he can be relied on to argue against insertions into the text (with a few exceptions in 2 Kgs 22:28–34), thus serving as a control for those who would fracture the book. For examples, see Walsh, *1 Kings*, 37–40, 104–5, 108–10, 117–18.

61. Seibert, *Scribes*.

62. Tamás Czövek writes about the charisma of the successive kings Saul, David, and Solomon. Solomon's character changes gradually over time, until his rule develops the characteristics of an exploitative, self-indulgent monarchy of which Samuel warned in 1 Sam 8. Solomon's charismatic independence allows him to reorganize Israel's society, but as his charisma becomes less and less controlled, he becomes more and more separated from Yahweh. Czövek, *Leadership*.

63. Savran, "Kings."

64. Viviano, "Lost," esp. 342–46. The stories of all three follow the same pattern of positive tales followed by negative tales, but Solomon is judged to be the worst, as only in his case is the kingdom split at the end.

how 1 Kgs 1–14 draws on Exodus motifs. The language used for Solomon's building activities parallels that used in Ex 1:11, so that Jeroboam (יִרֶב הָעָם, "the people multiplied" (Ex 1:20)) is, in many ways, a new Moses (although Jeroboam reverts to another Exodus theme, the calf tradition).[65] Jacques Cazeaux argues that the Solomon story, like the accounts of Solomon's predecessors Saul and David, constitutes criticism of the concept of a monarchy. The monarchy stresses centralization instead of a twelve-tribe federation, and the numerous Egyptian influences on Solomon in particular pave the way toward disaster.[66]

The literary critic's focus on synchronic readings helps us to better appreciate the complexity of an author's work. Bible scholars sometimes do not give ancient authors sufficient credit for being able to write diverse works. Knoppers notes that "whereas source criticism and historical criticism see tensions, repetitions, and stylistic variations as keys to uncovering disparate sources or layers of composition, [narrative critics] account for the same features by recourse to self-conscious authorial techniques of repetition, point of view, reported and reporting speech, and word plays."[67] The difference between what may be sophisticated writing technique versus clear evidence of textual intrusion needs to be carefully considered by proponents of both the Göttingen and Cross schools.

Structural Approaches to 1 Kings 1–11

An important point of discussion over the past 25 years has been the literary structure of the MT of 1 Kgs 1–11. While Noth argued that the Solomon narrative should be read as favorable in 1 Kgs 1–8 and unfavorable in chapters 9–11,[68] most scholars prefer to read Solomon positively through 1 Kgs 10.[69] Kim Parker argues that, far from being a disorganized collection of sundry materials, 1 Kgs 1–11 is carefully arranged. He cites Alter and Long in suggesting that the person who put together the final form of the narrative could well have intended to maintain tension

---

65. Frisch, "I Kings 1–14."
66. Cazeaux, *Royauté*.
67. Knoppers, *Two Nations*, 28.
68. Noth, *ÜS*, 60.

69. Brettler, 88n. Brettler cites the following specific examples: Benzinger, *Könige*, 76; Montgomery and Gehman, *Kings*, 231; Porten, "Structure" 97, 128; Gray, *Kings*, 270; Würthwein, *Könige 1–16*, 130; Nelson, *Redaction*, 113; Long, *1 Kings*, 121–22.

between positive and negative throughout.[70] Marc Brettler and Amos Frisch respond to Parker with breakdowns of their own. Brettler locates the main break at 9:26, where Solomon begins to expand his wealth by building ships. The prior section is marked by the account of Solomon's Egyptian wife finally moving into the city of David, thus completing in 9:24–25 the account begun in 3:1–2.[71]

Frisch prefers to end the Solomon narrative at 12:14. He argues that the succession drama after Solomon is as much a part of the Solomonic narrative as is the account in chapters 1–2 which precedes Solomon's ascension, especially as 1 Kgs 12 contains the fulfillment of Ahijah's prophecy in chapter 11. Frisch centers the Solomon narrative at the building and dedication of the temple (6:1—9:9). Pericopes which follow tend to portray Solomon negatively, while those which precede this show him in a positive light.[72] In response, Parker argues that a king's death notice normally ends the record of his reign in Kings, whereas the prophecy-fulfillment schema of 1 Kgs 11–12 should be able to cross over multiple reigns. Parker also notes an interesting difference of opinion on the center of the Solomon narrative: while Frisch believes that the account revolves around the temple, Parker holds that the main topic is Solomon himself.[73]

The most important issue separating Parker and Frisch is, according to David S. Williams, whether 3:1–15 is linked to a distinct 9:1–9 (Parker), or to 11:1–13 (Frisch). Williams argues that while 3:1–15 has greater linguistic affinity to 9:1–9, the structural arrangement linking

---

70. Alter, *Art*, 88–113; Long, *I Kings*, 18–21; Parker, "Repetition." Parker explains that 1 Kgs 1–11 is framed by accounts of succession issues involving prophets in 1 Kgs 1–2 and 11:14–43. Chs. 3–8 are favorable to Solomon; 9:1—11:13 is unfavorable. In Parker's analysis, each large division begins with a dream sequence (3:1–15; 9:1–10a), followed by sections on domestic/ foreign policy ("women and wisdom" 3:1–28; 10:1–13 and "administration and wisdom" 4:1—5:24, "wealth and wisdom" 10:14–29) and labor relations ("Contract with Hiram" 5:15–27; 9:10b–14; "Corveé" 5:28–33; 9:15–28). Each half ends with a section which Parker labels "Solomon's attitude toward God" (chs. 6–8; 11:1–13).

71. Brettler "Structure." Brettler determines that 9:26—10:29 has been arranged to place Solomon in conflict with an early form of Deut 17:14–17, "the law of the king." So, for example, the Queen of Sheba account is not about Solomon's wisdom, but his wealth.

72. Frisch, "Structure". See also Frisch, "Rejoinder."

73. Parker, "Response," argues further that Frisch's correlation of chs. 1–2 with 11–12 seems forced: the conflict between Adonijah and Solomon does not match up well with that of Jeroboam and Rehoboam.

3:1–15 with 11:1–9 is strong as well, so that perhaps Dtr intended to imply a dual link.[74]

A Diachronic Approach

Thomas Römer develops his ideas about the Solomon narrative in an article written for a Jacques Vermeylen *Festschrift*.[75] As per his monograph *The So-Called Deuteronomistic History*, Römer postulates Josianic, neo-Babylonian, and Persian editions of the Solomon story. While his scheme essentially follows the DblR theory, he attributes a relatively small amount of material to his seventh-century Dtr, arguing that most of chapters 8–10 and all of chapter 11 were composed during the exile. Römer's pre-exilic edition of the Solomon story seeks only to remember Solomon's greatness; unpleasant episodes were inserted later.

First Kings 1–11 and Wisdom

Stefan Wälchli creates a portrait of wise king Solomon through redaction-critical analyses of 1 Kings 2:1–9; 3; 5:9–26; 10:1–13, 23–25; and 11:41. Solomon is similar to the ideal ancient Near Eastern wise king as portrayed in contemporaneous texts from Egypt, Mesopotamia, and Canaan. The original Solomonic narrative (SG) was developed in the 8th century, when Hezekiah's royal bureaucracy in Jerusalem would have justified such an effort to depict a Solomon seeking wisdom in order to create an enlightened bureaucracy. This was followed by DtrG and DtrN redactions, as per the Göttingen approach.[76]

Ronald Clements suggests that the attribution of wisdom to Solomon here is simply the author's way of using ancient Near Eastern cultural symbols to demonstrate Solomon's wisdom. Clements notes that Solomon's wisdom accounts for the great wealth (clearly connected to wisdom in the Queen of Sheba narrative) needed for his building projects.[77] André Lemaire, however, states that the wisdom tradition must

---

74. D. Williams, "Once Again."
75. Thomas Römer, "Ambigu."
76. Wälchli, *Salomo*.

77. Clements, "Wisdom," thus rejects Albrecht Alt's argument for the historicity of 1 Kgs 5:13.

be pre-deuteronomistic, as wisdom is not a factor in the DH at all after Solomon.[78]

R. P. Gordon argues that the seemingly paradoxical lack of wisdom references in the construction of the temple in 1 Kgs 6–7 (especially compared to the abundance of wisdom references in the Exodus construction of the tabernacle) is mostly due to the fact that Israelites built the tabernacle, whereas foreigners did most of the technical work for the temple. Solomon's wisdom has more to do with his securing of the throne: 1 Kgs 2 should not be dissected from chapters 3–11.[79]

Steven Weitzman focuses on Solomon's search for wisdom, paying attention to both positive and negative aspects of this desire.[80] Iain Provan argues that Solomon's wish for supernatural wisdom in 1 Kgs 3:4–15 contrasts with the teachings of Proverbs that wisdom is to be attained through hard work, careful observation, and self-discipline. The concept of "wisdom," as demonstrated in 1 Kgs 2–11, must logically be connected to the term as it is used in the SN, which in many ways criticizes wisdom of the wise which is not rooted in God and Torah.[81] Johnny Miles relates the concept of wisdom in Prov 1–9 to Solomon, with similar results: through his wisdom Solomon attains the throne through multiple executions, enters into foreign alliances, and values his palace ahead of the temple, slowing his construction of the latter.[82] Yet the relationship of wisdom to God and Torah seems problematic throughout the Hebrew Bible, even in Proverbs.

David Jobling concludes the Solomon narrative negatively correlates wisdom with sexuality. Jobling offers four reasons: (1) 1 Kgs 11, Solomon's downfall, does not mention wisdom; (2) Solomon "proves" his wisdom through women in 3:16–28 and 10:1–13, so that women are a vehicle for demonstrating wisdom rather than sexual prowess; (3) a "golden age" concept of wisdom as a sex substitute may be present, so that Solomon's Egyptian wife has his attention during the day, while

---

78. Lemaire, "Wisdom," 106–18, dates the Solomon wisdom tradition to the time of Solomon's son Rehoboam, where a court official might have inserted 1 Kgs 10:8, extolling the wise servants of Solomon whose counsel Rehoboam refused to heed.

79. The reference to Solomon's neglect to ask for the death of his enemies in 3:11 is perhaps an implied criticism of his actions in ch 2. Gordon, "Divided," esp. 99–101 and 103–5.

80. Weitzman, *Solomon*.

81. Provan, "Seeing."

82. Miles, *Proverbs 1–9*, 42–43.

Lady Wisdom has his ear at night; (4) his wisdom is quantified before his fall (5:12), whereas his women are quantified after (11:3).[83] Claudia Camp, however, believes that Solomon's wisdom with respect to women is better described as "managing sexuality," a concept that seems to fit the struggle for Jewish identity in the Persian period, in which the MT of 1 Kgs 1–11 realized its final form.[84] The story of Solomon and the Two Prostitutes has Solomon using his newly-received wisdom to order the chaos represented by women who are not under the authority of a man (father, husband, brother, or son); and the Queen of Sheba (1 Kgs 10:1–13) symbolizes wisdom personified, testing Solomon's wisdom.[85] Following his earlier important articles on the structure of 1 Kgs 1–11, Kim Ian Parker describes how Solomon lives up to the idea of an ideal king in 1 Kgs 3–8, where his wisdom and justice are subject to Torah. Dtr then shows how folly and tyranny replace wisdom and justice in chapters 9–11.[86]

Other Synchronic Approaches

Walter Brueggemann portrays Solomon as the paradigm of royal power in the Old Testament, which includes roles as favored son, temple builder, wise king, and economic leader. Dtr functions as the voice of criticism. One of the notable features of this monograph is Brueggemann's effort to place Solomon within the DH, paying special attention to the failures of Solomon's father David in the SN.[87] Jung Ju Kang takes a "rhetorical"

---

83. Jobling, "Value."

84. Camp, *Strange Woman*, 144–90.

85. Ibid., "1 and 2 Kings," esp. 102.

86. Parker, *Wisdom*. Also see articles by Olley, "Structure;" Spina, "Confluence;" Miller, "Trickster." Olley argues that the intertwining of Solomon's wisdom and splendor with the seeds of his destruction in 1 Kgs 3–10 tells a people in exile that wisdom and wealth need to be used for the benefit of all, or the community will suffer. Spina concentrates on the merging of wisdom and Torah, a concept suggested at many points in the Solomon narrative (1 Kgs 2:5–9; 3:3–15; 10:1–13), but never quite accomplished by the king. While Solomon's wisdom places him squarely within the world's view of an ideal monarch, Dtr tries to show that the combination of wisdom with Torah could have elevated Solomon's kingdom above other world empires. Miller argues that a comparison of the Solomon narrative with the Lenape (Delaware) Indians' Wehixamukes (a Native American "trickster" figure) shows that the seeming disparate materials of 1 Kgs 1–11 form a coherent whole.

87. Brueggemann, *Solomon*.

approach to highlight Solomon's sin throughout 1 Kgs 2–11, resulting in Yahweh's punishment: the division of the Kingdom.[88] For Kang, Solomon was fatally flawed from the start, serving to demonstrate for Dtr the consequences of sin.[89] And a number of writers have contributed shorter pieces on various synchronic approaches to 1 Kgs 1–11.[90]

Part III—Works Pertaining to Specific Chapters of 1 Kings 1–11

First Kings 1–2

Gilliam Keys argues that, on stylistic grounds, 1 Kgs 1–2 does not fit well with the larger SN. Among other things, while repetition is a key feature of 1 Kgs 1–2, it is missing in 2 Samuel; actions in 1 Kgs 1–2 require several verses each to describe, whereas the variety of action is much greater in 2 Sam; similes and metaphors are used regularly in 2 Sam, but are missing in 1 Kgs 1–2.[91] Sophia Bietenhard posits that the character of Joab in 2 Sam 2—1 Kgs 2 developed over three pre-deuteronomistic phases. First Kings 1–2, completed during the reign of Josiah, was strongly pro-Solomon, and transformed the character of Joab from David's

---

88. Kang, *Persuasive*.

89. Ibid., 263–302.

90. Jerome T. Walsh, "First Kings 1–5;" Lasine, "Desire;" Hays, "Subtlety;" Avioz, "1 Kings 8;" Power, "Subversion;" Weyde, "Relationship;" Davies, "Discerning;" Jeon, "Re-Evaluation;" Cohn, "Characterization;" Younger, "Evaluation." Walsh attests to the narrative complexity of 1 Kgs 1–5 by analyzing these chapters section by section, showing how each passage presents Solomon both positively and negatively. Lasine writes of inherent ambiguity in 1 Kgs 3–11 which allows the reader to read these narratives as either positive or negative, depending on the larger context and the readers' orientation. Avioz contends that 1 Kgs 8, when read in light of the larger narrative of 1 Kgs 1–11, ironically criticizes Solomon: Solomon tends to ask YHWH to do things that Solomon should be doing himself. Power lists Solomon's shortfalls from the start through the lens of Deut 17:14–20. Weyde, however, argues that Solomon actually affirms Deut 17:14–20 early on, only failing later in his reign. Davies describes Solomon as a "New Adam," drawing parallels between Gen 1–11 and 1 Kgs 1–11. Jeon's "retroactive re-evaluation technique" calls for the reader to look back at prior references to Pharaoh's daughter after reading through 1 Kgs 11. Cohn notes the lack of access to Solomon's private thoughts, or even to his voice. Younger argues that the Solomon story needs to be read in light of ANE royal texts, noting, for example, the function of incomparability statements in contemporaneous ANE royal chronicles.

91. Keys, *Wages*, 54–70.

contrast/ opponent to his enemy.[92] The isolation of the character of Joab in 1 Kgs 1–2 helps to explain the purpose of those chapters if they were indeed composed independently from 2 Sam and 1 Kgs 3–11. Richard S. Hess argues on literary and historical grounds that 1 Kgs 1:1–4 does not highlight David's impotence to show him unfit to rule, but rather points to a general malaise accompanying the King's deterioration.[93] Sara M. Koenig, Michael S. Moore, and Mignon R. Jacobs have published describing the role and character of Bathsheba in 1 Kgs 1–2,[94] and Lesleigh Cushing Stahlberg has published a review of work done on Abishag the Shunammite.[95]

In a similar vein, Thilo Rudnig concentrates on the literary development of 2 Sam 9–20 and 1 Kgs 1–2, concluding that, rather than being a "Succession Narrative," these chapters result from a multilayered process of theological reflection which ran well into the post-exilic period. The intrigue in 1 Kgs 1 through which Solomon attains the throne can be ascribed to an antimonarchical reworking of the text. Rudnig also discovers layers devoted to theodicy, so attributing the remark that Joab had shed innocent blood (1 Kgs 2:5) and Benaiah's efforts to remove Joab from the altar (1 Kgs 2:30) to a redactor interested in highlighting Yahweh's righteousness in correlating deed with consequence.[96]

David M. Gunn and Dana Nolan Fewell demonstrate that the phrases "to be king after (David)" and "sit on (David's) throne," repeated throughout 1 Kgs 1–2, work to bind these chapters together.[97] These phrases take on a dubious tone through 1 Kgs 1–2, so that, instead of celebration at the end of 1 Kgs 2, the reader is left with a sense of the overtones of power struggle, duplicity, and fear.[98]

92. Bietenhard, *Heerführertraditionen*, 229–52.

93. Richard S. Hess, "1 Kings 1:1–4."

94. Koenig, *Bathsheba*, 77–104; Moore, "1 Kings 1:11–31;" Jacobs, "Mothering." Koenig develops the character of Bathsheba, describing her transformation from passive and quiet to an intelligent, articulate "player" in the Solomon intrigue of 1 Kgs 1–2. Moore describes parallels between the account of Bathsheba in 1 Kgs 1, and the tale of Anat in the Ugaritic Aqhat legend. Both act to persuade the king to correct an injustice, in order to preserve a house for the main protagonist (Solomon/Ba'al).

95. Stahlberg, "Abishag."

96. Rudnig, *Redaktionskriticshe*. Rudnig's redactors have very limited thematic agendas, so that Rudnig finds about 13(!) layers, which seems far too specific to be of much use.

97. Gunn and Fewell, 151–55.

98. Ibid.

Jeffrey S. Rogers concludes that 1 Kgs 2 contains very little deuteronomistic editing, perhaps only 2:3–4. David's final instructions to Solomon fit in well with David's general political acumen: far from the weak-minded David of 1 Kgs 1, this David gives sharp advice to his son on how to secure the throne.[99] James S. Ackerman also agrees that Dtr's additions to 1 Kgs 1–2 are minimal: only 2:1–4, 10–12, and 27b. But when he applies Meir Steinberg's "gap" methodology to the SN, he concludes that the original text reflects a David who, as suggested in the Mephibosheth/Ziba account, no longer knows right from wrong on his own, and so is prone to "guidance" from others, including Bathsheba and Nathan.[100] Along similar lines, Jean Koulagna holds that 1 Kgs 1–2 was composed as an exilic introduction to the older Solomon narrative in order to disqualify Solomon as an ideal candidate for the throne.[101]

Rogers and Ackermann share similar understandings of deuteronomistic editing in 1 Kgs 1–2, yet with different conclusions as to David's cognitive strength. This difference of opinion perhaps highlights a difficulty in reconciling the pre-Dtr David in 1 Kgs 1 with the pre-Dtr David of 1 Kgs 2. Otto Kaiser addresses this by postulating a series of redactions to the two chapters. He makes a "last testament of David" out of 2:1–2 and 5–9, added to the SN prior to Dtr additions in 3–4 and wisdom glosses in verses 6 and 9.[102]

Further work on 1 Kgs 1–2 has been published by Tomoo Ishida, Gary Rosenberg, and Iain Provan.[103]

---

99. Rogers, "1 Kings 2."
100. Ackerman, "Court History."
101. Koulagna, "1 Rois 1–2."
102. Kaiser, "Verhältnis."

103. Ishida, "Political," writes a "political analysis" of Solomon's accession in 1 Kgs 1–2. He argues that while the author was aware that Solomon had gained the throne through court intrigue, he did not intend to denounce Solomon or the Davidic dynasty, but instead focuses on the establishment of Solomon's throne. Rosenberg, *Allegory*, 170–1, observes Joab's "powerlessness" to alter the direction of David's kingdom, despite his repeated decisive action. His death at the altar of the tabernacle can be read as either an offering upon it, or a stain on the unity of Israel and Judah. Provan, "Barzillai," holds that 1 Kgs 2:5–9 places Barzillai between similar discussions of Joab and Shimei to reflect peace in the midst of troubles involving Israel (represented by Shimei) and Joab (Judah).

First Kings 3:1–15

David M. Carr discerns four layers within the text of 1 Kgs 3:2–15. The original *Vorlage* was a dream sequence promoting Solomon's right to receive a "hearing heart" in order to rule, and rewarding him with riches and honor because of his cultic piety. Dtr then neutralized the royal ideology of this text by converting the story into Solomon's request for legal wisdom, with reward contingent on his obedience to the Deuteronomistic program. Two later Dtrs then concentrated on cult centralization, promoting Solomon's heroism by modifying Dtr's complaint (3:3) that Solomon used *bāmôt*, as at Gibeon.[104] A. Graeme Auld makes a somewhat different breakdown by assuming that the accounts of 1 Kings, 3 Kingdoms, and 2 Chronicles all come from a common source, per the thesis of his earlier monograph *Kings Without Privilege*.[105]

Helen Kenik argues that 1 Kgs 3:4–15 should be added to the list of passages composed by Dtr. Kenik posits that Dtr used the Egyptian *Königsnovelle* form, and added traditional words, phrases, technical terms, and motifs. This method of construction allows Dtr to combine older traditions in new ways, in order to present a theology of kingship under the Torah. As an alternative, Choon-Leong Seow traces elements of the dream to Ugaritic texts, along with Phoenician, Aramaic, and Moabite inscriptions. Seow finds many parallels in the Kirta epic in particular.[106]

R.W.L. Moberly correlates the description of wisdom given Solomon with other Old Testament passages, including Pss 21 and 72, Isa 11:1–5, and Deut 1:9–18.[107] Literary dependence, however, may be more apparent than real, as wishes for wisdom, long life, and death of enemies seem to be common hopes for kings in the ANE.

Carole Fontaine uses "syntagmatic analysis" to compare 2 Sam 11–12 (David and Bathsheba) to 1 Kgs 3. Both sequences feature an act of choice (whose object is wisdom or folly, 1 Kgs 3:3–9); the consequences of that choice (3:10–15); and an evaluation of the act and consequence in the form of a court judgment scene, in which a child's life is at stake (3:16–28). Fontaine holds that "Yahweh's gift to Solomon . . . transforms

---

104. David M. Carr, *Dream*.
105. Auld, "Solomon at Gibeon."
106. Seow, "Dream."
107. Moberly, "Solomon and Job."

the negative example of a foolish ruler into the paradigmatic example of the 'wise king,' Solomon."[108]

First Kings 3:16–28

A number of articles over the past quarter century address the question of whether it was the true mother to whom Solomon gave the living child. E. and G. Leibowitz, Herbert Rand, and Gary Rendsburg hold that certain grammatical features indicate to the reader that the second woman to speak must be the true mother.[109] Stuart Lasine, Adele Reinhartz, Moishe Sternberg, and Ellen van Wolde argue the impossibility of discerning which one of the two women is the true mother.[110] But Moishe Garsiel (and, to a lesser extent, Karel Deurloo) carefully identifies the narrative markers which point the reader toward the traditional interpretation, that the first woman to speak is, in fact, the true mother, to whom the living child is restored.[111]

Stuart Lasine relates the story of Solomon and the Two Prostitutes to 2 Kgs 6:26–30, where Jehoram hears the plea of a woman who, with her neighbor, had cannibalized her son, and now demands her neighbor's child also. This story's message of hopelessness is strengthened by its similarity, inviting comparison to the Solomon story, where a judge with godlike wisdom is able to reveal truth (as demonstrated further by Hayyim Angel).[112] In response, Hugh S. Pyper proposes reading the Solomon story in light of the Jehoram narrative, instead of the other way around. This method reveals a Solomon who makes arbitrary decisions based on dubious reasoning. Jehoram is more realistic, at least showing empathy through the revelation of his underlying sackcloth.[113] Gina Hens-Piazza, drawing on the earlier work of Phyllis Trible, is even more forceful,

---

108. Fontaine, "Bearing," esp 62 and 70; Ibid., "Response." Fontaine's follow-up article argues further that this gift of wisdom changes the voyeuristic David of 2 Sam 11 into 'ideal king' of 1 Kgs 3:6, and forestalls Dtr from connecting the seeds of Solomon's downfall in 1 Kgs 3:1–2 to the problems of David's fall in the Court History.

109. Leibowitz, "Judgment;" Rand, "Pronunciation;" Rendsburg, "Guilty."

110. Lasine, "Detective;" Lasine, "Riddle;" Adele Reinhartz, "Anonymous Women;" Reinhartz, *Anonymity*, 108–9; Sternberg, *Poetics*, 66–70; Ellen van Wolde, "Embeddedness."

111. Garsiel, "Revealing;" Deurloo, "King's Wisdom."

112. Angel, "Cut," 189–94; Stuart Lasine, "Jehoram."

113. Hugh Pyper, "Judging."

arguing that the king's actions in themselves are foolish, and that his "wisdom of God" becomes apparent only through the mother's compassion and self-sacrifice.[114] As a counter-reply to Pyper, Lasine carefully argues that intertextual readings need to consider the structure of the texts being compared: if Dtr intended the reader to consider 1 Kgs 3:16–28 ahead of 2 Kgs 6:26–30, then the reader is not meant to read the second passage back into the first.[115]

Phyllis Bird argues that Solomon's wisdom is to see a mother past the stereotypical lying prostitutes, as prostitution was a legally recognized institution in monarchical Israel.[116] Along these lines, Avaren Ipsen discerns from conversations with Los Angeles prostitutes that the plot of the story *requires* the women to be prostitutes, since this is the only context in which women would not have a male relative, and thus could approach the king for justice (the matter would otherwise be handled by the man in the family).[117]

First Kings 4–5

Most useful for this study is a volume by Y. Avishur and M. Heltzer. In a revised and expanded version of their earlier Hebrew text, they look to seals and inscriptions to furnish information about the titles and functions of various officials. The authors treat Biblical references as historically accurate.[118] Edward Lipiński searches out historical evidence behind the "Hiram of Tyre" passages in 1 Kgs 5, 7, and 9, and includes an examination of Josephus and his "sources."[119] Christoph Berman describes

---

114. Hens-Piazza, *Sociorhetorical*, 153; Trible, *Sexuality*, 31–34.

115. Lasine, "Justice."

116. Phyllis Bird, "Harlot."

117. Ipsen, "Prostitutes," 142; Lopez and Burns, "Wise Women;" Beuken, "I Kings iii 16–28." Lopez and Burns observe that while the terms בין (understanding) and רחם (compassion) often apply to men directly, they must be applied to women's organs, as in this pericope (her eyes and bowels, respectively). Further, at the end of this story, wisdom is stripped from the true mother (who has no other male figure to protect her) in order to enhance the king's reputation. Beuken holds that the structure of the text marks verse 26b, "because compassion for her son burned within her," as the high point of the story. The king's wisdom results from his heeding the true mother, who is compared to lady wisdom, and rejecting the other woman, who is like lady folly.

118. Avishur and Heltzer, *Administration*.

119. Lipiński, "Hiram." Lipiński concludes that Dtr reworked all of these passages, none of which can be traced to a source involving Hiram I, ruling in the tenth century BCE.

the literary layers of 1 Kgs 5 which introduce and explain the concept of forced labor for construction, later expanded in 1 Kgs 9.[120] Paul Ash, Richard S. Hess, Pamela Tamarkin Reis, Graham I. Davies, and Jeffrey K. Kuan also have published on 1 Kgs 4–5.[121]

First Kings 6–7

Victor Hurowitz examines more than 20 examples of ANE building accounts to develop a picture of the typical ANE temple construction narrative. He finds a remarkably consistent pattern, where accounts include (1) a decision to build; (2) preparations for building; (3) building description; (4) dedication; (5) prayer or blessing of the king; (6) blessings and/or curses for future generations.[122] He concludes that this pattern fits the Solomonic temple quite well.[123] Hurowitz then compares details of the Solomon temple narrative (1 Kgs 5:15—9:25) with other ANE temple-building texts. He concludes that it is neo-Assyrian, rather than neo-Babylonian, sources whose parallels are closest to the Solomon narrative, thus implying that Dtr used a pre-existing story, and wrote under Assyrian influence.[124] More recently, Hurowitz devotes attention to the

---

120. Berner, "Egyptian Bondage."

121. Paul S. Ash, "List.;" Hess, "1 Kings 4:7–19;" Reis, "Tax Collectors;" Davies, "'Urwot;" Kuan, "Third Kingdoms 5.1." Ash argues that "Solomon's District List" in 1 Kgs 4:7–19, traditionally thought to be authentic, is riddled with improbabilities, inconsistencies, and textual issues, to the point that the information is almost certainly not historical relative to Solomon. Dtr probably inserted his version of a list which had been transmitted orally, and whose original purpose is unknown. But Hess finds this list comparable to administrative texts from Ugarit and Alalakh, and so may well be archival. Reis suggests that the proper names of the five governors who are listed as "ben ---" were deleted by the author as a form of disparagement. Davies shows through extensive word studies that 1 Kgs 5:6 should be rendered, "Solomon had 4,000 teams of horses for his chariotry; that is, 12,000 horses." The similarity of the Hebrew אֻרְוֹת to the Akkadian *urû* suggests that אֻרְוֹת in this context refers to a team of horses, rather than to a stall as in 2 Chr 32:28. Kuan suggests that some variant LXX readings of 3 Kgdms 5:1, which state that Hiram anointed Solomon as king, point to Solomon as Hiram's vassal. In chapter 4 I will show why this possibility is unlikely.

122. Hurowitz, *Exalted*, 32–64.

123. Ibid., 106–10.

124. Ibid., 313–16. Hurowitz, "'Solomon Built." This article represents a summary and update of Hurowitz's monograph. In another article, Hurowitz, "Golden Vessels," Hurowitz further proposes that 1 Kgs 7:48–50, rather than constituting the work of a priestly redactor, actually help us to understand the cult from which P was derived. The passage describes the altar, the table of showbread, lampstands, then describes

specifics of temple design, making comparisons with Assyrian texts and archaeological finds, while discussing later temple developments and "divine presence."[125]

Consistent with his previous work, John Van Seters holds that 1 Kgs 5–8 is essentially Dtr's composition supplemented by a number of later additions. The description of temple and furnishings simply attempts to create an "ideological continuity" between the beginning and end of the monarchy, with a view toward possible restoration.[126] Van Seters' student Mark McCormick builds on this, showing how the descriptions of the temple and its furnishings reflect social ideas and royal propaganda. McCormick compares Solomon's temple with that of Sennacherib in Nineveh, and examines the role that Sennacherib's temple played in the life of Assyria.[127] Wolfgang Zwickel offers perhaps the most complete up-to-date description of the temple, combining archaeological data with his reading of 1 Kgs 6–7.[128]

Among shorter studies, Martin J. Mulder shows how the symbols described in 1 Kgs 7 reveal a temple not devoted exclusively to Yahweh, but rather containing Canaanite symbols. The Yahweh of the temple is a Canaanite deity; only later does the temple symbolize exclusive Yahweh worship.[129] According to Elizabeth Bloch-Smith, while the temple featured no explicit royal imagery, its proximity to the palace and its carefully chosen courtyard symbols communicated to worshippers Yahweh's endorsement of the king.[130] John M. Monson and George M. Hollenback have also contributed articles on 1 Kgs 6–7.[131]

---

accessories for each of the three, suggesting their use in the cult practice.

125. Victor Hurowitz, "Aspects."

126. Rupprecht, *Tempel*; Van Seters, "Temple," esp. 49–51. Van Seters also includes a helpful critique of Rupprrecht's contention that 1 Kgs 6–7 really amounts to temple refurbishing rather than temple design.

127. McCormick, *Palace and Temple*.

128. Wolfgang Zwickel, *Tempel*.

129. Mulder, "Exclusivity."

130. While Garden of Eden imagery is evoked through Temple furniture and architecture, even more important to Solomon is the concept of YHWH's defeat of the chaotic forces of nature (symbolized by the molten Sea), His enthronement, and His support of the monarchy. Bloch-Smith, "Solomon's Temple"; Bloch-Smith, "King of Glory."

131. Monson, "Temple;" George M. Hollenback, "Molten Sea." Monson gives an overview of the archaeological background of the temple description in 1 Kgs 6, positing that this description fits well with what is known about the culture and politics of

First Kings 8

E. Talstra performs a sustained synchronic literary analysis of 1 Kgs 8 and finds five linguistic strata. He concludes from this that, contra Noth, 1 Kgs 8 is not entirely a composition of Dtr, but rather has a pre-deuteronomistic layer, followed by three deuteronomistic strata, and a "post-deuteronomistic" layer.[132] Talstra's distinctions, however, largely rely on small changes in subject, terminology, and word order, so it is unfortunate that he does not consider whether a single author may have varied these elements on his own. Thomas Römer identifies the same five layers, fitting the Dtr elements into his Josianic, Babylonian, and Persian redactors as per his DH monograph.[133] Marc Brettler finds that 1 Kgs 8 contains no fewer than four deuteronomistic layers. He bases his conclusion largely on his analysis of the relationship of Solomon's seven petitions to various themes in 2 Sam 7 and throughout Deuteronomy.[134]

On the other hand, Gary Knoppers argues that Solomon's prayer in 1 Kgs 8 was composed as a literary unity, with a chiastic structure centered on Solomon's seven petitions of 8:31–51. Dtr constructed it in the seventh century to highlight the gap between the idealized Solomonic era and the problems of Josiah's day. The temple is not part of the problem in Josiah's Judah, but rather is part of the solution.[135]

Sandra Richter argues that so-called "name theology" has historically misunderstood the translation and concept of the phrase לְשַׁכֵּן שְׁמוֹ

---

the 10th century BCE. Hollenback suggests a re-calculation, based on the Old Babylonian liquid measure *sila*, of the Hebrew *bath*, in order to reconcile the dimensions of the molten Sea in 1 Kgs 7:23 (while suggest a capacity of 1,500 *baths*) with its stated capacity in 7:26 (2,000 *baths*).

132. Noth, 60; Talstra, *Prayer*, 252–56.

133. Römer, "1 Kings 8;" cf. Römer, *So-Called*; "Ambigu," 108–16.

134. Brettler, "1 Kings 8:15–53."

135. Knoppers, "Propaganda;" Hoppe, "Afterlife;" Hoffmann, "Patterns;" Knoppers, "Rejection." Hoppe essentially confirms Knoppers' analysis of the prayer's chiastic structure, but uses this information to posit its creation by an exilic Dtr. Its petition-oriented center highlights its importance as a place of prayer, rather than as a place of sacrifice. This gives the temple a lasting usefulness even in a place and time where it does not exist, and so cannot maintain its cultic function. Hoffmann further shows how the entire composition is meaningful to the exilic community. Knoppers follows his earlier work with a second article in which he reiterates the temple's enduring value, even into the exile. Solomon's seventh petition (1 Kgs 8:46–51) hints at the "resacralization" of the temple: the site remains important, even in exile. The second dream sequence (9:2–9) has been re-worked to show that there was nothing inherently wrong with the temple cult, but rather with the people's lack of fidelity to YHWH.

שָׁם שָׁמָּה (which appears in Deut 12:11; 14:23; 16:2, 6, 11; 26:2) and its derivatives, which appear in, among other places, 1 Kgs 8:16, 29 and 9:3. Richter argues that the idea is that Yahweh is asserting a claim to the nation of Israel.[136] Finally, Martin Rösel concludes that the Hebrew *Vorlage* of 3 Kgdms 8:53b–c (which corresponds to MT 1 Kgs 8:12–13) cannot be accurately constructed, much less used to determine pre-Solomonic temple ideology.[137]

First Kings 9–10

D. G. Schley argues that comparisons of 1 Kgs 10:26–29 to the LXX and to 2 Chr 1:16b and 9:28 show that these verses, combined with 10:23–25, function as a eulogy celebrating Solomon's success.[138] Yutaka Ikeda describes the political background of Solomon's trading activities. The Queen of Sheba visited in order to negotiate Solomon's overland route to the Red Sea (per Herodotus, the canal was only begun during the reign of Pharaoh Necho II (610–595 BCE), and not completed until the reign of Darius). The gold and spices Solomon receives from her demonstrate his wisdom in the form of business acumen.[139] Alice Ogden Bellis and Dory Previn have also published on the Queen of Sheba.[140]

First Kings 11

Most important for this study are articles by Knoppers and W. Boyd Barrick. Knoppers shows that in 1 Kgs 11:1–13, Dtr blends the theologies of Deut 7:1–4, 9–10, where marriage to foreigners brings swift retribution,

---

136. Richter, *lesakken semô sam*, esp. 96–107 and 153–99. The concept going back to Welhausen has been thought to mean "to cause his name to dwell there," but Richter shows convincingly that this term is derived from Akkadian inscriptions, where its meaning is closer to "to put his name there," i.e., as an inscription (215–17). John Van Seters suggests, however, that a building constructed to house the name may simply indicate the appropriate place for a writing which contains the name (i.e., the Ark of the Covenant, which holds the Decalogue, in 1 Kgs 8).

137. Rösel, "I Regnum 8,12f."

138. Schley, "I Kings 10:26–29."

139. Ikeda, "Red Sea Trade."

140. Bellis, "Sheba;" Previn, "Sheba and Solomon." Bellis relates a number of historic re-tellings of the Queen of Sheba story, wryly commenting that "our readings of the story say more about us and our issues than about the story itself." Previn offers a dramatized account of the encounter between Solomon and the Queen of Sheba.

THIRTY YEARS OF SOLOMON SCHOLARSHIP

with Josh 23:11–13, which suggests that punishment for sin may be delayed. Solomon's deferred punishment reflects the selective manner in which Dtr uses Deuteronomy.[141] Barrick agrees with Knoppers (and Noth) that 1 Kgs 11:1–13 was composed by Dtr, finding nothing historical in that section. The Josianic Dtr introduced the tale of Solomon's wives (with Deut 17:17) in order to blame him for the schism between Israel and Judah, and a post-exilic Dtr re-worked the passage to stress the problem of alien wives (as per Neh 13:26).[142]

Diana Edelman holds that of Solomon's three enemies in 1 Kgs 11, Hadad, Rezon, and Jeroboam, only the last was likely historical. First Kings 11:14–40 features the common pattern of three-time repetition, so that Hadad and Rezon, pale imitations of Jeroboam, were inserted to strengthen Dtr's doctrine of immediate retribution.[143] Mark Leuchter, drawing extensively on the work of Katherine M. Stott, argues that 1 Kgs 11:41, which references "the Book of the Acts of Solomon," places Solomon in a category of evaluation similar to succeeding kings, yet distinguishes him from the "mythical" King David.[144]

Part IV: 1 Kings Commentaries

Martin Mulder's commentary on 1 Kgs 1–11 stresses the detailed analysis of text and syntax problems, with many word studies. One major strength is its 75(!) pages of commentary on the temple description and its furnishings in 1 Kgs 6-7, which features much comparative material on temple furnishings throughout the ancient Near East.[145] Pierre Buis stipulates four redactions: late 8th century; priestly redaction (which shows up in 1 Kgs 6:12 and 8:4–13); a seventh-century deuteronomistic redaction (during or immediately following Josiah); and an exilic redaction which added accounts of the last four kings of Judah, while making minor changes elsewhere.[146]

---

141. Knoppers, "Solomon's Fall."
142. Knoppers, *Two Nations*, 166–68; Barrick, "Loving."
143. Edelman, "Adversaries."
144. Leuchter, "Implications," 129–30; Stott, *Written Documents*.
145. Mulder, *Kings*, esp. 300–374.
146. Buis, *Rois*.

Marvin Sweeney, Simon J. De Vries, Mordechai Cogan, and Gina Hens-Piazza advocate other versions of the DblR.[147] Burke O. Long, Donald J. Wiseman, Paul R. House, Walter Brueggemann, Alice L. Laffey, Terence E. Fretheim, and Richard Nelson, however, write largely in the vein of Noth and Van Seters, considering how issues like temple and fidelity to the law would have resounded with an exilic audience.[148] As referenced earlier, the commentaries of Volkmar Fritz, Choon-Leong Seow, and Jerome T. Walsh stress literary issues.[149] Finally, Michael S. Moore organizes his devotional commentary on 1–2 Kgs *Faith Under Pressure* according to his understanding of the topics of various passages in Kings, rather than by the usual chapter-by-chapter approach.[150]

General Observations

The above survey points to several ideas pertinent to this study. First, with respect to the structure of 1 Kgs 1–11, scholarship has shown less and less comfort with the idea of reading 1 Kgs 3–10 (or even 3–8) as wholly positive toward Solomon. This state of affairs has come to the place where one major scholar confidently claims that all readers of the Solomon story are struck by the ambiguities of this king.[151] There are hints of problems at the highest level throughout 1 Kgs 3–10, even though Israel reaches her peak in the midst of Solomon's reign. Scholars who use literary criticism highlight Solomon's problems through 1 Kgs 3–10 without much consideration as to whether his difficulties were first reported by a pre-exilic, exilic, or post-exilic Deuteronomist (except for Siebert, who argues for a specifically pre-deuteronomistic "subversion" of the Solomon narrative).

Second, while Noth argued for an exilic DH, most scholars now hold that substantial Deuteronomistic authoring and/or editing of Kings took place prior to the exile. As explicated most thoroughly by Schniedewind and by Finkelstein and Silberman, the growth of Jerusalem and

---

147. Sweeney, *Kings*; De Vries, *1 Kings*; Cogan, *1 Kings*; Hens-Piazza, *Kings*.

148. Long, *1 Kings*; Wiseman, *Kings*; House, *Kings*; Fretheim, *Kings*; Brueggemann, *Kings*; Laffey, *Kings*; Nelson, *Kings*. Although Nelson is one of the most prominent advocates of the double redaction theory, here he works sychronically for the benefit of his teaching/ preaching audience.

149. Fritz, *Kings*; Seow, " Kings;" Walsh, *1 Kings*.

150. Moore, *Faith*.

151. Römer, "Salomon," 98. "Tout lecteur de l'histoire de Salomon dans la Bible hébraïque est frappé par l'ambiguïté de ce roi."

the urbanization of Judah in the late eighth and seventh centuries BCE probably fostered literary activity, thus engendering the composition of large portions of the Hebrew Bible.[152] The Solomon narrative in particular contains a number of elements that apparently draw on ninth-seventh century vocabulary and ideas.[153] Nevertheless, the fact of the *terminus a quo* for the final form of the DH requires at least one exilic and/or post-exilic edition of the DH, in addition to the pre-exilic edition(s).[154]

One of the natural breaking points within 1 Kgs 1–11 occurs between chapters 2 and 3. The style and substance of chapters 1–2 seems so different from that of chapters 3–11 that scholars have long identified chapters 1–2 as the end of the SN, rather than the beginning of the Solomon story. Yet Keys and others have cast serious doubt on the idea that 1 Kgs 1–2 was part of the original SN.

Scholars who work on Kings are now divided into two camps: those who accept 1 Kgs 1–2 as an essential part of the Solomon story as composed by the original Dtr (including Nelson, O'Brien, Knoppers, Parker, and Kang), and those who see these chapters as a later addition (Van Seters, McConville, Römer, Brueggemann). Sweeney observes that the addition of 1 Kgs 1–2 changes the way we read 1 Kgs 3–11, and goes so far as to suggest that chapters 1–2 were added during the time of Josiah.[155] But if 1 Kgs 1–2 depends on the SN, the presence of 1 Kgs 1–2 in a Josianic edition of the DH requires a Josianic (or earlier) dating for the SN. Yet if the objections of Van Seters and Römer against the inclusion of SN in the Josianic DH are found to be persuasive, then 1 Kgs 1–2 also cannot have been part of the Josianic Solomon narrative.

Sweeney proposes that 1 Kgs 1–2 changes the story of Solomon from positive to negative. If we can locate 1 Kgs 1–2 after 586 BCE, then we may be able also to explain the presence of seemingly contradictory elements within chapters 3–11, by relating these chapters to 1 Kgs 1–2 and the SN. A diachronic reading of the Solomon narrative, based on the idea that the Josianic form of 1 Kgs 3–11 did not know the SN or

---

152. Schniedewind, 379; Finkelstein and Silberman, 130–34.

153. Smith, *Memoirs*, 11–18, points to Akkadian loan-words and a temple plan in 1 Kgs 6–7 that most logically date to the eighth–seventh centures BCE.

154. Knoppers, "Theories," 81–83, offers more on the trend toward the acceptance of multiple post-exilic editions.

155. Sweeney, *Josiah*, 103. Sweeney, however, holds that most of the SN and 1 Kgs 3–11 are pre-exilic.

1 Kgs 1–2, will help us to unravel the meaning behind the final form of 1 Kgs 1–11.

Conclusions and Prospect

Scholars who read 1 Kgs 1–11 synchronically tend to have trouble finding ideological consistency. Most therefore accept that much of 1 Kgs 1–11 was composed during the reign of King Josiah, with additions made after 586 BCE. As the negative portrayal of David in the SN also seems to be ideologically inconsistent with the wholly positive portrayal of David after 1 Kgs 2 (and largely positive portrayal prior to 2 Sam 11), we should consider whether we can correlate the SN with post-586 BCE changes to the Solomon story which immediately follows.

The key section which will help us to identify this relationship is the section which connects the SN to the Solomon story: 1 Kgs 1–2. Scholars curiously cannot agree on whether to attach these chapters to the preceding SN, or to the Solomon story proper. Perhaps Dtr intended for us to do both? This is the question that compels this book.

But before we consider the effect 1 Kgs 1–2 has on the Solomon story, we need to search for indications of literary layers in 1 Kings 1–11 as a whole. Which parts of the Solomon story can be attributed to the source materials of a Josiaic Dtr? What parts of 1 Kgs 1–11 were written by this Dtr, and what should be attributed to his exilic successor? The next chapter seeks to answer these questions.

Excursus: 1 Kings 1–11 and 3 Kingdoms 1–11

One topic not broached by Noth in *ÜS* was the differences between the Septuagint (LXX 3 Kingdoms) and the Masoretic Text of DH. In recent years, scholars have argued over three main positions with respect to the text of 1 Kings: that 3 Kingdoms follows a midrashic version of the MT, that the MT revised a Hebrew text similar to the *Vorlage* of 3 Kingdoms, or that 3 Kingdoms and 1 Kings are revisions of some older text form.[156] A. Graeme Auld and Frank Polak have written in favor of this third option, that *1* Kings and 3 Kingdoms separately originate from an older Hebrew text type.[157] Auld notes that neither 3 Kingdoms nor 2 Chron-

---

156. See discussion in Keulen, *Versions*, 305.
157. Auld, *Privilege*, 10; Polak, "Septuagint," 139-64.

icles begin the account of Solomon's reign with a note on his Egyptian marriage, nor does either interrupt the account of the building of temple and furnishings by mentioning the building of Solomon's palace and the temple completion date.[158] This suggests that 1 Kings contains substantial late additions. But Van Seters answers that the author of Chronicles simply used an early version of 1 Kings that did not yet contain, among other things, the SN (particularly the intrigue of 1 Kings 1–2), and the references to Solomon's marriage to Pharaoh's daughter.[159]

Zipora Talshir holds that the omissions and rearrangements cited by Auld represent methods by which the editors/ revisers of LXX and Chronicles solved problems.[160] But Polak, who does not use Chronicles in his study, finds primary text and revisions in both 1 Kings and 3 Kingdoms. He argues for a redaction history consisting of four strata: a Solomon narrative corresponding to other historical reports in Kings (fortifications, relationship with Hiram, Egyptian connection, construction accounts); a "wisdom redaction" centering on wealth and wisdom, along with deuteronomistic additions; a "main recension" reflected by MT; and a "late recension" reflected by LXX.[161]

Julio Trebolle Barrera, Steven McKenzie, and Adrian Schenker take the view that 3 Kgdms reflects a Hebrew *Vorlage* prior to that of MT 1 Kings. Trebolle holds that the incorporation of the "supplementary" materials in 3 Kingdoms 2:35a–k, 46a–l and 12:24a–z into the main body of Kgs triggered the MT's rearrangement of the LXX *Vorlage*.[162] Building on and responding to the work of Auld and Polak, Trebolle argues that most divergences between 1 Kgs 3–10 and 2 Chr 1–9 can be accounted for by the latter's apparent reliance on 3 Kgdms 3–10, less the miscellanies

---

158. Auld, 22–27. Auld, "Solomon," later uses text-critical evidence, including comparisons with 2 Chronicles, to demonstrate that while Dtr shaped Kings, Joshua, Judges, and Samuel, much of what is normally thought to be deuteronomistic editing really belongs to Dtr's sources.

159. Van Seters, "Shared Text." For example, Van Seters notes that the reference to Pharaoh's daughter in 2 Chr 8:11 is at first glance similar to 1 Kgs 9:24, where Solomon's refusal to bring her to the City of David in 2 Chr 8:11b contradicts the information in Kings which placed her in residence in the city of David near the Ark for 20 years.

160. Talshir, "Pseudo-Connections."

161. Polak, 162–64, cf. 145. Polak is equally comfortable attributing additions to *1 Kings* ("*6:11–14*, not represented in LXX, is most probably secondary in MT, as it is totally out of context") and *3 Kingdoms* ("the additions 2:35 a-k, l-o, 46 a-l are secondary").

162. Trebolle, *Recension*, 9–10.

(partially reproduced in 2 Chr 8:3–12). Trebolle theorizes the following composition history of 1 Kgs 3–10: Hebrew version of LXX less miscellanies; Hebrew version of LXX with miscellanies; Hebrew version with miscellanies material distributed throughout 1 Kgs 3–10 (MT).[163]

In his comparison of 1 Kings 8 with its parallels in LXX and 2 Chronicles, McKenzie observes that 3 Kingdoms and 2 Chronicles rarely agree versus 1 Kings, while 1 Kings and 2 Chronicles share a number of significant agreements against 3 Kingdoms. Second Chronicles' dependence on 1 Kings points to the composition order 3 Kingdoms, 1 Kings, 2 Chronicles.[164]

Schenker takes a different approach: he examines the versions in their entirety for coherence, and then tries to determine whether the explanation for differences may be some narrative strategy or literary tendency.[165] Schenker concludes that LXX presents a more harmonious sequence than the scattered MT material, and is thus likely to reflect the more primary text. The MT "revision," at the expense of narrative clarity, emphasizes the extent of Solomon's dominion over his kingdom[166], his righteousness and fidelity to the law[167], and the avoidance of any suggestion that Solomon appointed the priesthood.[168] A problem with Schenker's method is that, while he is trying to establish the primacy of the (theoretical) Hebrew *Vorlage* of the LXX, he does not work with this, but instead solely analyzes the Greek text. Talshir points out that a Hebrew original's stylistic points may not necessarily be clear in its translation.[169]

Talshir, Percy S.F. van Keulen, and Andrzej S. Turkanik argue instead that the Hebrew *Vorlage* of 3 Kingdoms was a midrashic revision of a text form similar to MT. Talshir follows the view of D.W. Gooding that the text type of LXX is derived from that of the MT,[170] but she di-

---

163. Trebolle, "Textual Tradition," esp. 493 and 497.
164. McKenzie, "1 Kings 8."
165. Schenker, *Septante*, 1–4.
166. Ibid., 22–27, 25–59.
167. Ibid., 60–76, 121–25.
168. Ibid., 28–37, 146–47.
169. Talshir, "Design" 42–44. Talshir illustrates the problem with a discussion of 3 Kgdms 12:24d–f alongside its presumed Hebrew *Vorlage*. Verses 24d and 24f begin with *kai* and a verb, suggesting the Hebrew *waw* consecutive, while 25e has *kai Shousak*, thus likely indicating a different verbal form. This breakup of a *waw* consecutive indicates a flashback in Hebrew, but not so in the Greek translation.
170. D.W. Gooding, "Third Book."

verges from her predecessor by holding that the revisions were made in the *Vorlage*, not in the LXX itself.[171] The 3 Kingdoms *Vorlage* rearranges some of MT's problematic sequencing and refines the interpretation of Ahab, Jeroboam, and Solomon.[172]

Keulen argues that while 3 Kingdoms occasionally attests a text form older than 1 Kings, 3 Kingdoms is secondary almost everywhere, including in all the Deuteronomistic passages.[173] Third Kingdoms tends to group together themed texts which appear scattered in 1 Kings.[174] Following Gooding, Keulen holds that the revision was performed on a Greek text by a single reviser, who was working in an authoritative scribal community in an early stage of the Greek text transmission.[175]

Turkanik takes up the work of J.W. Wevers, who also had sought to explain the Greek translators' interpretation of MT (thus presuming that MT was the basis for LXX).[176] Turkanik identifies a weakness in Keulen, that Keulen used Rahlf's edition, rather than the more scholarly Larger Cambridge Septuagint.[177] Turkanik nevertheless comes to many of the same conclusions as Keulen, while continuing to hold that the LXX translators worked from the MT, rather than a separate Hebrew *Vorlage*. Talshir, however, while agreeing that LXX ultimately depends on MT, cannot discern a motive for a translator to make these changes. She therefore attributes them to an editor who created the LXX translator's Hebrew *Vorlage*.[178] T.M. Law further explains that the idea that the LXX changes were made by Greek translators or copyists violates what we know of the work of translators and redactors, that ancient translations tended to move toward their *Vorlagen*, rather than away from them.[179]

Study of the text history of 1 Kgs 1–11/3 Kgdms 1–11 must be tempered by Trebolle's advice:

> One thing is clear: in order to reconstruct the history of the *redaction* and composition of the books it is necessary first to

---

171. Talshir, *Alternative*.
172. Ibid., 13–14.
173. Keulen, *Versions*, 305.
174. Ibid., 300.
175. Keulen, *Versions*, 303.
176. Wevers, "Exegetical Principles."
177. Turkanik, *Kings*, 6.
178. Talshir, "Review of *Two Versions*" 6.
179. Law, "Plea."

reestablish correctly the history of the *recension* of the text. The type of text on which the Old Greek is based occasionally shows knowledge of a text in which not all of the Deuteronomic additions had yet been made or in which these had been arranged according to a different compositional plan.[180]

Law further offers that since the Hebrew *Vorlage* of the Old Greek of 3 Kingdoms is not a direct literary ancestor of MT, we generally should not use the LXX to correct MT Kings.[181] Therefore, for this study, I make only limited use of the work done on 3 Kingdoms.

---

180. Trebolle, "Redaction," 22–3.
181. Law, 294.

3

The Diachronic History of 1 Kings 1–11

The whole of the historical tradition in the Old Testament is contained in a few large compilations. These works have collated and systematized the extremely diverse material of traditional tales and historical reports and enclosed them in a framework, determined in each case by their own particular concerns. Therefore, whoever wishes to investigate the individual elements of this historical tradition ... must first construct for himself an exact picture of the extent and nature of these collections and of the degree to which they have re-worked the older, traditional material, or at least have colored it in some way by insertions into a particular passage.[1]

THUS BEGINS MARTIN NOTH'S *Überlieferungsgeschichtliche Studien*. While Noth proposed that a single author/editor should receive credit for putting together the Deuteronomistic History, most scholars since find theological distinctions significant enough to posit two or more deuteronomistic historians. As seen in chapter 2, scholars who propose compositional models tend to address the entire corpus of Deuteronomy through Kings, while those working on 1 Kings 1–11 alone generally use a synchronic approach.[2] Rather than debate the number of

---

1. Noth, *Deuteronomistic*, 4.
2. Parker, *Wisdom*; Kang, *Persuasive*; Brueggemann, *Solomon*; Seibert, *Subversive*; and Weitzman, *Solomon*, are full-length examples. Exceptions include Knoppers, *Two Nations*; Pekka Särkiö, *Weisheit*; Wälchli, *Weise*; and Römer, "Ambigu." See ch. 2, part

Deuteronomistic historians and their locations, these scholars argue that, whatever the composition history of the text, it is the "final form" itself which is most important. But if diachronic readings prove useful for interpreting the DH as a whole, then it stands to reason that an examination of literary layers within individual sections of the DH will prove useful for the interpretation of those sections.

As per the introduction to chapter 1, synchronic readings struggle over texts that seem to teach different things at once.[3] But if textual discord is the result of additions to a text, then we can best figure out the theology of the *final* author/editor if we can determine what he was starting with, and what he added. The final author/editor may not necessarily agree with the teaching of an inherited text, but his additions to a text certainly do reflect his views. So when we find apparent thematic contradictions, the latest of these positions will reflect the position of the final author.

I therefore use diachronic analysis to identify the textual layers of 1 Kgs 1–11. My analysis of 1 Kgs 1–11 proceeds as follows. With Noth, I agree that there are at least three basic layers: Dtr's source material, the text created by Dtr, and additions to the text made after Dtr completed his work.[4] To these, I add a fourth: a second Dtr ("Dtr2," succeeding the first Dtr, "Dtr1"), who comprises "deuteronomistic" revisions made after the completion of Dtr1's work, but prior to the final additions. My Dtr1 and Dtr2 most closely match those of the "double redaction" theory ("DblR").[5]

When I add Dtr2 to Noth's hypothesis, I stipulate that Dtr1 is pre-exilic, while Dtr2 was written during the Babylonian exile. Hypothesizing a pre-exilic Dtr1 makes it easier to allow Dtr1 to draw on Assyrian-influenced ideology, even beyond the ideas which may have been transmitted through the pre-exilic documents hypothesized by Noth. With respect to Solomon, Assyrian parallels foster Dtr1's construction of a king who looks like a prototypical Assyrian monarch. Cross, Nelson, and Friedman

---

II for articles devoted to 1 Kgs 1–11, most of which take a synchronic approach.

3. In chapter 2, I referenced several works in which commentators try to take synchronic approaches, but must at some point resort to diachronic analyses. Two good examples are Robert Alter, *David*, xii–xiii, and Seow, "Kings."

4. In *ÜS* Noth proposes numerous post-Dtr additions, beginning with Josh 13–22 (40–41).

5. Cross, *Canaanite*, 274–89; Friedman, *Exile*; Friedman, "Egypt;" Nelson, *Double*; Nelson, "Compelling."

did not go in this direction, but more recent treatments of the DH stress the connection to Assyrian writings.[6]

Also following Noth, I prefer to attribute texts to Dtr1's source material, unless there is a compelling reason to do otherwise. Dtr1 was responsible for arranging this material and making insertions that fit his theology. We can identify Dtr1's insertions through his reliance on certain stock phrases, rife in the DH,[7] and his interest in promoting the key ideas that David is the ideal king and that Israel needs to follow the Law of Moses. Dtr1 is also generally credited with creating chapters 8 and 11. I attribute to Dtr2 material that seems theologically at odds with that of Dtr1, yet nevertheless supports the basic Dtr1 program. Passages that may not initially appear to be theologically opposed to the work of Dtr1 but are strongly connected by style or vocabulary to passages that are clearly the work of Dtr2, should be credited to Dtr2 as well. Finally, there are a small number of passages that feature unusual vocabulary and/ or distinctive ideology, which I attribute to (a) post-Dtr editor(s).[8]

First Kings 1–2

In 1926 Leonhard Rost published a monograph which developed the idea that 2 Sam 9–20 and 1 Kgs 1–2 constitute a single narrative, the "Succession Narrative." Rost argued that differences in style and theology argued for the likelihood that 1 Kgs 1–2 originated from a different hand than that of 1 Kgs 3–11.[9] Rost's work continues to sway the majority of Bible scholars to this day, although, as we saw in chapter 2, a number of scholars argue in favor of reading 1 Kgs 1–11 as a closed unity.[10] Certainly, the study of 1 Kgs 1–11 as a unity is helpful from a "history of interpretation" viewpoint. But while by the time the canonical books were formed Kings was meant to be understood as a single work in its own right, distinct

---

6. For example, see Römer, *So-Called*.

7. The most complete compilation of "Deteronomistic" phraseology appears in Weinfeld, *Deuteronomic*, 320–65.

8. The only passages in this category are 1 Kgs 3:10, 15b (the only passages in 1 Kgs 1–11 which refer to the deity as "Adonai"), 6:11–13, and the "priestly" editing of 8:1–11.

9. Rost, *Überlieferung*.

10. Knoppers, 6–10, offers an interesting approach, arguing for the compositional unity of 1 Kings 1–14 while still holding to the importance of recognizing at least two Deuteronomistic Historians.

from Samuel, the examination of the composition history of these texts nevertheless enhances our understanding of the theological intent of 1 Kgs 1–11.

First Kings 1–2 features a number of thematic differences from 1 Kgs 3–11. In 1 Kgs 1, David seems unaware of what is going on around him, and he is rather easily manipulated by Nathan and Bathsheba. David's apparent pursuit of personal vendettas in his final instructions to Solomon in 2:5–11 is further unsettling. These characterizations of David do not fit well with the ideal king consistently cited from 1 Kgs 6 forward (6:12; 9:4–5; 11:4, 13, 34; etc.). Considering the importance of David's model reign to the rest of Kings, it is hard to accept that, whatever his sources, the Deuteronomistic Historian would have permitted such negative portraits of David to remain in his work, particularly at the last stage of David's life.[11] More plausibly, 1 Kgs 1–2 in its final form was added to an already existing text.

Furthermore, the account of the means by which Solomon becomes king in 1 Kgs 1–2 tends to undermine the prophecy-fulfillment scheme often noted in the DH.[12] One of the key events in the DH is Solomon's construction of the temple in 1 Kgs 6, fulfilling the prophecy of 2 Sam 7:13. First Kings 1, however, calls into question Solomon's legitimacy as rightful heir to David's throne, which should make the reader wonder whether Solomon really was the appropriate temple-builder. By way of contrast, 1 Chronicles offers an alternative to the succession narrative drama: in 1 Chr 28:5–6, David simply names Solomon as his heir. First Chronicles leaves no doubt that Solomon is Yahweh's choice to rule Israel.

Thus, while the contents of 1 Kgs 1–2 fit into the storyline of 2 Sam—1 Kgs, the presentation of David in 1 Kgs 1–2 is seriously at odds with his portrayal in 1 and 2 Kings after 1 Kgs 3. This marks 1 Kgs 1–2 as a Dtr2 addition.[13] Still, part of 1 Kgs 1–2 must be attributed to Dtr1.

---

11. Robinson, *Kings*, 24, notes the contrast between the "senile" David and the vigourous Moses of Deut 34, who retains his capacity to exercise his authority to the time of his death.

12. Nelson, "Compelling," 319–37. Nelson offers the following examples: (1) An unnamed prophet in 1 Kgs 13 predicts that Josiah will desecrate and demolish Jeroboam's renegade altar at Bethel; fulfillment is reported 300 years later in 2 Kgs 23:15–18. (2) Prophecy made in Joshua 6:26 of death to sons of whoever rebuilds Jericho; fulfilled in 1 Kgs 16:24. (3) Construction of the temple by David's son in 2 Sam 7:13, fulfilled in 1 Kgs 8:20. (4) The fall of Israel due to the sins of Jeroboam in 1 Kgs 14:15–16, fulfilled in 2 Kgs 17.

13. Romer, "Ambigu," 116–19, following Kunz-Lübke, *Salomo*, 81–87, aruges that

While 1 Kgs 1–2 in total is incompatible with the overall themes of 1 Kgs 3–11, 1 Kgs 3–11 combined with 2 Sam does not offer any account of how Solomon came to succeed David on the throne. It seems likely that Dtr1 originally addressed the transfer of power in some way. John Van Seters argues that the original transition from David to Solomon comes in 2:10–12. The words "David slept (שָׁכַב) with his ancestors ... and (Solomon's) kingdom (מַמְלַכְתּוֹ) was firmly established (כּוּן)" in 2:10–12 closely follow 2 Sam 7:12, "When ... you lie down (שָׁכַב) with your ancestors, I will raise up your offspring after you ... and I will establish (כּוּן) his kingdom (מַמְלַכְתּוֹ);," thus turning 1 Kgs 2:10–12 into the fulfillment of 2 Sam 7:12.[14]

Van Seters also attributes 2:1–4 to the Dtr responsible for 2:10–12, on the basis of deuteronomistic language in 2:3–4.[15] Yet the conditional promise in 2:4, "If your heirs take heed to their way . . .," stands in opposition with the unconditional promise of 2 Sam 7:16. To solve this problem, Nelson links 2:4b, "if your heirs take heed to their way, to walk before me in faithfulness with all their heart and with all their soul, there shall not fail you a successor on the throne of Israel," to similar promises in 8:25 and 9:4, all of which he attributes to his Dtr1.[16] But in contrast to the latter two verses, 2:4 does not identify David as the one Solomon should imitate. This weakens the link between 2:4 and the others, increasing the possibility that 2:4 could just as well have come from a subsequent Dtr who was less interested in promoting David as the ideal king.

Looking at 2 Samuel and 1 Kings as they appear in the MT, David's farewell speech in 1 Kgs 2 is redundant, as 2 Sam 23:1–7, which is separate from the Succession Narrative, also purports to give the last words of David.[17] The section 2:1–9 thus represents a new "farewell speech" of David, most probably originating from a different hand than that of the speech of 2 Sam 23.

---

the succession of Solomon in 1 Kgs 1 is based upon accounts of the ascension of Assarhaddon to the Assyrian throne in the early 7th century BCE. But we can still date 1 Kgs 1 to the 6th century as long as we can theorize that its author knew of the outlines of the Assarhaddon account. The gripping intrigue of this story certainly permits its endurance to the time of the Baylonian exile.

14. Van Seters, "Perspectives."

15. Ibid., 77–79.

16. Nelson, *Deuteronomistic*, 99–105.

17. While a number of older exegetes have argued for a late date for this pericope, more recent commentators tend to date this before the exile, even to the early monarchy. For a detailed discussion, see McCarter Jr., *2 Samuel*, 476–86.

We must also consider here the problematic beginning of 1 Kgs 3. First Kings 3:1 begins with a *waw*-consecutive, וַיִּתְחַתֵּן ("and he became the son-in-law of"), unusual for the beginning of major narrative sections. Sweeney, following the Latin Vulgate, argues that the unit properly begins at 2:46b, וְהַמַּמְלָכָה נָכוֹנָה בְּיַד־שְׁלֹמֹה, "and the kingdom was established in the hand of Solomon."[18] Cogan further stipulates that 2:46b functions as a *Wiederaufnahme* which, with 2:12b, brackets stories of the king's rivals.[19] Cogan of course is correct with respect to the text as it now stands. But the repetition of 2:12b at 2:46b in the MT does not preclude the possibility that 2:46b once existed on its own, prior to the addition of 2:12b–46a. First Kings 2:46b works well as a summary to the events preceding, but it also serves as a fine opening for the narrative of chapter 3. The likeliest possibility, therefore, is that 2:46b was originally the work of Dtr1, only later taking on a dual function after Dtr2 made his additions.[20]

Taking all of the above into account, the connections of 2:10–12 to 2 Sam 7 identify it as the work of Dtr1, while the rest of 1:1—2:46a belongs to Dtr2. This leaves us without a logical beginning to Dtr1's Solomon story. I propose that this has been lost, as each of the other "chapters" of the Deuteronomistic History (Deuteronomy (1:3), Joshua, Judges, and Samuel) begins with וַיְהִי, "and it happened…." We do not find any occurrence of this word in 1 Kgs 1–2 which might serve as a plausible start to a new major section of the DH.[21]

First Kings 3:1–3:3

First Kings 3:1 is entirely absent from the Septuagint. Its nearest equivalent appears in 3 Kgdms 4:34, "and Solomon took the daughter of Pharaoh to himself as a wife, and he brought her into the city of David until his completion of the house of Yahweh and his own house and the wall of

---

18. Sweeney, *Kings*, 72. Note that while the first word begins with ו, it is attached to a noun, not a verb.

19. Cogan, *Kings*, 180.

20. Omanson and Ellington, *1 Kings*, 102, gives more about options for treating 1 Kgs 2:46b.

21. Wissmann, "Criteria," 256. Wissmann accounts for the lack of a suitable beginning to 1 Kgs by suggesting that 1 Sam—2 Kgs was originally a single book. He bases his argument on three observations: the system of judgment formulae of kings reaches back to 1 Sam 13:1 and 2 Sam 2:10–11, 5:4–5; David is frequently mentioned in 1–2 Kgs, and the motif of the *bāmôt* is part of both Samuel and Kings.

Jerusalem." Sweeney writes, "By rewriting the text, the LXX emphasizes Solomon's power and greatness in an attempt to alleviate any doubts about him."[22] But Sweeney does not consider whether this argument might be reversed, so that the editor of the MT could have done the "rewriting" to strengthen doubts about Solomon. Montgomery cites several older scholars, including Burney and *BHK*, who favor the LXX placement.[23] Montgomery himself, however, prefers the MT treatment as an illustration of 2:46b, "So the kingdom was established in the hand of Solomon," recognizing as well similar notices for David in 2 Sam 3:2ff and 5:12ff.[24]

The first word of 1 Kgs 3:2 is the particle רַק, which normally functions as a restrictive ("only," "but, except") or clarification ("however," as in 3:3b).[25] Sweeney argues that 3:2 as is begins the case against Solomon and his toleration of the *bāmôt* later destroyed by Hezekiah.[26] 1 Kgs 3:2 criticizes the "people" who sacrifice at the *bāmôt*. Elsewhere in Kings, the people's use of *bāmôt* is consistently offered as a criticism of the current monarch; this seems to be a serious problem for Solomon as well.[27] But if we remove 3:1, we are still left with 2:46b, "So the kingdom was established in the hand of Solomon," or LXX 2:46l, "Solomon the son of David reigned over Israel and Judah in Jerusalem." In both of these cases, the succeeding רַק of verse 2 is awkward, referring to the people rather than to Solomon, his building, or the nation at large.[28] Because of this most commentators regard 3:2 to be a gloss on 3:3.[29] This could be attributed

22. Sweeney, 78.
23. Montgomery and Gehman, *Kings*, 102; Burney, *Kings*, 27, 47.
24. Montgomery, 102.
25. Waltke and O'Connor, *Syntax*, 669–70.
26. Sweeney, 78–79.
27. One possible argument is that Solomon, in building the temple, provides a solution for the peoples' illicit activity. This conclusion is never explicitly stated; furthermore, "bad" kings are criticized not so much for the failure to promote centralized worship at the Jerusalem temple, as for failing to destroy the *bamot*—something Solomon also fails to do.
28. McConville, "Narrative," 31–49. McConville argues that רַק is appropriately placed in 3:2, as it anticipates its use later in Kings when praise for a king is modified with a note that he did not eliminate the high places (2 Kgs 12:3, 14:4, etc.). רַק certainly does function in this way through 1–2 Kgs, and can be seen to be anticipatory in the final form of the text, but these observations do not preclude the likelihood, on literary grounds, that 3:2 was added later, perhaps by a scribe who appreciated the רַק connection to later passages in 1–2 Kgs.
29. See especially Noth, *Könige*, 49; Provan, *Hezekiah*, 68–69; Eynikel, *Josiah*, 50–60; Cogan, 184; Day, "Gibeon," 132.

to a post-Dtr editor, but without a compelling reason to do so, I prefer to attribute 3:2 to Dtr2.

Verse three remarkably comments about Solomon: לָלֶכֶת בְּחֻקּוֹת דָּוִד אָבִיו, "(he was) walking according to the statues of his father David." Cogan correlates the "statutes of David" here with "the statutes of Yahweh" in which David walked in 3:14.[30] But while both verses refer to David, they do so in different ways: in 3:14, David is walking in the statutes of Yahweh, whereas in 3:3, Solomon walks in the statutes of David. Simon De Vries more persuasively links the "statues of David" to 2:2-4. He views this connection positively, as the opening וַיֶּאֱהַב שְׁלֹמֹה אֶת־יְהוָה, "now Solomon loved Yahweh," sounds laudatory. De Vries shows that in Deuteronomy the verb אהב with Yahweh as object "implies moral concern and commitment, rather than mere affection."[31] Nevertheless, Walsh shows that elsewhere in the Hebrew Bible the phrase "walking in the statutes of . . ." indicates righteousness only when the statutes in question are those of Yahweh. Occasions in which someone "walks in the statutes of" a human being always refer to unrighteous behavior.[32]

Walsh further points out that, in the text's final form, fidelity to David's statutes may not be such a good thing: the commands which Solomon had most recently carried out were the executions of Joab and Shimei as per 1 Kgs 2—commands issued by David specifically in his role as Solomon's father![33] Therefore, in the final form of the text, the observation that Solomon walked in the statues of David is best taken as an ironic criticism of Solomon, dependent on 1 Kgs 2 for its interpretation. But if we remove לָלֶכֶת בְּחֻקּוֹת דָּוִד אָבִיו from the text, we are left with a grammatically coherent, theologically consistent construction, compatible with Dtr1's ideology. Therefore the simplest explanation for the final form of 3:3 is that לָלֶכֶת בְּחֻקּוֹת דָּוִד אָבִיו was added only after chapters 1-2 had become associated with chapter 3. These additional words may thus fit the agenda of a Dtr2 looking to discredit Solomon's devotion at this stage.

One other piece of evidence supports the conclusion that 3:2, 3aβ are the work of Dtr2. Commentators often highlight connections between 3:1-3 and 9:24-25: both passages reference Pharaoh's daughter and her

---

30. Cogan, 185.
31. DeVries specifically cites Deut 6:5; 10:12; 30:16, 20. DeVries, *Kings*, 51.
32. Walsh, *1 Kings*, 73.
33. Ibid.

entrance into/ exit from the city of David, Solomon's acts of sacrifice, and Solomon's other building projects.[34] 3:2 and 3aβ, however, do not have parallels in 9:24–25, buttressing the theory that they were later additions.

First Kings 3:4–15

First Kings 3:4–15 gives the famous dream sequence in which Solomon asks for, and receives, wisdom. Arguing for the narrative unity of this passage, Helen Kenik stresses its logical and stylistic consistency.[35] Yet while various "consistencies" certainly are features of a unified composition, they can also be the work of a skilled editor, who is careful about integrating revisions seamlessly. This passage contains indications of several hands at work.

First, the passage features three separate names for the deity. Most strikingly, the introduction of אֲדֹנָי in verses 10 and 15b[36] almost certainly points to a post-Dtr hand: while the term אֲדֹנָי יְהוָה does occasionally appear in Kings (including 1 Kgs 2:26 and 8:53), אֲדֹנָי alone appears in only three other places in 1–2 Kgs as a title for God (1 Kgs 22:6; 2 Kgs 7:6, 19:23).[37] First Kings 3:10, 15b are certainly important to the theology of the narrative's final form. 3:10, "It was pleasing in the eyes of *Adonai* that Solomon had asked this," turns what may be a dubious request[38] into something approved by Yahweh. And 3:15b, "He came to Jerusalem . . . ,"

---

34. Kang, *Persuasive*, 162–65. Kang offers a thorough analysis of the possibilities along with their various proponents.

35. Kenik, *Design*, 49. "The cohesion between the forms has been effected by the fact that the content runs in continuous discourse. The narrative was written in continuous prose, one idea or motif leading to the next in a progressive build-up to a central point, then descending with statements that balance or contrast."

36. BHS indicates that many manuscripts have יְהוָה here, so many English translations follow the KJV by rendering this word as "Lord," including NRSV, JPS, and ESV. NASB and NIV have "Lord." The preference for יְהוָה may be due to v. 15's unique construction אֲרוֹן בְּרִית־אֲדֹנָי in which יְהוָה or הָאֱלֹהִים elsewhere appears in place of אֲדֹנָי. But it is hard to see why the principle of *lecto dificilor* should not apply here.

37. אֲדֹנָי alone does not seem to have been used as a substitute for the divine name in pre-exilic texts. See Carr, *Dream*, 24; Mulder, *Kings*, 146–47.

38. For example, Eslinger, *Hands*, 134–35, argues that Solomon essentially asks for the same knowledge which caused Adam and Eve to be expelled from the garden. Nevertheless, this parallel seems awkward, as Gen 2–3 uses different terminology. Adam and Eve do not ask for wisdom, but simply eat from the tree of the "knowledge of good and evil." "Wisdom" per se in this passage is never characterized as something bad, but rather as something that could potentially conflict with divine law.

"sanitizes" Solomon's actions by having him offer sacrifices at the correct central location, Jerusalem, rather than the cult center Gibeon.

A comparison of this text with its parallel in 2 Chr 1:1–13 bears this out. While 2 Chr 1 tends to put Solomon in an unequivocally positive light, it does not contain any direct parallel to 3:10, that is, a direct notice that Yahweh was pleased to hear Solomon's request. And while 2 Chr 1:13 brings Solomon to Jerusalem, 2 Chr 1 does not mention Solomon's sacrifices at all. According to 2 Chr, Solomon returns to Jerusalem in order to commence his reign over Israel. It seems likely, then, that the author of Chronicles added 2 Chr 1:13 to his version of Dtr1 in order to establish the idea that Solomon in fact reigned from Jerusalem, not Gibeon. Subsequently, an editor of 1 Kgs 3 adjusted verse 15 in order to return Solomon to Jerusalem, perhaps relying on the information provided in 2 Chr 1.

Also noteworthy are the appearances in verses 5 and 11 of the standalone אֱלֹהִים, (*Elohim*) "God" (e.g., not part of phrase such as "Yahweh my God" or "God of Israel"), to refer to the deity. Outside of these passages, there are only four other occurrences in 1 Kgs 1–11 in which אֱלֹהִים stands alone. Three of these (3:28, 4:29, and 10:24) refer specifically to the wisdom which God had given Solomon. The fourth, 8:27, is used in an instance in which Solomon compares Yahweh to a generalized conception of a god. This points to an overriding feature of 1 Kgs 1–11: even though 3:4–15 uses the words יְהוָה and חָכְמָה ("wisdom") prominently, they are never directly linked in the same phrase. Instead, 1 Kgs 1–11 consistently correlates wisdom to אֱלֹהִים.

First Kings 3:4–15 is one of four episodes in 1 Kgs 1–11 (including 6:11–13; 9:1–9; 11:11–13) in which Yahweh speaks directly to Solomon. In all four, Yahweh stresses the need for Solomon to "walk in my ways (i.e., the ways of Yahweh), keeping my statutes and commandments as your father David walked..." (3:14a). None of the other three passages refers at all to either אֱלֹהִים or חָכְמָה. This is particularly notable in light of the construction in 3:5, where Yahweh appears to Solomon, yet אֱלֹהִים speaks (here and in verse 11). This suggests that the phrases containing אֱלֹהִים and חָכְמָה belong to a different literary layer than those containing the divine name. Dtr's preference for the Divine Name rather than [39]אֱלֹהִים supports the notion that, in 3:4–15, Dtr edited an older passage featuring אֱלֹהִים.

---

39. See Weinfeld, *Deuteronomic*, 320–365.

In his response to Yahweh's offer, Solomon utilizes the divine name only in verse 7, saying "O Yahweh my *Elohim*, you have made your servant king in place of my father David, although I am only a little child; I do not know how to go out or come in." While on its face "I do not know how to go out or to come in" may seem *apropos* as a request for wisdom to judge, elsewhere in the Hebrew Bible this phrase refers to military activity.[40] This suggests that Solomon desires military acumen. Yet verse 9 indicates a wish for juridical ability. A synchronic reading therefore pushes us to give juridical meaning to a military phrase. A diachronic reading, however, allows us to conclude that verse 9 came from a different hand than that of the author of verse 7.

Disagreements among the numerous commentators points to the difficulty of ferreting out the specific work of Dtr.[41] Burney, followed by Montgomery and Gehman, sees signs of Dtr's work in verses 6, 8a, 12b, 14, and 15. Noth lists verses 6–8, 13b, and 14; Long adds to this 12b and 15.[42] Carr and Sweeney are even more specific and detailed, while Weinfeld and Van Seters simply observe the hand of Dtr working through the entire section.[43]

While arguing for internal consistency, Kenik finds concentric layers in 3:4–15. The outermost, verses 4 and 15b (". . . and he came to Jerusalem . . ."), sets the limits of the narrative; the next layer, verses 5a ("in Gibeon the Lord appeared to Solomon in a dream by night") and 15a, announces the onset of the dream.[44] While the layers could be part of the original design, this structure invites us to consider the possibility that the inmost account was appropriated to serve in a new context. The fact that 5a (along with verses 1–3) uses *Yahweh*, while 5b–14 uses *Elohim*

---

40. The most descriptive usage of this term occurs in 2 Chr 1:10, which is followed by a description of armaments in 1:14–17. Other occurrences include 1 Sam 18:13b–14; 1 Sam 29:6; 2 Sam 3:25; Num 17:17; Deut 31:2; Josh 6:1; 14:11. See Van der Lingen, "*bw'—ys*", 59–66.

41. While I attribute Dtr's work in 3:4–15 to Dtr1, I use the general term Dtr here to reflect the views of scholars who may see Deuteronomistic influence in this section as the work of a later Dtr. I don't know of any scholar who argues for the work of more than one Dtr in this passage (aside from the late אֲדֹנָי passages in vv. 10 and 15).

42. Burney, 55; Montgomery and Gehman, 107–8; Noth, *Könige*, 50–52; Long, *I Kings*, 63.

43. Burney, 28–34; Montgomery & Gehman 105–8; Long 63; Weinfeld, *Deuteronomic*, 246; Van Seters, *History*, 307–8.

44. Kenik, 53.

(with the exception of the construction יְהוָה אֱלֹהָי "*Yahweh Elohay*" in verse 7) points to different writers for the two layers.

First Kings 3:4–15 is thus most likely the result of (at least) three separate efforts: a story in which Solomon asks *Elohim* for wisdom, and receives his wish; further expansion from the hand of Dtr1, in which Yahweh promises loyalty to Solomon in exchange for the king's fidelity; and later editorial comments, featuring the use of *Adonai* (thus, not from Dtr2), designed to improve Solomon's image.

It seems clear, therefore, that the source material for Dtr1 included verses 4, 5b, 9, 11, 12a, 13a, and 15a. These verses together teach that Solomon's pursuit of wisdom led to his wealth and fame. Dtr1 then contributed verses 5a, 6, 7, 8, 12b, 13b, and 14. First Kings 3:5a references Yahweh; verses 6 and 14 stress David's exemplary relationship with Yahweh; verse 7 cites Solomon as successor to David; verse 8 hearkens back to Deut 1:9–12; and verses 12b and 13b add incomparability formulae to the gifts received by Solomon.[45] These additions render this section more harmonious with 9:2ff and 11:9ff. A later editor then theologically purified the account through the supplement of verses 10 and 15b, as per above.

First Kings 3:16–28

I will argue later that the story of Solomon and the Two Prostitutes is related not only to the account of the wise woman of Tekoa, but also to several other episodes within 2 Sam 11–1 Kgs 2, all of which were demonstrably inserted into the DH after Dtr1 had completed his work. The question, then, is whether this account belongs to the same literary layer as the SN passages, or whether it precedes them. Two pieces of evidence suggest that 1 Kgs 3:16–28 was added to the DH after Dtr1 had completed his work.

First, the Solomon story of 2 Chronicles omits the account of the Two Prostitutes, just as most of the Succession Narrative (with the exception of the Ammonite war account of 2 Sam 10:1–11:1 and 12:26–31) is also missing from 1 Chr. The Succession Narrative (SN) portrays David badly, making it understandable for a pro-David author of Chronicles to omit this section. But given the popular appeal of Solomon and the Two Prostitutes, it is hard to imagine why the author of Chronicles would

---

45. A deuteronomistic feature pointed out by Knoppers, "Incomparability."

have excluded it from his work. Considering the similarities between 1 Kgs 3:16–28 and various parts of the SN, the most likely possibility is that these accounts were unavailable to the author of Chronicles.[46]

A second issue is that the text suggests that it is natural that a case involving a question of identity would be brought before the king. George E. Mendenhall argues that, in some other setting, the case would be brought "before Yahweh"—by oath, or by the casting of lots.[47] The MT in fact does favor the "before Yahweh" approach in 1 Kgs 8:31–32. Solomon of course does make a perjury "test," but his test seems far more drastic than what 8:31–32 has in mind, and he does not directly invoke Yahweh. As I will argue later in this chapter that 1 Kgs 8:31–40 is the work of Dtr1, it would seem very inconsistent to have the king making a perjury determination earlier, without any comment.

Thus, the insertion 1 Kgs 3:16–28, with its strong relationship to other accounts in 2 Sam 11–1 Kgs 2, belongs to Dtr2. I will argue in a later chapter that this story was not created by Dtr2, but rather was adopted from some foreign source. Dtr2 then replaced the original narrated explanation of how these women came before the king with the testimony of the first woman in 3:17–21. He notably did not insert the name "Solomon" into this account at all, just as the name "David" does not appear in the story of the wise woman of Tekoa in 2 Sam 14:1–20. This is striking, as 3:16–27 uses הַמֶּלֶךְ ("the king") ten times (!) to refer to Solomon. I will demonstrate in chapter 7 how Dtr2 further chiastically shaped the crux of this story, verses 23–27, around the feelings and actions of the true mother.

First Kings 4–5[48]

After a short section listing the Solomonic officials, 4:7–19 describes the regions responsible for supporting Solomon's household. Solomon divides Israel into twelve districts, distinct from the tribal boundaries. While commentators tend to cite this as an example of the oldest archival

---

46. See Nelson, "Compelling," 330. Nelson argues that differences between Kings and Chronicles suggest that the Chronicler had only the work of Dtr1 at hand.

47. Mendenhall, "Shady," 324. Of course, the identification of the women as "prostitutes" might be seen as necessarily obviating the idea that oaths might work, but this does not explain why some other method, like lots, might not be tried.

48. Throughout this book I use chapter and verse numbering of the Hebrew (Masoretic Text) for 1 Kgs 4 and 5.

documents used by Dtr,[49] Nadav Na'aman demonstrates from his examination of ANE archives that non-literary texts typically were kept for only a few generations before being discarded. We therefore cannot assume or conclude that biblical authors, including the author(s) of Kings, consulted archives and retrieved information from centuries-old documents.[50] William G. Dever notes that of the fifteen place-names on the list, thirteen have been identified with known archaeological sites, with remains of towns occupied during the divided monarchical period. Since a number of them were probably not well settled, or even within Israelite territory in the tenth century, Dever suggests that the list reflects glorified seventh-century BCE ideals.[51] This suggests that Dtr1 created and shaped a list that demonstrated Solomon's efforts to press tax districts on Israel.[52]

First Kings 4:20—5:14 provides a positive picture of Solomon. Alongside descriptions of his provisions, property, dominion, and wisdom, are comments in 4:20 and 5:5 indicating that the people of Israel and Judah were numerous, secure, and happy. First Kings 5:15–32, however, turns negative, particularly when read in light of 4:1—5:14. It is unlikely that this was ever intended to be part of the account of Solomon's downfall, since the narrator gives no clearly negative evaluations in chapter 5. Details of the story itself, not some evaluation, put Solomon in a negative light. This shift in narrative technique lends itself to the conclusion that Dtr1 turned 1 Kgs 5:15–32 from positive to negative (or vice versa).

First Kings 5:15–26 reports the account of Solomon's negotiations with King Hiram of Tyre for lumber. Victor Hurowitz lists a number of parallels between Solomon's words in 5:17-19 and certain ANE texts, concluding that 5:17-19 adheres to the form of a "decision to build" speech, especially when read in light of 2 Sam 7 and 1 Kgs 8:14-19.[53] But the decision to build is not presented as the main point of the text. The

---

49. Gray, 130-31; Cogan, 217-18; Hess, "District List," 279-92; Fritz, 47.

50. Na'aman, "History of Solomon," 131-32, accepts that scribes used the library in Jerusalem for source material, while objecting to the idea that archived documents were copied. See also Van Seters, "Temple," 49.

51. Dever, "Textual Criticism," 227; Dever., *Archaeology*, 138-44. Dever notes as well that a number of the sites appear to have been abandoned during the Persian and Hellenistic periods, further buttressing a pre-exilic date for this list.

52. 4:13 contains a note about Ben-Geber's "villages of Jair, son of Manasseh, which are in Gilead." Gray, 135n, suggests that this may be a deuteronomistic expansion based on Deut 3:4, 14. But if all of 4:7-19 is from Dtr1, then perhaps Dtr1 simply correlates his list to the information given in Deuteronomy.

53. Hurowitz, *House*, 131-67.

account instead reads as a description of trade negotiations in the context of peaceful relations between Tyre and Israel.

These negotiations do not go well for Solomon. Solomon initially proposes that Israelites join the Sidonians (generally understood as a term for Phoenicians in general[54]) in cutting timber. He notes that the Sidonians have special skill in this area, and so by referring to this skill directly, reveals the possibility that the Israelites may gain some new technological ability. Hiram apparently catches on to this wrinkle in Solomon's proposal, and so changes the terms, proposing that the Sidonians cut and ship the wood to Israel by themselves, so as to retain their technological secrets.

Hiram's proposal prevails. Even worse, the end result effectively makes Solomon into Hiram's vassal. First Kings 5:2–3 describes the daily provisions provided Solomon by his district governors listed in 4:7–19, "thirty cors of choice flour, and sixty cors of meal," in addition to sundry cattle and fowl. This adds up to 32,400 cors of grain per 360-day year. In 1 Kgs 5:25 Solomon agrees to give Hiram 20,000 cors of wheat annually: nearly 2/3 of the grain Solomon himself was to receive annually from his own vassals![55] Having his proposals rebuffed while effectively becoming Hiram's vassal places Solomon in a poor light.

Solomon nevertheless acts according to his original suggestion in verse 28, sending Israelite laborers to Lebanon. Their function there is not specified, but this arrangement seems much closer to Solomon's proposal in verse 20, "my (Solomon's) servants shall join your servants," than Hiram's rejoinder in verse 23, "My (Hiram's) servants shall bring it down to the sea from the Lebanon." Montgomery and Gehman resolve this discrepancy by stressing the Sidonians' skill in cutting lumber, proposing that the Israelites provided the unskilled supporting labor,[56] but this seems unlikely in view of Hiram's explicit comments in verse 9 to the effect that Hiram's servants would be doing transport as well as cutting. More probable is that the original report of the agreement, perhaps favorable to Solomon in keeping with the thrust of 4:20—5:14, was later adjusted to put Solomon's "wisdom" into question.[57]

54. Cogan, 227.
55. Walsh, *1 Kings*, 96–99 gives more on this.
56. Montgomery and Gehman, 137.
57. On literary grounds, a number of commentators view 26a as a later gloss, although Mulder deems it "integral to the narrative." See Gray, 149; Würthwein, 55–56; De Vries, 80; Mulder, 218.

The most likely adjustment is that Dtr2 added verses 25b–26a: "Solomon gave this to Hiram year by year. So the Lord gave Solomon wisdom as he promised him." First Kings 5:25b–26a follow the same form as 5:24–25a: two summary statements joined by a ו translated "so" in the NRSV, and "and" in the KJV and JPS). As the statements of 25b–26a are linked,[58] Dtr2 probably added them at the same time. Verse 26a, which reads וַיהוָה נָתַן חָכְמָה לִשְׁלֹמֹה כַּאֲשֶׁר דִּבֶּר־לוֹ, further mimics the construction of verses 24–25a. The construction ו + subject + qal perfect third masculine singular of *natan* + direct object + ל + indirect object, is essentially the same as used in verses 24–25a to describe Hiram's supply of cedar and cypress to Solomon, and Solomon's supply of food to Hiram.[59]

O'Brien argues that verses 22 and 23 preserve part of the original text of 1 Kgs 5. He finds no deuteronomistic language in these verses, noting as well that Hiram's proposal stands in contrast to the general principle through chapters 5–7 that Israelites do the building. Hiram also speaks of cedar and cypress, rather than cedar only, and asks for food for his household, rather than wages for his servants.[60]

The chief difficulty with O'Brien's thesis is that in the final form of the text Hiram's proposal clearly rules the day. In verses 24–25 Hiram meets Solomon's needs for cedar and cypress, while Solomon provides food for Hiram's household. If a deuteronomistic editor emended the text to stress that Israelites alone acquired materials for and built the temple, then he did a very poor job, since the resulting text, reinforced by the summary in 5:32, leaves us with the impression that Hiram's men cut the wood and brought it to the sea.

More likely, Dtr1's source materials reflected true negotiations: Hiram makes a counter-offer to Solomon's proposal which is implicitly accepted. Hiram's mention of cypress in addition to cedar in verse 22 may be an editorial supplement intended to increase Hiram's participation in the venture and perhaps better justify Solomon's exorbitant annual payment in verse 25. O'Brien argues for the deuteronomistic authorship of 5:17–21, pointing out a number of deuteronomistic features for this section.[61] Only verse 20 lacks both a reference to divinely-procured rest

---

58. Walsh, 98–99.

59. In verse 24 the MT gives the participle form נֹתֵן, perhaps to strengthen the case for an ongoing reciprocal trading arrangement. The pointing nevertheless could just as well be rendered נָתַן as in vv. 25–26.

60. O'Brien, *Reassessment*, 149–50.

61. Ibid; De Vries, 80–81. Cogan also credits the section to Dtr. Montgomery and

and some encomium to Yahweh or David. First Kings 5:20 nevertheless requires the three verses preceding as introduction, and provides context for Hiram's reply in verse 21.[62] O'Brien notes that Dtr follows the same path he had taken in 3:4–15, in which he retains the outline of a story, while adding substantial dialog.[63] The consistency in method and message with 3:4–15 further identifies this as the work of Dtr1.

First Kings 5:27–31 contains other problematic constructions. As related earlier, verses 27–28 describe a relatively mild *corveé*: Solomon draws thirty thousand men from all Israel to cut and deliver lumber from Lebanon, with the proviso that the workers get two months off after each month of service. These workers are organized under a single leader. Verses 29–30, however, abruptly introduce a much harsher levy: seventy thousand porters and eighty thousand stoneworkers, with 3,300 שָׂרֵי הַנִּצָּבִים, "chief officers" (NRSV "supervisors"). This latter arrangement is undoubtedly what causes Brueggemann to conclude that the labor policies of Solomon and the Pharaoh of Ex 1:11 (who set שָׂרֵי over the Hebrew slaves) are so similar that one must be modeled on the other.[64]

Working from Noth's commentary on Kings, Christoph Berner argues for the composite development of 5:27–32.[65] Berner proposes that the original consisted of 5:27–28 aα (the first two words only of verse 27, וַיִּשְׁלָחֵם לְבָנוֹנָה, "and he sent them to Lebanon"), and most of the last part of 5:32 וַיָּכִינוּ הָעֵצִים לִבְנוֹת הַבָּיִת, "and they prepared the timber to build the house" (omitting the word וְהָאֲבָנִים, "and the stones").[66] The result is a grammatically cohesive sentence. Berner argues that 28aβ–b, which explains the rotating shifts, interrupts this sentence and thus represents a later addition.[67] Yet the inclusion of all of verse 28 still renders the text grammatically correct.

Alternatively, the additions 28aβ–b and 29–32* may stem from different redactional layers.[68] If we simply remove references to the stone-

---

Gehamn accept Dtr authorship for all but the "outlines" of the account. See Cogan, 231; Montgomery and Gehman, 136.

62. O'Brien, 149.

63. O'Brien, 150n.

64. Brueggemann, 126.

65. Montgomery and Gehman, 136, and Mulder, 221, further draw attention to the unartful addition of vv. 15–17.

66. Berner, "Bondage," 225–26; Noth, *Könige 1*, 92–94; Würthwein, 56–57.

67. Berner, 226n.

68. Ibid.; Würthwein, 51n. Berner argues for yet another layer for the note about

cutters and laborers in verses 29–32*, then we are left with a picture of a Solomon who includes "all Israel" in the work of temple construction in a non-oppressive manner. The section that references stone workers, who clearly lack the "rotation" benefit, seems thematically inconsistent with the more humane treatment of the woodcutters. Moreover, the larger passage of 1 Kgs 5 addresses wood acquisition, so that the sudden introduction of stone workers is jarring, the likely result of Dtr2's intrusion.

Also problematic is the opening phrase of verse 30 לְבַד מִשָּׂרֵי הַנִּצָּבִים לִשְׁלֹמֹה, "except for the chief officers belonging to Solomon." Verse 29 begins וַיְהִי לִשְׁלֹמֹה, "and Solomon had," followed by the introduction of porters and stoneworkers. In this context, לִשְׁלֹמֹה in verse 30 is unnecessary (with whom else could the "chief officers" be associated?), and awkward, repeating the name "Solomon" from verse 29. However, the 3,300 supervisors could very well be associated with Adoniram and the shift workers from verse 28. Adoniram could hardly be expected to manage 30,000 workers by himself, and the terms of Solomon's arrangement with Hiram, in which Tyrians would do a substantial portion of the lumber preparation and transportation, surely required some level of "supervision" by Solomon's workers to ensure smooth progression of the work. The attribution of the 3,300 to Solomon thus shows that the king actively involved himself in setting up the process by which material moved from Tyre to Israel, and did not simply delegate this task to others.

With the above in mind, the following diachronic history for 1 Kgs 5 seems most probable. Verses 15–16, 22–25a, 26b, and 32 (which appears after 6:1 in LXX) were likely source material. Dtr1 supplied the dialog in verses 17–21, along with the information about rotational workers and supervisors in verses 27–28 and 30. Dtr2 then added the critical language of verses 25b–26a, and the information about stoneworkers in verses 29 and 31.

First Kings 6–7

With the exception of 6:11–14, for which see below, these chapters are devoid of deuteronomistic language. Van Seters argues that in these chapters Dtr is trying to recapture the glory of the temple after its destruction in 586. To support his view, Van Seters cites repetitions of some furnishing descriptions in 2 Kgs 25:13–17, and further notes that all of

---

Adoniram in 14b.

our descriptions of Herod's temple come from works of Josephus written after its destruction in 70 CE.[69] But Cogan points out that the references to bronze oxen in 1 Kgs 7:25, 44, said to have been shipped to Assyria in the 8th century (2 Kgs 16:17), are unlikely to have been remembered or invented by an exilic Dtr.[70] It seems more reasonable therefore to attach some description of the temple to the account of Solomon's negotiation for building materials.[71] These chapters therefore can be identified as Dtr1 source materials.

In terms of narrative continuity, the most outstanding section of 1 Kgs 6 occurs in verses 11–14, where Yahweh promises to establish Solomon and the children of Israel if Solomon follows Yahweh's commands. As these verses do not appear in LXX or Josephus, most commentators view them as a late insertion into the Hebrew text, intended to stress the importance of adherence to law over and above the fulfillment of temple functions. Verse 11 reads וַיְהִי דְבַר־יְהוָה אֶל־שְׁלֹמֹה לֵאמֹר, "and it happened that the word of Yahweh (came) to Solomon, saying," language suggesting the mediation of a prophet. Outside of this passage, Solomon, from the time he takes his throne, is unique among the major kings of Israel and Judah[72] in that he never interacts with prophets. This fact further points to a relatively later date for this section. The absence of these verses from LXX, along with a significant theological divergence from the rest of 1 Kgs 1–11, identifies 6:11–14 as a post-Dtr insertion.[73]

First Kings 7:1–12a moves away from the temple to the palace complex, and the House of the Forest of Lebanon (hereafter designated "HFL"). The LXX places this section immediately after the section on temple furniture, rendered in the MT in 7:13–50. D.W. Gooding, who held that the 1 Kgs *Vorlage* of the LXX is later than that of the MT, understood the LXX to be separating the "profane" palace and court from the temple sections of chapters 6–7, and thus rejected the LXX order as

---

69. Van Seters, *History*, 310, 310n.

70. Coogan, 273.

71. Campbell and O'Brien, *Unfolding*, 334–35 offer more on this point.

72. "Major" kings include Saul, David, Jeroboam, Rehoboam, Ahab, Jehu, Hezekiah, and Josiah.

73. The refrain of 6:14, וַיִּבֶן שְׁלֹמֹה אֶת־הַבַּיִת וַיְכַלֵּהוּ, "so Solomon built the house and finished it," appears in 6:9b in MT and LXX, and 6:3b in LXX. In verse 9, this phrase marks the transition from the discussion of stone to the discussion of timber. MT perhaps moved the other occurrence of the phrase from v. 3 to its present position in v.14.

a "reverent" revision.⁷⁴ Julio Trebolle, however, cites textual corruptions related to the transposition of texts in arguing for the priority of the LXX *Vorlage*. 7:12b in the MT refers to the temple court and entryway, which does not correlate well with the description of the palace in verses 2–12a. Verse 12b does, however, flow logically from 6:36, transitioning from the דְּבִיר ("inner sanctuary," 6:19–32) with its doors, and the הֵיכָל ("main temple room," 6:33–35) with its doors, to the temple court and its pillars.⁷⁵

Walsh regards 7:1–12a as an intrusion, since chapters 6–7 focus on the temple. Besides the text evidence above, Walsh points out two anachronisms. First, the temple furnishings would have been completed prior to the construction of the other buildings, as per the implications of 6:38–7:1: temple, then palace. Second, according to 3:1 and 9:24, the palace for Pharaoh's daughter (7:8b) was constructed only after the temple had been completed, and thus should chronologically occur after 7:13–50.⁷⁶

Further evidence for the superiority of the LXX here comes from Josephus' *Antiquities*, which discusses the construction of the palace and administrative buildings only after recounting Solomon's prayer (*Ant.* 8:130–140). Josephus is generally favorable towards Solomon, so his decision to report Solomon's non-temple building activity only after the temple narratives could not have been part of some agenda to place Solomon in an unfavorable light (since the MT's placement of 7:1–12a renders Solomon's "other" building activities less noticeable). More likely, Josephus' source for Solomon's other building activities came from a text like the LXX in which temple and non-temple construction were already segregated.⁷⁷

If Dtr1 created a unified text which lacked clear marks of insertions, then the rearrangement must have occurred later. We see insertions in chapters 3–11 which stress some theological agenda. It therefore seems appropriate to attribute to this same hand the movement of 7:1–12a to its

74. Gooding, "Timetabling," 155–56.
75. Trebolle, "Redaction," 25–28.
76. Walsh, 105–6.
77. Feldman, "Portrait," 103–67; Nodet, "Text," 41–68. Because of this and other text similarities to the LXX, many scholars have concluded that Josephus used a copy of the LXX as his text. However, Nodet demonstrates that Jospehus almost certainly used a Hebrew version of at least 1–2 Kings (as Josephus claims in *Antiquities* 1:5), since Josephus renders translations of MT proper names into forms which are quite distinct from those appearing in the LXX. Feldman argues for both the LXX and a Hebrew text, noting similarities in the construction accounts of LXX and Josephus.

MT placement in the midst of the "temple" section of the Solomon story, 5:15 through 9:9.

First Kings 8

First Kings 8 consists of a long speech by Solomon, surrounded by a narrative frame describing the ceremonial transport of the Ark of the Covenant to the temple. The frame consists of verses 1–11 and 62–66. Numerous aspects of verses 1–11 point to the work of a post-Dtr editor who was partial to P theology[78], rendering impossible attempts to reconstruct the oldest account.[79] While P-like influence in 1 Kgs is rare, the perceived theological import of 1 Kgs 8 evidently attracted a priestly editor, who perhaps desired to stress "the legitimacy of the Solomonic Temple as heir to the desert Tabernacle."[80] Since this ideology is difficult to attribute to Dtr1 or Dtr2, our best bet is to conclude that specific P elements in 1 Kgs 1–11 were contributed by a post-Dtr editor.[81] It nevertheless does seem probable that Dtr1 included something of the transfer of the Ark to the temple. A solemn assembly marking the temple as Israel's new shrine seems appropriate.[82] Campbell and O'Brien argue that 8:1a, 1c, (thus, "then Solomon assembled the elders of Israel ... that they might bring up the Ark of the Covenant of the LORD out of the city of

---

78. These include the following. First, while קהל often appears as a verb in P, verses 1 and 2 feature the only instances in Kings (other than 12:21) using a verbal form. Second, the phrase "all the heads of the tribes, the leaders of the ancestral houses of the Israelites" shares strong affinity with Numbers 3:30, 35; 7:2; 30:1. Third, in verse 4, the phrase אֹהֶל מוֹעֵד, "tent of meeting," appears at least 133 times in the Old Testament, including 120 times in P, but only here in Kings. Notably, אֹהֶל מוֹעֵד does not appear in 2 Sam 6 or 1 Kgs 1–2, which discuss the previous locations of the Ark. Fourth, verse 5 uses עֵדָה to refer to the Israelite assembly; the only time this word appears in 1 Kings 1–11 (is appears frequently in the hexateuch). Verse 5 also stands in conflict with verse 63: the former states that the number of sheep and oxen sacrificed was too great to count, whereas the latter gives specific numbers. Fifth, הֶעָנָן, "the cloud," which often represents God's presence in P, appears in DH only in 1 Kgs 8:10–11. Gray 204–12 has the best English description of the P work on 1 Kgs 8:1–11, but see also Würthwein 86–89, Hurowitz 262–66, Mulder 377–96, and Cogan 277–93.

79. Römer, "1 Kings 8," 69.

80. Cogan, 291.

81. As per Römer, 69.

82. Wiseman, *Kings*, 117.

David, which *is* Zion"), 2, and 6 are free of priestly influence, and so serve as a suitable introduction to Solomon's speech.[83]

Fritz credits verses 62–66 to Dtr as an expansion of Dtr's source material from verse 5.[84] This passage does not feature characteristic deuteronomistic language, however, so it seems more likely that Dtr1 followed his usual method in the Solomon narrative, adopting a frame from his sources, then adding dialog. Long, Noth, and Mulder hold verse 62 to be a resumptive repetition of verse 5, but Cogan stresses changes in language from verse 5 to verse 62.[85] First Kings 8:62 thus most likely continues the frame of Dtr1's source. Jones, De Vries, and O'Brien find 8:64 to be out of place,[86] but it appears as a reasonable explanation of verse 63, that the huge number of sacrifices taking place required more space, and thus a sanctification of the court in addition to the temple.[87] Buis and Römer see verse 64 as a priestly insertion (Römer also places verse 63 in this category), but their evidence is scanty, limited to a few words.[88]

Solomon's discourse itself has historically been taken to illustrate theological development in the concept of Yahweh's presence within Israel. Verses 12–13 suggest that Yahweh himself will physically sit or otherwise reside in the temple, but Solomon in verses 14–21 explains that the temple is being built for the *name* of Yahweh. The author of 1 Kings 8:14–21 thus likely intended this passage to serve as an explanation of a popular ANE ideology, expressed in 8:12–13, by which "temples are erected to connect the godhead to a certain place."[89] The Old Testament sometimes promotes this idea, as 8:12–13 alludes to other Old Testament passages, particularly Ps 132:13–14 and "songs of Zion" Pss 46, 48, and

---

83. Campbell and O'Brien, 349–50.

84. Fritz, 101–2.

85. Noth, *Könige*, 190–91; Long, 106; Mulder, 450–51; Cogan, 288–89.

86. O'Brien sees "consecration" in 8:64 vs. "dedication" in v. 63, but different terms for the different objects should not be seen as indication for a different authorial hand. See Jones, 207; O'Brien, 153; De Vries, 127.

87. Mulder, 452; Cogan, 289.

88. Buis, 88; Römer, 69.

89. Römer, 69, cites Keel, "Beobachtungen," 9–22, to suggest that the LXX of 12–13, which appears in LXX only after v. 53, reflects "the installation of the storm-god YHWH by the solar-god who grants him a place in the Jerusalem temple, in which the two deities co-existed." However, Rösel, "Rekonstruktion," 402–17, cautions that we do not have sufficient resources to accurately determine the Hebrew *Vorlage* of LXX here, much less determine the theology behind it. Fritz, 91–92, also cites Eissfeldt, "Wohnsitze," 502–6, to show that this idea is well-attested in Ugaritic texts.

76. In contrast, 8:14–21 reflects "nominal realism," the idea that the name of an item or person in fact exists along with the item or person itself. Thus (unsurprisingly in the context of Dtr language) Yahweh's name in the temple represents his presence.[90]

First Kings 8:31 begins seven specific petitions directed toward Yahweh. There has been much discussion about whether the seven petitions were composed as a unity, the debate often centering on the appropriateness of these petitions in a pre-exilic setting. Knoppers, for example, argues for the compositional unity of 8:31–53 on stylistic grounds.[91] But while some of the petitions seem appropriate with respect to a standing temple, others make more sense for the aftermath of the temple's destruction.[92] This suggests that someone "added on" petitions to those which originally called for a physical temple. The final form may be stylistically appealing, but this does not negate the possibility of an older, shorter, less attractive version.

The petitions, along with their introduction in verse 30, introduce concepts of forgiveness and repentance. As these ideas are very important to a number of post-exilic texts (including Ezra 9 and Neh 9), some scholars argue that most or all of 1 Kgs 8 is exilic or post-exilic.[93] Claus Westermann's categorization of the "long prose prayers" of 1 Kgs 8, Ezra 9, and Neh 9 within his stages of the development of Hebrew Bible prayer has further solidified their identification together.[94] Westermann argues that within these prayers "we no longer find the unity coming together in worship and the civil community held together by state and monarchy."[95] Yet 1 Kgs 8:31–53 is not completely devoid of references to the monarchy, as Solomon refers to his role as temple builder in verses 43, 44, and 48.[96]

However, literary and thematic links between 1 Kgs 8:31–53, Ezra 9, and Neh 9 do not necessarily prove that Solomon's prayer was entirely written after 586 BCE. Moshe Weinfeld argues that 8:31–53 is not strictly

---

90. Richter, *Name*, 14–17.

91. Knoppers, "Prayer," 229–54.

92. Römer, "Redaction," 71, dates all seven petitions to the exilic and post-exilic periods, since they do not mention sacrifice. But since Römer's Josianic section (8:14–21) also does not mention sacrifice, this "argument from silence" is not strong.

93. Levenson, "Temple," 142–66; O'Brien, 153–58; Werline, *Prayer*, 18; Boda, *Praying*, 47–61.

94. Westermann, *Elements*, 155–56.

95. Ibid., 156.

96. See chapter 7 for comments about the significance of these references.

a prayer, but is instead "a discourse on the function of prayer in Yahweh's chosen place."[97] This difference between 1 Kgs 8 and Ezra 9 / Neh 9 lends support to the majority of scholars who, in the observation of Samuel E. Balentine, hold 1 Kgs 8 as "one of the earliest" Hebrew Bible passages to use confession as a major prayer theme.[98]

Following Cross, many DblR advocates agree that the MT of 1 Kgs 8:31–53 should be dated to the exile (or later).[99] But this conclusion does not discount the possibility that this passage went through some redactional process, as argued by Cross himself.[100] Brettler reasons that since prayer was recited at the First Temple, we should allow that part of this section may have been written by a pre-exilic Dtr.[101] Cogan further points out that 8:31–45 points to a standing temple, a present Davidic dynasty, and Israelites living in the land.[102] Thus, the idea that 8:31–53 represents one of the initial Hebrew Bible passages to work with confessional prayer, combined with indications that the First Temple is still standing, allows us to date at least part of this section to the time of Dtr1.

The first two petitions actually require the petitioner's presence in the temple. In verse 31, the petitioner must swear "before your altar in this house," and in verse 33, the defeated Israelites "confess your name, pray and plead with you in this house." These petitions therefore point to a pre-exilic composition: the temple is standing, and a reference to military activity seems out of place in a post-exilic setting. Given these facts, it is particularly noteworthy that the hypothetical supplicant of the fifth and sixth petitions does not offer prayer in the temple itself. Instead, according to the fifth petition, the foreigner בָּא וְהִתְפַּלֵּל אֶל־הַבַּיִת הַזֶּה, "comes and prays toward this house"—that is, he journeys on account of the fame of Yahweh, yet is not expected to offer his prayer within temple grounds.[103]

97. Weinfeld, *Deuteronomic*, 37.

98. Balentine, "Ready," 12.

99. Cross, 278, and others scholar below. Römer, "Ambigu," 115, argues for the unity of most of 8:31–51 in part due to their apparent similarity to the curses of Deut 28. However, the difficult situations of 1 Kgs 8 comprise only a part of the list in Deut 28, so 1 Kgs 8 could have been expanded simply by drawing more from its Deut 28 "source." Furthermore, Römer's argument works only if Deut 28 is based on 1 Kgs 8, instead of the other way around.

100. Ibid.

101. Sarna, "Superscriptions;" Milgrom, *Leviticus 1–16*, 19; both cited in Brettler, "1 Kings 8:15–53," 25.

102. Cogan, 293.

103. Isaiah 56:6–8 similarly opens up the covenant of Yahweh to foreigners,

And while in the second petition, the militarily defeated Israelites swear before the altar in the temple, in the sixth petition, the army need only pray toward the chosen city and the temple therein.

A second point to consider is that in each of the last three petitions, Solomon refers to the temple as the "house that I have built" (verses 43, 44, 48). These are the only instances in verses 31–53 in which Solomon refers to himself. In this manner, this section stands in contrast to verses 14–30 and 56–61, in which Solomon references himself repeatedly.

A third feature to consider is the nature of the fourth petition. Unlike the others, this is phrased as a "catch-all," mentioning famine, plague, infestation, sickness, enemy threat, and other nasty eventualities. Knoppers identifies petition four as the center of not only the seven petitions, but of seven "literary frames" of 1 Kgs 8. The problem with this idea is that the seventh petition is given a disproportionate amount of space as compared to its predecessors—six verses, as opposed to two or three for petitions one, two, three, five, and six.

Brettler, seconded by Judith H. Newman, instead proposes that the first four petitions were designed as a unity, featuring increasing length for each petition: one and two are about the same length; three is longer; four is longer still. The fifth petition, however, breaks the pattern. Brettler further points out features of petition four (verses 37–40) which suggest that this section originally concluded the "petition" section of Solomon's speech. וְסָלַחְתָּ . . . וְאַתָּה תִּשְׁמַע in verse 39 mirrors the last two words of verse 30, וְסָלַחְתָּ וְשָׁמַעְתָּ, so that this concept holds the section together. In verse 38, וּפָרַשׂ כַּפָּיו hearkens back to Solomon's spreading of his hands in verse 22, thus suggesting the closing of the section. Finally, the fourth petition ends with a motive clause beginning with לְמַעַן : motive clauses often end units in the DH.[104]

De Vries identifies only the final two petitions as additions, since each begins with the particle כִּי ("when," routinely identified by its pronunciation "ki"). In his view, since petition six "closely repeats the substance of" petition two, it serves as an exilic revision, while petition seven

---

perhaps building on an early form of the idea in Isaiah 55:5 (thus, Deutero-Isaiah). Watts, *Isaiah 34–66*, 253, notes that the key idea in v. 7 that the temple is a "house of prayer" echoes 1 Kgs 8:27–30. Since the temple is clearly standing in Isa 56 but is unreferenced in 1 Kgs 8:41–43, Isa 56 perhaps depends on 1 Kgs 8 theology.

104. Brettler, 25–26; Newman, *Praying*, 48ff. On motive clauses in the DH, Sonsino, *Motive Clauses*, cited in Brettler, 26n.

is clearly exilic.¹⁰⁵ Yet as Levenson points out, the other five petitions have no uniform start, and the fourth petition also begins with a "ki" clause.¹⁰⁶ Thus, while כִּי may signal an addition, other factors may also be at work.

The most feasible solution therefore is that of Brettler, that the first four petitions belong to Dtr1, and the final three, to Dtr2.¹⁰⁷ This explains why petitions one and two clearly presume a standing temple, while five and six do not.¹⁰⁸ Petitions three (lack of rain) and four (catch-all) do not require the supplicant's presence in the temple because of their frequent and general nature. Small Israelite farmers might often want for rain,¹⁰⁹ and in any case Dtr would have the individual approach Yahweh (rather than other deities) for all manner of difficulties, so that repeated trips to Jerusalem to address these issues would be impractical. Serious oaths (petition 1) and military setbacks (petition 2), however, are infrequent enough that personal visits to the temple would be indicated.¹¹⁰

---

105. De Vries, 126.

106. Levenson, 155.

107. Brettler, 25–27. Brettler actually suggests that while petitions 1–4 were originally composed as a unity, petitions 5–7 were composed by at least two other Dtrs. Yet Brettler nevertheless notes similarities between petitions 5–7 which are absent in petitions 1–4.

108. Battle against enemies might at first glance seem out of place in the exile (petition six, vv. 44–5), but the phrase "if your people go out to battle against their enemy" can certainly refer to local bands, or even be taken metaphorically. Given our limited data on the exilic situation, it is hard to say that this phrase could not have originated from an exilic setting.

109. My experiences pastoring small churches in rural Virginia have made this abundantly clear to me. While Richmonders are very happy with dry weather, every summer, week after week the folks in Farmville and Lawrenceville would ask for prayer for rain!

110 While Jon Levenson holds that this section represents an exilic unity, he (unintentionally?) presents further data pointing to the 4/3 breakdown. One of his arguments for the exilic origin of 1 Kgs 8 is its seven verbal parallels with Deut 4 and 30, which Levenson also dates to the exile. However, of the seven, five come from petition 7, one comes from petition 5, and one comes from 1 Kgs 8:23. Levenson's parallels include 1 Kgs 8:23 / Deut 4:39; 1 Kgs 8:41 / Deut 29:21; 1 Kgs 8:47 / Deut 4:39, 30:1; 1 Kgs 8:48 / Deut 30:10; 1 Kgs 8:51 / Deut 4:20; 1 Kgs 8:52 / Deut 4:7. See Levenson, 160–62.

First Kings 9:1–9

First Kings 9:3–9, represented as a single speech by Yahweh, is clearly a composite text. Gray states that the "admonitory purpose" of 9:1–9 requires the passage to be read as a whole, but then recognizes 9:6–9 as a deuteronomistic expansion of verses 1–5.[111] Brueggemann similarly reads 9:1–9 as a unity intended to bring Solomon "fully and without qualification" under the Torah, but then immediately admits that the statement in its entirety is not aimed primarily at Solomon, but has the Babylonian exile in view.[112] 9:1–9 may function as a coherent unity, but verses 6–9 nevertheless expand upon verses 1–5.

Knoppers attributes verses 4–5 to a different author from that of verses 1–3, based on different subject matter and the fact that "the phraseology" of verses 4–5 repeats that of 1 Kgs 2:4 and 8:25–6.[113] However, while I agree that 2:4 comes from Dtr2, Dtr2 could have simply copied a phrase used by Dtr1. As he expanded the DH, Dtr2 certainly could have utilized phrases and ideas from Dtr1. The cleanest way to reconcile 9:1–9 with 2:4 is to posit that Dtr2 copied language from 9:4 as he wrote 2:4.

First Kings 9:6 begins אִם־שׁוֹב תְּשֻׁבוּן אַתֶּם וּבְנֵיכֶם, "if you or your sons turn in any way," utilizing the second person plural pronoun. It thus must be aimed at more than just Solomon and his descendants. Furthermore, the tone of the passage changes at verse 6: where 9:3–5 represents a conditional promise (rewards for faithfulness), verses 6–9 contain a conditional threat: punishment for failure to follow Yahweh. Römer, who does not consider the above argument, takes 9:1–9 as a unified section, based on his observation that 9:6b, ". . . and do not keep my commandments and my statutes that I have set before you . . . ," repeats language from 3:14.[114] But, again, there is no particular reason to discount the possibility that the author of a later diachronic layer at times adopted language from the earlier layer. More telling is the dissonance with 9:1–9. It is therefore best to read 9:3–5 as God's response to Solomon, and 9:6–9 as a widening of this response toward the people in general.[115]

---

111. Gray, 236.
112. Brueggemann, 122–23.
113. Knoppers, *Two Nations*, 109–10.
114. Römer, "Ambgiu," 106–8.
115. See O'Brien, 160, for further linguistic and stylistic features which point to a different author for 9:6–9.

Yahweh's statement in verse 3, "I have put my name there forever; my eyes and my heart will be there for all time," is in tune with the theology of 8:14–21: Yahweh's name represents His presence in the temple. This contrasts with verse 7, in which, as punishment for rebellion, Yahweh states, "the house that I have consecrated for my name, I will cast from my sight."[116] Yahweh's presence is not in view here; the issue instead is his attention, as in the seven petitions of 8:31–53.

First Kings 9:10–14

In *ÜS*, Noth marked the beginning of Solomon's downfall at 9:10. Yet he stated also that the only "blot" on Solomon's image in chapters 9–10 is the section 9:10–14, in which "Solomon fails to pay back Hiram properly."[117] Noth's conclusion that the Solomon narrative turns at this point was no doubt influenced by his earlier contention that shifts in the DH are marked by major speeches, as in 1 Kgs 8.[118] While some continue to argue that Solomon's downfall begins at 9:10,[119] most no longer stress the DH speeches as markers of shift in emphasis.

First Kings 9:10–14 resumes the accounts of Solomon's dealings with Hiram from chapter 5. Verse 11 introduces the idea that Hiram supplied gold to Solomon, beyond cypress and cedar. In exchange Solomon gives over twenty עִיר, "cities" from Galilee. Many commentators read this section as a criticism of Solomon, since he surrenders Israelite territory to Hiram, perhaps violating Deut 17:15b, "you are not permitted to put a foreigner over you, who is not of your own community."[120] But the structure of the story highlights not Solomon's surrender of territory, but Hiram's reaction to the cities he has received. Hiram is clearly dissatisfied, as he has sent 120 talents of gold to Solomon—an exorbitant sum for the territory surrendered.

The jolting nature of verse 14 has engendered various theories about the composition history of 9:10–14. Coogan asserts that verses 12–13

---

116. Coretese, *Deuteronomistic*, 97. Cortese contends that in the era of a standing temple, the threat of the temple's destruction sounds too much like blasphemy for an Israelite to utter it.

117. Noth, *Deuteronomistic*, 60–61.

118. Ibid., 5–10.

119. These include Savran, "Kings," 157; Mulder, *Kings*, 20; Bruegggemann, *Solomon*, 78; Sweeney, 140 52.

120. Walsh, *1 Kings*, 120; Jones, *Kings*, 213.

intrude into the natural flow of verses 11 and 14, thus introducing conflict into the otherwise cordial relationship between Hiram and Solomon. Würthwein and Kuan see verse 14 as the later interpolation, developing the introduction of the term זָהָב, "gold," in verse 11.[121] The presence of a פ in the MT, separating verse 14 from its predecessor, buttresses this view.[122] These composition reconstructions lead to a similar result, in that Solomon profitably trades cities for gold. If verse 14 was an addition, it shows that Solomon was the ultimate benefactor from his exchange with Hiram. If instead verses 12–13 were inserted, then the passage stresses the idea that Solomon got a good deal. And if the section was composed as a unity, then the concept that wisdom leads to material benefits holds as well. Thus, Nelson's conclusion that this transaction serves to highlight Solomon's wisdom holds in all cases.[123] Furthermore, whatever the composition history, the editor(s) of chapters 9–11 (and of the Solomonic narrative as a whole) never develop the idea of any sort of rift between Solomon and Hiram, as all of Solomon's other interactions with Hiram are cordial.[124]

This section represents the first time in 1 Kings in which Solomon acquires gold for something other than temple usage. Solomon gets more gold in 9:28; then chapter 10 refers to gold no fewer than twelve times, describing Solomon's acquisitions and luxury. 9:10–14 thus serves as a turning point in the narrative, bringing gold into view. Again, this is not necessarily critical toward Solomon. Modern Israelis and Bible exegetes may look upon the sale of irreplaceable land with horror, but we cannot automatically assume that the ancients shared this same value system.[125] And the simple fact that Solomon becomes exorbitantly rich should not be a difficulty in light of 3:13.[126]

121. Würthwein, *Könige*, 106–8; Kuan, "Third," 38.
122. As per *BHS*.
123. Nelson, *Kings*, 63–64.
124. Jobling, "Value," 470–92. Jobling further suggests that while it is unclear who gains the advantage in this trade, the deal was in any case "hard-headed."
125. Contra Jones, 213. Sweeney stretches Deut 17:15 by claiming that Solomon's placing of these cities under foreign control violates the intent of that passage. Sweeney later cites the ceding of these cities as consitituing a burden on the northern tribes, thus factoring into the split in 1 Kgs 12. But without an understanding of how these cities came under Solomon's control in the first place, we cannot assume that the northern tribes objected to Solomon's deal here. Sweeney, *Josiah*, 95, 100.
126. Parker, 94–95, does not address this aspect of 3:13, while strenuously objecting to the fact that Solomon's wisdom leads to wealth in 1 Kgs 10.

There is no particular justification, therefore, for attributing 9:10–14 or parts of it to a different hand or time than that of the earlier account of Solomon's dealings with Hiram in chapter 5. Literary considerations alone satisfactorily explain Dtr1's introduction of gold in chapter 9.

First Kings 9:15–25

The *corveé* in MT 9:15–25 invites comparison to that of chapter 5, the chief difficulty being verses 21–22, which specify that "(and) from the sons of Israel, Solomon made no slaves" (וּמִבְּנֵי יִשְׂרָאֵל לֹא־נָתַן שְׁלֹמֹה עָבֶד). This directly contradicts 5:27, which specifies that forced laborers came from "all Israel" (מַס מִכָּל־יִשְׂרָאֵל). Gray draws a distinction between מַס; (in 4:6 and 5:27), and מַס־עֹבֵד in 9:21–22, arguing that only the latter represents "permanent serfdom," as the former indicates "occasional regimentation" (specifically, temple construction).[127] Cogan, however, points out that the comparisons of Josh 16:10 with Judg 1:30–35 and 1 Kgs 9:21 with 2 Chr 8:8 demonstrate that the two terms mean the same thing.[128] The term מַס־עֹבֵד is significant, however, in that the two instances in which it is used feature the phrase עַד הַיּוֹם הַזֶּה, "until this day." מַס־עֹבֵד closely follows Deuteronomy 20:10–11, which stipulates that residents of surrendering Canaanite cities will become forced laborers and will serve (יִהְיוּ לְךָ לָמַס וַעֲבָדוּךָ).[129]

As everything in 1 Kings 9:16–21a is grammatically subordinate to the verses concerning forced labor in 21b–22, Walsh deems the principle subject of the entire section 9:15–25 to be forced labor.[130] However, the corrupted nature of the text, combined with the length and variety of the interruptions in 16–21a, suggest that the author intended to communicate more. Cogan's assessment of verses 16–25 as a "miscellaneous collection of short notices" regarding building projects and forced labor seems more accurate.[131]

The intrusion of verses 16–19 into the MT (they are absent in LXX) points to a reworking of 9:15–25.[132] Sweeney nevertheless asserts that the

---

127. Gray, *Kings*, 155; House, *Kings*, 158.
128. Cogan, 229.
129. Geoghegan, *"Until This Day"*, 80–81.
130. Walsh, 122–23.
131. Cogan, 307.
132. The MT is unclear here, as 9:15 (LXX 10:22) specifies that the arrangement

point of the distinction between 5:27 and 9:21–22 is that Israelites are subject to forced labor only with respect to building the temple, while the forced labor of the foreigners was more comprehensive.[133] Therefore, the distinctions between the *corveés* of chapters 5 and 9 do not necessarily point to different stages in the history of the composition of 1 Kgs 1–11. Since the themes of 5:27–32* and 9:15–25 can be easily reconciled, it seems safe to conclude that Dtr1 arranged 9:15–25 from various source materials.[134]

First Kings 9:24 informs us that, in the midst of the building activity, the daughter of Pharaoh moved into the palace constructed for her by Solomon. Paul R. House observes that this verse pulls together statements from 3:1, 7:8, and 9:15.[135] Solomon's marriage to the daughter of Pharaoh is thus a continual source of concern through the Solomon narrative. There is no particular reason to suggest that someone other than Dtr1 contributed this wrinkle to the story. Dtr1 apparently spreads mentions of this woman throughout the narrative to help us keep her in mind.[136]

Moore highlights the idea of "raising up" throughout the larger section 9:10–25. First Kings 9:11 utilizes a form of the verb נָשָׂא, "he raised up," to describe Hiram's furnishing of wood and gold to Solomon. In 9:24, the daughter of Pharaoh "went up" from the City of David to her own house (enhancing her stature?), and in 9:25, Solomon "offers up" sacrifices. These instances of "raising up" occur within a passage generally devoted to building activity, featuring the verb בָּנָה, "he built (up)."[137] Therefore, "raising up" of structures, materials, queen, and sacrifice unifies this section.

---

with the Canaanites included the construction of the temple as well as Solomon's other building projects. Furthermore, Joshua 9:27 specifies that מַס־עֹבֵד; must permit temple service.

133. Sweeney, *Kings*, 145; cf. Jones, 214; Berner, 227.

134. For a fuller argument of this point, see Noth, *Könige*, 208-9, and Knoppers, *Two Nations*, 123-24. Walter Dietrich, "History and Law," 340-41, prefers to read 9:15–24 as a Deuteronomistic expansion, negative toward Solomon, of 5:27–32. But the idea that this passage is more critical to Solomon than 5:27–32 is difficult to advance givien the note in 9:22 that Solomon did not enslave Israelites.

135. House, 158-59.

136. As noted earlier, the LXX combines the MT passages into one, placing it after 4:34.

137. Moore, *Faith Under Pressure*, 198-99.

First Kings 9:26-28

This short passage describes Solomon's further accumulation of gold, again with his associate Hiram. One of the main text questions occurs in verse 28, with respect to the amount of gold imported: LXX^B reads "120" talents of silver, whereas LXX^{LUC} agrees with MT and the other ancient witnesses on 420. Debate over the correct amount typically centers on the unlikelihood of the extraordinarily high amount of 420 talents, versus the more reasonable lower figure.[138] From a literary perspective, the higher number reduces the significance of the 120 talents of 9:14. This in turn makes the surrender of Israelite land more noteworthy, since the wealth Solomon gains from this venture obviates the desire to trade territory for gold. If LXX^B represents the original reading, then the MT revision to 420 puts Solomon's actions of 9:15-25 in an unfavorable light. But in either case, it is hard to identify this section as anything other than Dtr1 source material.

First Kings 10:1-13

First Kings 10:1-13 gives the account of the Queen of Sheba's visit to Solomon. While commentators often struggle to date this story,[139] De Vries, seconded by Mulder, suggests that the "pragmatic, judicial wisdom" in view in 10:9 makes a pre-exilic date likely.[140] First Kings 10:1a ends with the phrase לְשֵׁם יְהוָה, "due to the name of the Lord," which most commentators take as a marginal gloss due to its absence from the parallel passage in 2 Chr 9:1 and its "harsh" placement.[141] Montgomery and Gehman apply the term *ad majorem gloriam Dei* to this phrase, which seems to fit the overall program of Dtr1.[142]

First Kings 10:9 suddenly introduces Yahweh at the end of the Queen's speech. It thus seems to follow Dtr1's pattern of retaining the form of his source material, while adjusting the dialog.[143] Dtr1's edit-

---

138. See comments by Cogan, 306-7; Mulder, 503-4; Keulen, *Versions*, 181-88.

139. Römer, *So-Called*, 100n, remarks that this passage looks like something from "Thousand and One Nights." He nominally attributes it to his Assyrian Dtr, then states that its setting makes the Persian period more likely.

140. De Vries, 138; Mulder, 507.

141. Cogan, 311.

142. Montgomery and Gehman, 228; Noth, *Könige*, 224; Mulder, 511.

143. Noth, 226; Mulder, 519; Fritz, 118.

ing here cleverly promotes his agenda. While the Queen is impressed primarily by Solomon's wisdom and resulting wealth,[144] Dtr1 does not promote Yahweh as the source of Solomon's wisdom. Instead, the Queen remarks on Yahweh's love for Israel, along with His desire that King Solomon "execute justice and righteousness."

First Kings 10:11–12 looks like an interpolation: while verses 1–10 and 13 focus on the Queen of Sheba's visit to Solomon, verses 11–12 suddenly announce the return of Hiram's fleet from Ophir, loaded with "almug wood" and precious stones, followed by an account of the use of the almug wood.[145] Most commentators regard the presence of these "unrelated" verses within the Queen of Sheba account as evidence for a general reworking of the passage, perhaps to portray the Queen's visit as part of a broader depiction of Solomon's international relations.[146] Yet we have no textual evidence for a re-ordering of materials, unlike the situations in chapters seven and nine.

A better possibility is that the addition to the text comes in verse 13. Without this verse, 10:1–10 presents a wholly positive picture of Solomon: the Queen of Sheba is doing all the giving, whereas Solomon merely dispenses wisdom.[147] Solomon relinquishes nothing of his material wealth, instead demonstrating in various ways his superiority above his contemporaries. The Queen of Sheba account, considering verses 1–10, thus serves only to exemplify the overarching point of 10:23–25, in that the whole earth, like the Queen, seeks Solomon's presence to hear his wisdom.[148] But if verse 13 is an addition, it can only reduce Solomon's stature: now Solomon is also giving materially out of his accumulated wealth.

The syntax of verse 13 matches the distinctive grammatical construction of 5:24–26a: *waw* + subject + perfect of *natan* + ל + indirect

---

144. Fewell and Gunn, *Gender*, 175, comment that at this juncture "it would appear that wealth and wisdom are correlates."

145. The type of wood referenced by the term אַלְמֻגִּים is probably lost to us; the term appears only here and in the parallel passage in 2 Chr 9:10, and in 2 Chr 2:7. Mulder, 519–21.

146. So Sweeney, *Kings*, 147–49. According to DeVries, 138, "gold" is the key word for 9:26—10:29.

147. The suggestion of Ikeda, "Red Sea Trade," that the purpose of the Queen of Sheba's visit was to negotiate a trade agreement with Solomon seems speculative, and certainly not the thrust of 1 Kgs 10:1–13.

148. The strongly positive depiction of Solomon in 10:23–25 is an important argument against Noth's breakdown of 1 Kgs 3–8 positive, 9–11 negative.

object + direct object. Furthermore, 10:13 and 5:25b–26a function in like fashion, clarifying their preceding passages in a way that reduces the reader's opinion of Solomon. Most likely, therefore, 10:13 is a secondary addition from the same hand as that of 5:25b–26a.

First Kings 10:14–22

This section centers on the House of the Forest of Lebanon (HFL), and Solomon's wealth stored there. This links this section to 7:1–12a, which, as we have seen, likely originated after Solomon's prayer in chapter 8. Verse 22 is the highlight of this section, describing Solomon's trading gains. The MT lists the fruits of Solomon's trade activities as luxury items: gold, silver, ivory, apes, and peacocks. The LXX, however, lists only materials useable for construction: gold and silver, wrought stones, and hewn stones. This change suggests that MT wishes to intensify the luxury of Solomon's kingdom, while the LXX offers a more pragmatic, construction-oriented view. The LXX thus corresponds nicely to its earlier description of the construction of the HFL in 3 Kingdoms 7. Following the LXX, this section clearly belongs to Dtr1's sources.

First Kings 10:23–29

First Kings 10:23–25 serves as a fitting bookend to the main "positive" section of the Solomon narrative beginning in chapter 3, as it hearkens back to God's promise to Solomon in 3:12–13 to grant unparalleled wisdom and riches. Noth views 10:27 as a later addition, since it "disrupts the train of thought."[149] But Schley shows that verses 26–29 are organized as a poetic eulogy, rather than a historical portrayal.[150] All together, the entire section 23–29 works to show that Solomon's wisdom results in unparalleled wealth: 24–25 shows how the world's desire to hear Solomon enriches him, and 26–29 shows how Solomon benefits from a practical "business" wisdom involved in leveraging trade routes and his solid relationship with Egypt. We can easily attribute all of 10:23–29 to Dtr1's sources.

---

149. Noth, 61, n. 57.
150. Schley, "Reconsideration," 595–601.

First Kings 11:1–13, 41–43

First Kings 11 references Solomon's wisdom only once, in verse 41. At the conclusion of the Solomon narrative, 11:41 tells us that we can read more of Solomon's wisdom in "the book of the Acts of Solomon." The special note of Solomon's wisdom here suggests that wisdom was associated with Solomon prior to the time of Dtr1. Gray suggests that the word וְחָכְמָתוֹ, "and his wisdom," might be an addition to the text, but he offers no reason, and there is no supporting textual evidence for this suggestion.[151] Thus, while we cannot specify the point at which the tradition of Solomonic wisdom developed, the appearance of וְחָכְמָתוֹ in 11:41 supports the notion that Solomon had been associated with wisdom by Dtr1's time.[152] Of course, as Lemaire points out, wisdom itself is not a *deuteronomistic* concern, since we do not see deuteronomistic references to wisdom outside of 2 Sam 9–20 and 1 Kgs 1–11.[153] But since 11:41 cites Solomon's wisdom as a component of Dtr's source material, Dtr1 clearly accepted Solomon as a "wise" figure.

First Kings 11:1–13 certainly contains strong deuteronomistic features. De Vries, Jones, Long, Montgomery, Gray, O'Brien, Würthwein, and Noth all agree that the reference to Solomon's 700 wives and 300 concubines in 3a serves as part or all of the pre-Dtr core of 11:1–13.[154] Knoppers, seconded by Van Seters and McKenzie, contends that even this information likely originates with Dtr, since he cannot imagine any source listing this.[155] The determination over whether these numbers come from Dtr1 or his sources is connected to other exaggerated claims throughout 1 Kgs 1–11. While some of this may come from Dtr1, I've shown above that there are good reasons to believe that many claims about Solomon's excessive gold and unparalleled wisdom come from Dtr1's sources. Dtr1's main task was organization, not invention. In 1 Kgs 11 Dtr1 presents

---

151. Gray, 298.

152. Soggin, "Solomon," 172; Jones, 120. Soggin identifies the time and place in which "Solomon was praised as a wise king in the distant past" as one in which there was "a craving for wise leadership." Jones suggests that the emphasis on wisdom in 11:41 combined with the repetition of Solomon's wisdom throughout 1 Kgs 1–11 shows that this was a dominating source behind the history.

153. Lemaire, "Wisdom," 114.

154. De Vries, 143; Jones, 232–33; Long, 121; Montgomery, 232; Gray, 274; O'Brien, 161; Würthwein, 131; Noth, 244.

155. Knoppers, *Two Nations*, 144–45; Van Seters, *History*, 311; McKenzie, *Trouble*, 56.

Solomon's excessive number of wives as a criticism of the king, but his source did not necessarily see this negatively. Dtr1 simply presented his information in a way which underscored his theological point. Therefore, while most of 11:1–13 was composed by Dtr1, the note about Solomon's wives should be credited to Dtr1's source material.

First Kings 11:14–40

This long section consists of several narrated events. Na'aman suggests that the material for this section originated as part of a broader narrative which included the basis for 2 Sam 8–10.[156] The narrative is based on historical events hinted at by inscriptions to Hazalel at Samos and Eretria. For Na'aman, an eighth century BCE date for this document is the only plausible means for a seventh–sixth century Dtr to be aware of these events.[157] However, Na'aman's evidence relies almost entirely on his reading of 2 Samuel. The part of 1 Kgs 11 related to the story continued from 2 Sam 8–10 merely involves Rezon's capture of Damascus in 11:23–24.[158] But this brief note could as well have been inferred from data available to Dtr1, as other material in this section was also adjusted to fit Dtr1's ideology.[159] Furthermore, as Edelman points out, the source identified in 11:41, "the book of the Acts of Solomon," with its references to Solomon's wisdom, can hardly be identified with an account of David's wars.[160]

Edelman instead proposes that the accounts of Hadad the Edomite and Rezon of Damascus in 11:14–25 were added some time after the work of Dtr1. This was done to fit the ideology of someone who subscribed to the Chronicler's theology of immediate retribution.[161] First Kings 11:26–40 satisfied Dtr1's need to demonstrate the fulfillment of Yahweh's word, but did not do so quickly enough for the taste of some subsequent editor. Knoppers points out, however, that Deut 7:1–6, the section prohibiting foreign marriage, when related to 1 Kgs 11:1–13,

---

156. Na'aman, "History of Solomon."
157. Nadav Na'aman, "History of David," 174–75.
158. Ibid., 175.
159. Na'aman, "History of Solomon," 61–63.
160. Edelman, "Adversaries," 172–73.
161. Ibid., 189. Moore, 204, further discusses relationships between the three accounts.

teaches *quick* retribution for intermarriage (verse 4).[162] This would permit Dtr1 to compose these additional stories, as per Edelman's suggestion, in order to more closely fulfill Deut 7:4, while still retaining the idea of the delayed punishment prophesied in 11:26-40 and effected in 1 Kgs 12. Thus, there is no strong reason to attribute any part of 1 Kgs 11 to Dtr2 or some succeeding scribe.

Diachronic Analysis: Summary

Compiling the above data, our four layers are as follows:[163]

- Source materials: 2:10-12; 3:1*, 3*, 4, 5b, 9, 11, 12a, 13a, 15a, 15c; 4:1-20; 5:1-16, 22-25a, 26b-28, 32; 6:1-10, 14-38; 7:12b-51, 1-12a; 9:10-28; 10:1-8, 10-12, 14-29, 11:3a.
- Dtr1 additions: 2:46b; 3:1*, 3*, 5a, 6-8, 12b, 13b-14; 8:1a, 1c, 2, 6, 12-40, 54-66; 9:1-5; 10:1*, 9; 11:1-43*.
- Dtr2 additions: 1:1-53; 2:1-9, 13-46a; 3:2, 3aβ; 3:16-28; 5:25b-26a, 29-31; 8:41-53; 9:6-9; 10:13. Dtr2 is also responsible for placing 7:1-12a, originally located after 1 Kings 9:9, in its current MT location before 7:12b.
- Post Dtr2 additions: 3:10, 15b; 6:11-14; 8:1-11*.

First Kings 3:4-15 contains multiple layers: Dtr1's source material regarding Solomon's dream and God's gift of wisdom to Solomon, Dtr1's reworking to include deuteronomistic elements, and later "clarifying" references to *Adonai*. The key idea expressed in 3:11-13a, that Solomon is to be granted wisdom and glory as his reward for requesting wisdom, does not appear to be a "deuteronomistic" theme elsewhere in the DH. The connection of wealth to wisdom thus came from Dtr1's source materials.[164] The entire section 3:4-15 reveals significant reworking by Dtr1, so that verses 11-13 were probably present in the earliest Dtr1 version of the Solomon narrative.

162. Gary N. Knoppers, "Solomon's Fall and Deuteronomy," in Handy, 407-8.

163. Campbell and O'Brien, *Unfolding*, 329-71, renders the most comprehensive breakdown for comparison that I know of.

164. Wälchli, *Salomo*, 24-127, and Särkiö, *Salomos*, describe the wisdom sources in greater detail, positing pre-Dtr wisdom redactions. But the information on Solomon's wisdom in 1 Kgs 1-11 is scanty enough that the safest course is simply to attribute all of these materials to Dtr1's sources.

In his assessment of the Solomon narrative, Ronald Clements makes similar findings regarding the Queen of Sheba narrative in 10:1–13. He suggests that this passage along with 5:15; 9:26–28; 10:14–15, 22, and 29 point to Solomon using his wisdom to take advantage of historic trading routes linking Mesopotamia and Africa, thus increasing his wealth, and the wealth of Israel.[165] The theme of "[the pursuit of] wisdom leads to wealth and fame" naturally links 3:4–15 to the contents of 9:10–10:29.[166]

First Kings 3:4–15 and 9:10–29 furthermore portray wisdom in positive terms. Yahweh/ Elohim seems pleased to grant Solomon wisdom, as well as wealth and honor, as a reward for seeking a לֵב שֹׁמֵעַ לִשְׁפֹּט אֶת־עַמְּךָ, "hearing heart to judge your people" (3:9). First Kings 4:1—5:14 and 9–10 favorably describes Solomon's wealth and fame. Chapters 9–10 also presuppose Solomon as builder of the temple and its furnishings, per specific references in 9:10, 25; 10:5, 12. And 1 Kgs 9:11–14, 27 and 10:11, 22 connect chapters 9–10 to the account of Solomon's acquisition of construction materials in chapter 5.

First Kings 1–2, however, undercuts this positive picture of Solomon by questioning his right to the throne. This transforms the accounts of Solomon's temple-building in chapters 5 and 8. If we assume that Solomon was David's legitimate heir, then chapters 5 and 8 describe Solomon fulfilling the charge made in David's day to construct a temple for Yahweh. When the question of Solomon's legitimacy is raised, however, chapters 5 and 8 can be read to show how Solomon tried to legitimize his position as lawful heir.

First Kings 7:1–12a seems awkwardly placed on thematic, grammatical, and chronological grounds. Its current location in the midst of temple construction accounts, however, does help to aggrandize Solomon's desire for power and influence, consistent with the apparent aims of Dtr2. Following LXX, it seems likely that Dtr1 originally placed this section between MT 7:52 and 8:1. The three secondary petitions of Solomon's prayer in 8:41–53, with their refrain "the house that I have built," also work to create an image of Solomon engaged in self-justification, and so fit Dtr2's agenda.

Furthermore, verses 5:25b–26a and 10:13 appear to be later additions to the accounts to which they are attached, and all work to the same

---

165. Clements, "Origins," 34.

166. Porten, 97, argues that the entire narrative of 1 Kgs 3–11 serves to fulfill 3:12–13. This seems overly broad, as large portions of the narrative, including the temple construction and dedication in chs. 5–8, do not appear to be linked to these verses.

purpose: to denigrate Solomon's wisdom. These verses are appended onto sections which, by themselves, illustrate some aspect of Solomon's wisdom. But in each case, the added verse changes the meaning of the prior section to raise doubts. The similarity in vocabulary and syntax between 5:26a and 10:13 suggests that these two verses came from the same hand (which I identify with Dtr2).

Toward a Double Redaction

The above analysis points to a Dtr1 who is generally positive toward the monarchy, and a Dtr2 who is quite willing to criticize it. Drawing on the work of Weberian sociologist A. Steil,[167] Thomas Römer proposes that an exilic "mandarin" class, composed of high-ranking officials with generally conservative views, produced a Dtr who was ambivalent about the idea of kingship. This mandarin Dtr thus explains the frequent interspersion of apparently pro- and anti- monarchic passages—for example, positive and negative depictions of kingship in 1 Sam 8–12, and the mix of "good" and "bad" kings found in 1–2 Kgs.[168] My Dtr2 fits this description, as the final form of 1 Kgs 1–11 maintains positive depictions of Solomon, with negative elements added to the work of Dtr1.

The DblR therefore acts as a helpful model toward understanding 1 Kgs 1–11. Dtr1 assembled sundry source documents, occasionally supplying linking mechanisms and editorial comments to buttress his ideology. His ideas included a generally positive view of Solomon's rule through 1 Kgs 10. A positive view of Solomon and his power fits the monarchical society of Dtr1. Dtr1 further accepted the idea that the pursuit of wisdom leads to more tangible benefits, although this idea does not play into his evaluation of Solomon. Dtr2 subsequently revised the work of Dtr1, questioning the legitimacy of Solomon's claim to Israel's throne, as well as the value of Solomon's wisdom. The final form of the MT then reflects a few later editorial adjustments.

Conclusions

Based on the above analysis, the DblR of 1 Kgs 1–11 seems feasible. Ideological discrepancies within this section can be sorted out by theorizing

---

167. Steil, *Krisensemantik*.
168. Römer, *So-Called*, 111–64.

work from two separate dtrs. Issues specifically pertinent to 1 Kgs 8 point to pre-exilic and exilic dtrs, since parts of the prayer require a standing temple and an army, while later parts of the prayer, along with 9:6–9, fit the exilic *Sitz im Leben*. Dtr1's work is ideologically consistent, and the Dtr2 passages can be ideologically separated from the work of Dtr1. We also can easily reconcile all of the passages from Dtr2 to each other theologically.

Having established literary "layers" of 1 Kgs 1–11, we are now in position to closely examine the theological ideas of the Josianic edition of the Solomon narrative.

4

Dtr1's Solomon Story

Dtr1 and Royal Power

THE 1 KINGS ACCOUNT of King Solomon is an account of his power. All other matters are secondary. We see nods in the direction of Solomon's wisdom, but as almost all diachronic analyses have shown, these references are easily identified as either Dtr source material or, possibly, a wisdom "redaction." Other matters involving Solomon directly relate to his power, including his building activity, his wealth, and his international renown. The DH thus distinguishes Solomon's story from the account of David in 1–2 Samuel, which regularly features David's personal drama and inner thoughts. Everything about Solomon is exterior, meant to shape the people's opinion of Solomon; all of his words and actions are public. Even the famous dream sequence of 3:4–15 is designed for public appreciation, justifying prominent aspects of Solomon's rule: Solomon is perfectly justified in seeking wealth and international acclaim, because Yahweh Himself promises these.

In this chapter, I will locate Dtr1 in history, then explore his ideas about King Solomon. In chapter 3 I discussed the main ideas of Dtr1's source material; we are now ready to address Dtr1's royal ideology.

Locating Dtr1

The DblR holds that Dtr1 did his work in the late seventh century BCE during the reign of King Josiah. Frank Moore Cross and his successors have argued that this location best suits the repeated emphasis on the eternal decree of Davidic kingship, first given in 2 Sam 7.[1] The Cross school thus holds to most of Noth's ideas about the original construction of the DH, only pushing its date back several decades to before the exile, during the reign of King Josiah. This means that most of what we might consider to be "deuteronomistic" theology applies to Dtr1. According to 2 Kgs 22:1, Josiah began his reign at the age of eight, probably around the year 640 BCE. Josiah died thirty-one years later, c. 609 BCE. Since Dtr1 ends with Josiah still alive in 2 Kgs 23:25, Dtr1 must have composed his work within the decade or two prior to 609.

Some scholars suggest that the appointment of Josiah was a move away from central control. Second Kings reports that Josiah was placed on the throne not by the urban elites, but by the עַם־הָאָרֶץ, "people of the land" (2 Kgs 21:24). Schniedewind thus argues that the broad social concerns of the book of Deuteronomy point to the work of an author outside of the Josianic scribes and the Jerusalem elites. Schniedewind's position depends on the contemporaneous existence of the so-called "Law of the King" of Deut 17:14–20, which severely limits the power and authority of the king in favor of the priests in charge of the law.[2] Yet the author of 2 Kgs apparently approves of Josiah's total control over Judean government and religion, while Deut 17:14–20 is the only passage in Deuteronomy which mentions the king. These considerations point to the likelihood that Deut 17:14–20 (or, at least, verses 18–19) was added subsequent to Josiah's reign, perhaps driven by a desire to critique King Solomon's style of rule.[3]

Deuteronomy's social concerns nevertheless remain intact without the "Law of the King," and do not preclude an ideology of centralized rule and worship. Outside of Israel in the late seventh century BCE, Assyria was being upstaged by the neo-Babylonian empire, thus creating expansion opportunities for Judah in the north. Second Kings 23:4–19 discusses Josiah's activity in Bethel and Samaria, likely enabled through Assyrian weaknesses. Concomitant with Judean expansion northward

---

1. Cross, *Myth*, 278.
2. Schniedewind, *Textualization*, 113.
3. McConville, *Deuteronomy*, 283–84.

would have been an increase in the non-Judean population newly subject to Judean rule. Judah had suffered great trauma and population loss a century earlier at the time of the invasion of Sennacherib of Assyria c.722 BCE. Pro-immigrant policies during a time of territorial expansion seem wise as long as immigrants can be assimilated into the host population. By stressing kindness toward strangers alongside a policy of strong centralization, Dtr1's Deuteronomy and DH promoted the probable aims of Josiah's administration. This suggests that Dtr1 was a scribe loyal to Josiah, who wished to stress that the future success of Judah lay in loyalty to Torah, a centralized cult, and the king.

Setting the Stage: 1 Kings 2:10-12; 2:46b—3:1, 3

As I demonstrated in the previous chapter, Dtr1's account of Solomon begins with David's death and Solomon's ascension to the throne. Some commentators find a need for some event to solidly establish Solomon's rule, leading to various proposals about the purpose of the dream sequence in 3:4-15*.[4] But the information presented in 2:10-12 is simple and direct, with the ending note that Solomon's kingdom "was established firmly," informing us that Solomon's transition was effective.[5]

While many commentators mark off sections within 1 Kgs 3, typically 3:1-3 and 4-15,[6] Dtr1's grammar signals his intent to present 2:46b—3:15* as one unit. 3:4 begins with a *waw* + imperfect verb, which, while certainly common in 1 Kgs 3-11*, typically does not begin a new section.[7] This suggests that we should consider the possibility that verse 4

---

4. Cogan, *1 Kings*, 189-91, provides a nice summary, along with critiques.

5. Auld, *Privilege*, 37-38, notes that the accounts of 2 Sam-1 Kgs and 1-2 Chr share thematic similarities. David chooses Solomon from among his sons; Solomon becomes king before David's death; the aged David wishes Solomon strength and offers advice; and, of course, both note David's death, the length of his reign, and Solomon's successful establishment. But, of course, while the Succession Narrative and 1 Chr share these elements, their narratives are quite different. It may be that the SN replaced something more favorable to David (and closer to the account of 1 Chron?) which is unrecoverable.

6. Gray, *Kings*, 114-17; Würthwein, *Könige*, 28-38; Long, *1 Kings*, 61-67; Mulder, *Kings*, 130-54.

7. Some commentators view 3:5 as the beginning of a new section, but this verse more likely represents simple development of the action of 3:4. See Buis, *Rois*, 53; Montgomery and Gehman, *Kings*, 105.

is meant to continue the story from verse 3.[8] In this case, the information from verse 3b that Solomonבַּבָּמוֹת הוּ מְזַבֵּחַ וּמַקְטִיר, "used to sacrifice and make offerings in the high places" does offer a natural lead-in to verse 4. The best solution therefore is to read the entire passage 2:46b—3:15* as the beginning of Dtr1's Solomon narrative.[9]

A number of commentators find 3:1 to be badly attached to this section, as Dtr1 does not immediately develop issues of family life and temple/ building construction.[10] Gray suggests that the marriage notice has been placed here to fit the historical situation: 9:24 indicates that Pharaoh's daughter lived in the city of David until Solomon completed the temple, and since the temple was started in the fourth year of Solomon's reign, the marriage must have taken place earlier.[11] Peter Leithart argues that Solomon's marriage fulfills the Abrahamic promise to "bless the nations."[12] But Dtr1 does not otherwise seem interested in the Abrahamic covenant, and the idea of "blessing the nations" seems out of place in a deuteronomistic context which elsewhere frowns on marriage to foreigners.[13] Martin J. Mulder's conclusion that 3:1–3 is "clearly tailored to what follows" seems more likely, although Mulder does not offer specifics.[14]

Martin Noth suggests that 3:1 was meant to highlight Solomon's prominent international position from the beginning.[15] Noth based his argument in part on an influential article by Abraham Malamat which argues that the marriage between Solomon and an Egyptian princess was an "absolutely unique event" in the annals of Egypt.[16] Kenneth Kitchen,

---

8. Jung Ju Kang sees a "shift in narrative technique" from v. 3 to v.4, while maintaining that vv. 3–4 remain connected by the theme of "sacrifice at the high places." Kang, *Persuasive*, 171–72.

9. Brueggemann, *Kings*, 43–9, (along with Sweeeny, 79), offers a unique approach, taking vv. 3–15 as a unit, with vv. 1–2 as its foil. Solomon indicates readiness to depart from Yahwism in vv. 1–2, then seemingly embraces Yahwism in vv. 3–15.

10. Cogan, 184. Sweeney, *Kings*, 78–79, and Fritz, *Kings*, 33–34, offer further comments. Barrick, "Loving," 428–30, argues that the 3:1b's "inverted quotation" of 9:15's sequence "house of the Lord, house, wall around Jerusalem" demonstrate the former's dependence on the latter. However, 9:15's reference to the millo (הַמִּלּוֹא) in the midst of the other terms throws doubt on the idea that one verse antedates the other.

11. Gray, 117.

12. Leithart, *Kings*, 43.

13. Seow, "Kings," 37.

14. Mulder, 130.

15. Noth, *Könige 1*, 49.

16. Malamat, "Aspects," 1–17.

seconded by John Currid, questions this, citing specific instances of Egyptian diplomatic marriage in the second millennium BCE.[17] Alan Schulman argues that Egyptian unwillingness to permit Egyptian princesses to participate in diplomatic marriages was indeed fixed policy under certain conditions, as suggested by Amarna letter no. 4 line 4.[18] (The Amarna correspondence of course took place in the fourteenth century BCE,[19] while 1 Kgs 3:1 was written much later, within the tenth–seventh centuries BCE, during which time a weaker Egypt was perhaps more willing to marry off princesses to foreign rulers[20]). Kitchen nevertheless agrees that Solomon's marriage in 3:1 was a "momentous" event.[21]

Choon-Leong Seow concurs with Noth that the marriage signaled Israel's entry into the realm of "world-class diplomacy."[22] Steven Weitzman takes this further when he suggests that this marriage is part of a picture of a Solomon who gets along with foreign rulers (Pharaoh, Hiram of Tyre, the Queen of Sheba), because he has become one of them, sharing their interests and values.[23] Yet while Noth's contention is possible, Solomon's international importance does not connect directly to anything else in chapters 1–3.[24]

Seow instead argues that the narrator intends 3:1–3 to be read "with the Torah of Moses in mind." Syncretism is the issue here: Solomon's rush to welcome his Egyptian bride is concomitant with his neglect to construct the temple and defense walls.[25] But Seow's "building delays" conclusions may be over-reaching, since it is hard to see anywhere in 1 Kgs 3–11 where Solomon runs into problems stemming from slow construction. Probably best is Walsh's conclusion that three themes introduced in 3:1–3 (foreign marriage, temple construction, and other

---

17. Kitchen, "Egypt and Israel," 111; Currid, *Ancient Egypt*, 164–65.

18. In Amarna 4 line 4, Babylonian ruler Kadasman-Enlil addresses Pharaoh Amenophis as follows: "you, my brother, when I wrote [to you] about marrying your daughter, in accordance with your practice of not giving (a daughter), [wrote to me], saying, "From time immemorial no daughter of the King of Egypt is given to anyone." Moran, *Amarna Letters*, 8. See also Schulman, "Diplomatic Marriage," 177–93.

19. Moran, xxxiv–xxxix.

20. Kitchen, *Third Intermediate*, 282.

21. Kitchen, "Egypt and Israel," 111.

22. Seow, "Kings," 37.

23. Weitzman, *Solomon*, 93.

24. Important, since Noth does not regard chs. 1–2 as a later interpolation.

25. Seow, 37.

building projects) "thread their way" through the Solomon account, marking both high and low points.²⁶

Buis argues that we should not understand 3:1 to be critical of Solomon's marriage. Egyptians do not appear on the list of peoples to be destroyed in Deut 7:1-2, and Egyptians furthermore may eventually be welcomed into the assembly in Deut 23:8.²⁷ But Solomon does not merely take an Egyptian wife; he seeks to become Pharaoh's son-in-law. First Kings 3:1 reports וַיִּתְחַתֵּן שְׁלֹמֹה אֶת־פַּרְעֹה מֶלֶךְ מִצְרָיִם, "Solomon made an alliance by marriage with Pharaoh the King of Egypt." The *hithpaʿel* וַיִּתְחַתֵּן, literally, "he became (someone's) son-in-law," consistently carries a negative connotation in the Hebrew Bible, implying the incurrence of an obligation to someone not under covenant with Yahweh. The practice is definitively condemned in Deut 7:3 and Josh 23:12, key deuteronomistic passages which forbid foreign marriage.²⁸ These two verses within their contexts share substantial interplay with the account of Solomon's downfall in 1 Kgs 11:1-4.²⁹ Thus, in terms of the narrative structure of Dtr1's account of Solomon, 3:1 serves as a beginning which corresponds nicely to the account of Solomon's fall in 1 Kgs 11. Furthermore, the proximity of 3:3 to 3:1 associates foreign intermarriage with infidelity to the Yahwistic cult, as is found in the larger contexts of the above passages: Deut 7:1-6,³⁰ Josh 23:6-13, and 1 Kgs 11:1-10. Therefore, the act of seeking to become Pharaoh's son-in-law must be read negatively, pointing to Solomon's improper desire for power and influence.

In 3:1b, Solomon undertakes various building projects, but the narrator lists the construction of Solomon's own house first, ahead of the temple and of the wall of Jerusalem.³¹ In verse 3, Solomon goes to a "high place" to offer his sacrifices, rather than to the altar in Jerusalem. This is preceded in verse 3 by the note that Solomon "loved Yahweh, to walk in

---

26. Walsh, *1 Kings*, 69.

27. Buis, 52.

28. See Walsh, 70 for a fuller discussion.

29. Knoppers, "Fall," 392-410, offers more on the relationships between these three passages.

30. McConville, *Grace*, 139-42. McConville reads 7:1-6 in particular as primarily referencing the overall struggle of Yahwism vs. "Canaanitism," in which intermarriage is but a part.

31. Walsh, 71-73, discusses these shortcomings of Solomon's behavior at some length.

the statutes (לָלֶכֶת בְּחֻקּוֹת) of his father David."[32] The concept of walking in the statutes of someone other than Yahweh consistently refers to unrighteous behavior.[33] To save himself from disaster, Solomon must walk in the statues of Yahweh alone.[34]

First Kings 2:46b–3:1, 3 clearly sets the tone for the rest of Dtr1's Solomon story. But while temple and other building projects are mentioned, the more important themes, heightened by the rest of 1 Kgs 3, are religious syncretism, illustrated by Solomon's marriage to an Egyptian and by sacrifices at the בָּמוֹת, "high places," and Solomon's striving for power, illustrated by the note that the kingdom was established "in the hand of Solomon," and, again, Solomon's desire for a marriage relationship with Pharaoh.

Granting Wisdom to Solomon: 1 Kings 3:4–15*

While this passage is best remembered for telling how Solomon came to be wise, there is more going on here. As per my previous chapter, the central story in which Solomon asks for wisdom at God's behest is part of Dtr1's source material. Dtr1 then shapes this narrative to fit his overall message, which here is to demonstrate Solomon's affection for syncretistic practices, and Solomon's desire for power.

Dtr1 stresses Solomon's tendency toward syncretism by locating this narrative at הַבָּמָה הַגְּדוֹלָה, "the great high place," in Gibeon (3:4). While some commentators excuse Solomon's actions here in light of the fact that the temple had not yet been built (as per 3:2), the larger narrative had solved this problem already by allowing David to sacrifice in Jerusalem, without the presence of a temple (2 Sam 6:17–18; 24:18–25).

---

32. The "statutes of his father David" perhaps refers to "the last words of David" in 2 Sam 23:1–7. As I mentioned in chapter 3, this pericope is usually thought to be quite old, and thus available to Dtr1. Verses 3–4 stress royal authority, and God's covenant with David in verse 5 is "everlasting," consistent with 2 Sam 7.

33. Ibid., 73. Second Kings 22:2 uses different language of Josiah, וַיֵּלֶךְ בְּכָל־דֶּרֶךְ דָּוִד אָבִיו, "and he walked in all the *ways* of David his father." At the beginning of this chapter I stressed David's role as the archetype for Israelite kings in the book of Kings. David as model of righteous behavior only begins in 3:14, which gives a much less ambiguous statement of this idea.

34. Ibid.

Dtr1 underscores the location (and so, its inappropriateness) by placing the phrase בְּגִבְעוֹן, "at Gibeon," at the start of 3:5.[35]

De Vries, following the work of Siegfried Herrmann, sees 3:4–15 as a legitimization story, perhaps motivated by the questionable means through which Solomon ascends the throne in chapter 2.[36] Burke O. Long, however, observes that Hermann's work relies on the fragmentary Sphinx Stele of Thutmose IV, which is probably not a legitimization account.[37] Furthermore, we must consider the grammar of verse 4b, which begins אֶלֶף עֹלוֹת יַעֲלֶה שְׁלֹמֹה, "Solomon used to offer a thousand offerings . . ." The imperfect יַעֲלֶה is most probably a frequentive, since the action is clearly past and the converted imperfect at the beginning of the verse makes it unlikely that this is an ancient preterite.[38] Since Solomon had sacrificed at Gibeon in the past, it is unlikely that the narrator expects us to think that Solomon undertook this particular venture with a special purpose in mind.

The key phrase of Solomon's speech comes in 3:9a:

וְנָתַתָּ לְעַבְדְּךָ לֵב שֹׁמֵעַ לִשְׁפֹּט אֶת־עַמְּךָ לְהָבִין בֵּין־טוֹב לְרָע
"And give your servant a hearing heart, to judge your people, that I may discern between good and evil."

W. Malcolm Clark has demonstrated the legal background of the last part of this sentence, לְהָבִין בֵּין־טוֹב לְרָע.[39] At a different juncture, the wise woman of Tekoa uses these words in 2 Sam 14:17 amidst her plea to David for a "just" (i.e., merciful) treatment of David's estranged son Absalom. Clark puts it, "the wise king hears the good and the evil, and because the wisdom of God is in him, he gives correct judgment."[40] This understanding seems to fit the context in other passages in which the phrase is used, such as 2 Sam 13:22 and Gen 31:24, 29. In these passages also, the phrase "good and evil" functions as a legal term.[41]

This observation gives us insight into the best understanding of the key word שָׁפַט. The usual translation of שָׁפַט is "judge," but it is often rendered as "govern," as in the NRSV, NIV, ESV, and Reina-Valera. Gerhard

---

35. De Vries, 1 Kings, 51.
36. Ibid., 47–48; Herrmann, "Königsnovelle."
37. Long, 1 Kings, 64–65; ANET 469.
38. Carr, Dream, 34n; Cogan, 185.
39. Clark, "Background," 266–278.
40. Ibid., 268–69.
41. Ibid., 269.

Liedke argues that שָׁפַט is the act of using legal means to restore people and communities to a place of שָׁלוֹם, "peace." A governor therefore performs שָׁפַט by enacting and enforcing laws which benefit the community, while a magistrate may do שָׁפַט by hearing a lawsuit.[42] So while Jones, Kenik, Buis, Walsh, Mulder, Fritz, and Omanson and Ellington prefer "govern," all note that the particular kind of "governing" in view retains a strong note of "judging" as well.[43] Most English translations nevertheless render this word "judge," as do Scott, Gray, Montgomery, Carr, De Vries, Leithart, Cogan, and Sweeney. Gray perhaps gives the best rationale for "judge," noting that, while the Ras Shamra texts indicate that the root שָׁפַט has the primary connotation of "rule," the last phrase of 3:11, הָבִין לִשְׁמֹעַ מִשְׁפָּט, "understanding to discern judgment," featuring the key 3:9 word שמע (hearing), points to hearing cases.[44]

Solomon's request for wisdom in 3:4–15 tells us something about his approach toward leadership. First, as I pointed out in the previous chapter, Solomon's comment in 3:7b (inserted by Dtr1) וְאָנֹכִי נַעַר קָטֹן לֹא אֵדַע צֵאת וָבֹא, "although I am only a little child; I do not know how to go out or to come in," points to Solomon's unfamiliarity with military matters. This distinguishes him from his royal predecessors David and Saul, both military men.[45] Second, citing his responsibility in verse 8 to a "numerous" people "beyond measure," and, in verse 9, "heavy" (דָּבֵד), Solomon asks of *Elohim* a לֵב שֹׁמֵעַ, "hearing heart," to aid him in his task of שָׁפַט. Solomon's approach fits the general ANE pattern, in which kings tend to personally administer justice.[46] But what does Dtr1 think of Solomon's request?

42. "jpv," *TLOT* III,1393–94.

43. Walsh, 75, prefers "govern" in order to reflect the broader concept of שפט as compared to the English "judging." However, his description of the "ancient ruler's duties" with respect to שפט include only the making of just decrees, and the making of judicial decisions that enforce those decrees. The concept of the English "govern," however, includes "the exercise of continual sovereign authority over" (*Merriam-Webster's Collegiate Dictionary, Eleventh Ed*)., which seems broader than the making of decrees and decisions. See also Jones, *Kings*, 127; Kenik, *Design*, 129–30; Buis, 54–5; Mulder, 145; Fritz, 38; Omanson and Ellington, *Kings* 113.

44. Gray, 126. See also Scott, "Beginnings of Wisdom," 270–71; Montgomery and Gehman, 108; Carr, 64; De Vries, 45; Leithart, 45; Cogan, 187; Sweeney, 74.

45. Mobley, *Empty Men*, 229–30. Going further back into the DH, this also distinuguishes Solomon from the judges, noted military leaders. Mobley thus highlights Solomon's ascension as the end of the heroic age, as Solomon becomes ruler without having had to first win at battle.

46. Levinson, "Reconceptualization," 515–16; Levinson, "Deuteronomy's Conception," 76.

We may be able to discern Dtr1's attitude by comparing 3:4–15 to Deut 1:9–17, which is clearly related. In Deut 1:10, as in 1 Kgs 3:8, the people are numerous, so that Moses describes his juridical responsibilities in terms of bearing heavy burdens. To assist, Moses seeks men who are "wise and discerning" (חֲכָמִים וּנְבֹנִים) in 1:13 to help him to settle disputes among the Israelites, just as in 1 Kgs 3:12 *Elohim* gives Solomon a wise and discerning (וְנָבוֹן חָכָם) heart. שׁפט in Deut 1 clearly has a juridical sense; therefore, 1 Kgs 3 most likely reflects the same idea.

Moshe Weinfeld argues that Deut 1:9–17 and 1 Kgs 3:4–15 share the deuteronomistic idea that the possession of wisdom is the main requirement for a competent jurist.[47] In his commentary on 1 Kings, Weinfeld further elucidates the dependence of Deut 1:9–17 on Ex 18:13–23 and Num 11:11–17, noting that Deut 1:10 diverts Ex 18's stress on moral qualities (Ex 18:13) to qualities of an "intellectual" nature (Deut 1:13, 15).[48]

In a similar vein, Parker argues that Solomon's request for wisdom in 3:9 is bound to ideals of justice, wisdom, and law, which are characteristic of the leadership of Moses.[49] Lyle Eslinger goes even further, suggesting that Dtr has Solomon presenting himself in 3:9 as a "New Moses."[50] However, these two models require the stipulation that 1 Kgs 3:4–15 depends on Deut 1:9–17, so that the two passages either originate from the same literary layer, or that Deut 1 was earlier. But it is hard to prove that Deut 1:9–17 was written at the same time or earlier than 1 Kgs 3:4–15.[51]

First Kings 3:4–15 does differ from Deut 1:9–17 and the texts from which it comes, Ex 18:13–23 and Num 11:11–17, in one important way. In these other texts, Moses' solution to the problems of leadership is to appoint others to assist him. Moses proposes shared leadership; Solomon seeks more ability for himself. So rather than present Solomon as a "new Moses" either positively (Parker) or negatively (Eslinger), Dtr1 distinguishes Solomon by highlighting Solomon's preference to work alone. While Moses effectively decreases central control through delegation, Solomon seeks to enhance his power as he takes on judicial responsibilities.

47. Weinfeld, *Deuteronomic,* 246.
48. Weinfeld, *Deuteronomy,* 139.
49. Parker, 71.
50. Eslinger, *Into the Hands,* 134.
51. As Weinfeld notes, the phrase בָּעֵת הַהִוא (the first words of Deut 1:9) usually signals an intrusive pericope (Weinfeld, *Deuteronomy,* 139).

Solomon's desire to act as judge moves toward conformity with typical ANE monarchs, who generally maintained the prestigious role of relieving the oppression of those who lacked power.[52] Deuteronomy, however, tends to push leaders in the opposite direction, arguing for shared leadership in passages such as Deut 1 and 16:18–18:21 ("the constitution of ancient Israel"[53]). Since the tradition of diverse leadership under Moses is referenced several times in the Pentateuch, it stands to reason that Dtr1 adopts and edits Solomon's dream account in a manner which highlights Solomon's alternative approach.

Elohim grants Solomon's request. But if we do not have verse 10, is this a positive development? In the same breath, in verse 13, *Elohim* also gives Solomon great wealth, contrary to the strictures of Deut 17:17. Perhaps, then, Solomon is to be a kind of experiment, similar to that of 1 Sam 8, where God grants a different request, giving the people of Israel the kind of king they seem to want. Just as Saul has a chance for success if he maintains fidelity to Yahweh's laws (1 Sam 12:14), so Solomon can gain long life if he matches the standard of obedience set by his father David (1 Kgs 3:14). But at this point, Solomon also has been promised fabulous riches, along with incomparable juridical acumen. What happens to a king when he does receive great wealth, and takes on the role of judge, contrary to Deut 17?

First Kings 2:46b—3:15*—Summary

Dtr1 thus constructs 1 Kings 2:46b—3:15 to lay out the issues which will become important in his King Solomon narrative. Dtr1's Solomon story of 1 Kgs 3–11* depicts numerous instances of centralized control and syncretism, within the central narrative of temple building and the accumulation of wisdom and wealth. Temple-building, wisdom, and wealth are positive aspects of the Solomon tradition, and appear with some frequency in the material which follows. However, none of these three aspects can be said to form the basis for a unified picture of 1 Kgs 4–11. The elements of the Solomon story which do appear consistently throughout these chapters are Solomon's royal power and acclaim, references to

---

52. Levinson, "Conception of Law," 76.

53. This term is often credited to McBride, "Polity," 229-44, although McBride actually applied it to Deut 5:1—26:15.

David as the standard of fidelity to law, and, to a lesser extent, his willingness to accept, and even stress, syncretism.

Royal Power

For Dtr1, the most important element of Solomon's reign is his royal power. Dtr1 consistently selects source materials which demonstrate Solomon's power and writes connecting sections to underscore Solomon's overarching power and influence. Power in itself not necessarily negative, but, as foreshadowed in 3:1 and 3:4–15, Solomon is capable of overreaching, particularly when it comes to his building activity and his assumption of cultic functions. As the following sections of this chapter will show, Solomon displays his power in four ways: empire administration, foreign comparisons, building activity, and cult leadership.

Power—Empire Administration

Dtr1 immediately establishes Solomon's power through his description of Solomon's governmental organization. After a short section listing the Solomonic officials, Dtr1 employs source material for 4:7–19, describing the districts responsible for supporting Solomon's household. Solomon divides Israel into twelve districts, thus making his imprint on Israelite society.[54] Egyptian parallels suggest that the point is to effect taxation, while destroying older tribal connections.[55] This idea of re-districting for tax purposes fits Baruch Halpern's thesis that Hezekiah and Josiah were involved in replacing traditional tribal boundaries with state-defined districts, in order to promote state control of society.[56] Long furthermore suggests that this passage is not meant to record the whole of Solomon's administrative apparatus, but merely a portion of it which contributes to Solomon's wealth and honor.[57]

In the context of Dtr1's Solomon narrative, this list therefore functions to demonstrate that Solomon successfully took control of the

---

54. McConville, *Earthly Power*, 152.

55 Heaton, *New Men*, 51–53; Currid, 165–67. Moore, *Faith Under Pressure*, 68–70, suggests that this model may have Mesopotamian precedents as well.

56. Halpern, "Sybil."

57. Long, 74.

northern tribes.⁵⁸ Southern control of the northern tribes is an issue which runs through Samuel and Kings.⁵⁹ Solomon's efforts to gain firm control over the northern tribes are therefore an element of his power. Wiseman suggests that the numbers 3,300 in 5:30 and 550 in 9:23, both multiples of eleven, further point to Solomonic control over northern levies, from which Judah therefore was implicitly exempt.⁶⁰ Solomon organizes Israel into districts apart from the traditional tribal boundaries, then further solidifies his influence by marrying off female court figures to two of his "governors" (4:11, 15).⁶¹

Solomon's construction of the temple further demonstrates his power. Abraham Malamat argues that Solomon's predecessor David displays royal power through territorial gains and spheres of influence,⁶² but Carol Meyers counters that once David had conquered his territory he needed still other means of persuasion to convince conquered peoples of the legitimacy of his position as ruler of an extended realm. This is why David brought the Ark of the Covenant to Jerusalem.⁶³ Meyers suggests that David did not regard his transfer of the Ark as sufficient itself to promote national unity, and so sought to build a temple for this key cultic object, as per contemporaneous ANE practice.⁶⁴ As temple construction would thus be the expected next step of a new emperor, Walter Brueggemann labels Solomon's temple construction a "generic achievement."⁶⁵ Solomon nevertheless exceeds David's accomplishments by actually engaging in construction.⁶⁶

---

58. Moore, 69.

59. Na'aman, "Rise of Jerusalem," esp. 36, represent the view that one "United Kingdom" consisting of northern and southern tribes was a myth, developed during or after Hezekiah's reign. If he is correct, then Dtr1, working sometime between Hezekiah and the exile, develops the myth by showing that the strong bond between north and south was a feature of Israel's "golden age."

60. Wiseman, *Kings*, 101, 127.

61. As mentioned in chapter 2, Avishur and Helzer, *Administration*, 70–71, have shown that the term בַּת־שְׁלֹמֹה in an administrative context most likely refers to a woman in Solomon's court, whether or not a daughter of Solomon.

62. Malamat, "Political."

63. Meyers, "Temple Builder," 362–63.

64. Ibid., 364.

65. Brueggemann, *Solomon*, 90–91.

66. Meyers, 370–72, offers the interesting proposal that David ordered the census of 2 Sam 24 as a precursor to organizing forced labor for the temple. The pestilence was seen by a reluctant populace as God's retribution for David's intent to draft slaves

Based on extra-biblical ANE comparisons, A.S. Kapelrud and Moshe Weinfeld suggest that Solomon's dream sequence at Gibeon in 3:4–15 was originally a dream in which God either commanded Solomon to build a temple, or approved Solomon's desire to do so.[67] Hurowitz has shown, however, that while such dreams occur with some frequency, a significant number of ANE temple building accounts do not contain a dream or other indications of divine initiative.[68] This leaves us without any evidence that God ever commanded or authorized Solomon's temple construction.

Instead of seeking approval or authority to build, Solomon simply decides that this is what he will do, making his announcement in 5:17–19. This contrasts with David's approach in 2 Sam 7:2, where David seeks the approval of the prophet Nathan. David proposes construction; Yahweh says, "No." Does Yahweh approve of Solomon's decision? First Kings 5 does not tell us; the reader must wait until chapters 8–9 for help in discerning Yahweh's verdict.[69]

Solomon further adds to his rationale for building, however, by explaining in 5:3–4 that his kingdom has achieved peace. Simply building the temple because of Yahweh's promise to David would tend to reduce Solomon in comparison to his father: the temple would result from David's accomplishments, not those of Solomon. Therefore, Dtr1 has Solomon relating that he has, in fact, achieved something that David had not. This "rest" which has been granted him by Yahweh enables Solomon to engage in negotiations with Hiram as an equal.

Power Among Monarchs

As I explained earlier in this chapter, Dtr1's notice of Solomon's marriage to Pharaoh's daughter, a rare achievement of contemporaneous royalty, signals Solomon's international prominence. Dtr1 re-emphasizes Solomon's international acclaim first through continued references to Solomon's relationship with Egypt and Egyptians. Dtr1 specifies that

---

for construction. Second Samuel 24 was moved only later on in the development of the book of Samuel to its present place.

67. Kapelrud, "Temple Building," 56–62; Weinfeld, *Deuteronomic*, 244–54.

68. Hurowitz, *Temple Building*, 165–66.

69. Solomon thus demonstrates the truth of the proverb "it is easier to get forgiveness than to get permission"!

Solomon exceeded "all the wisdom of Egypt" in 4:30 and later describes his trade in Egyptian chariots in 10:28–29. Dtr1's distributed references to Pharaoh's daughter (3:1, 7:8, 9:16, 9:24, 11:1) also keeps the reader cognizant of Solomon's relationship with Pharaoh.[70]

Dtr1 portrays Solomon as surpassing David in their respective relationships with Hiram of Tyre. This is evident at Hiram's first entrance into the Solomon narrative in 1 Kgs 5, which naturally draws comparison to 2 Sam 5:11–12. In 2 Sam 5:12, David understands that he has been elevated to the ruling level when Hiram builds a palace for him. Hiram has the capacity to elevate David, and thus appears as David's superior in the international realm. One might think that, since Dtr1 places Hiram above David, this same Hiram might at least begin interactions with Solomon with superior status to that of David's son. But the portrayal of the relationship between Hiram and Solomon, from their first contact in 5:15–23 through descriptions of their sea trade in chapters 9–10, is consistently one of equals.[71]

The sole exception to the equality of the two comes in 9:10–14, where Solomon bests his ally. Verse 11 introduces to the Solomon narrative the idea that Hiram supplied Solomon with gold, beyond the cypress and cedar specified in chapter 5. To pay for building materials, Solomon hands over twenty "cities" from Galilee. Many commentators read this section as a criticism of Solomon, since he gives over Israelite territory to Hiram, perhaps violating Deut 17:15b, "you are not permitted to put a foreigner over you, who is not of your own community."[72] But as explained in the previous chapter, this passage is actually an account of Solomon getting the better of Hiram in a business transaction. Solomon's success here renders him as, in Brueggemann's words, the "senior party" in the alliance.[73]

---

70. Sweeney, *Kings*, 78–79, finds all five of these references to be "intrusive," thus highlighting their deliberate placement.

71. Cogan, 232–33; Kuan, "Third Kingdoms 5.1;" Nam, *Portrayals*, 82–83. Cogan gives a number of reasons to think that Tyre was the superior power in terms of international commerce and its supply of building timber, while recognizing that Dtr nevertheless portrays the relationship between Hiram and Solomon as one of equality. Kuan, working with LXX^B and LXX^{LUC} which state in 5:1 that Hiram's servants anointed Solomon as king, posits that Solomon was Hiram's vassal. But Nam points out that Tyre's *economic* power did not necessarily translate into the *military* strength needed to establish "overlord" status.

72. Noth, *Könige 1*, 209–12; Jones, *Kings*, 213; Parker, "Repetition," 19–27; Walsh, 122.

73. Brueggemann, *Solomon*, 129.

In 1 Kgs 10, Dtr1 utilizes Solomon's encounter with the Queen of Sheba to establish Solomon as a major international figure beyond the greater region encompassing neighboring Tyre and Egypt. Verses 2 and 10 suggest that the Queen of Sheba carried items which were not typical of Israel; for this reason, a number of scholars conclude that one of the purposes of her visit was to negotiate a trade agreement.[74] Cogan, however, rightly rejects such "historical speculation" as straying from the facts at hand.[75] Würthwein, Fritz, and Walsh, hold that the purpose of this story is, in Fritz' words, to "glorify the unique wisdom of Solomon,"[76] but Mulder and Cogan cite the importance of Solomon's wealth to this section as well.[77]

Adele Reinhartz argues that the narrator presents the Queen of Sheba here as Solomon's full equal. The fact that she can test and judge Solomon's wisdom points to significant wisdom of her own, and, lacking the formal diplomatic tie of marriage, she maintains her own autonomy.[78] Yet other aspects of this narrative point to Solomon's dominance. First Kings 10:1–5 describes a queen and royal retinue designed to impress, and 10:2 suggests that the queen came to Jerusalem prepared to compare her wisdom, and that of her land, with the wisdom of Solomon. "But Solomon answered all her questions" (וַיַּגֶּד־לָהּ שְׁלֹמֹה אֶת־כָּל־דְּבָרֶיהָ). The *hif'il* of נגד, the first word of 10:3, points to the revelation of things unknown (the same word is used in Judg 14:12 to "solve" Samson's riddle).[79] The Queen of Sheba hopes to demonstrate equality, but Solomon proves to have greater wisdom.

First Kings 10:1–10 focuses on Solomon's effect on the Queen of Sheba during her visit. Moore locates three stages in her "education": interrogation, perceptional shift, and affirmation.[80] Solomon thus becomes

---

74. Gray, 259–60; Jones, 221; Ahlström, *Ancient Palestine*, 518–19; Ikeda, "Red Sea Trade," 113–32; House, *Kings*, 156; Brueggemann, *Kings*, 135; Sweeney, *Kings*, 150.

75. Cogan, 315.

76. Würthwein, 120–1; Fritz, 118; Walsh, 126.

77. Mulder, 507; Cogan, 314–15.

78. Reinhartz, *Anonymity*, 72.

79. Fewell and Gunn, *Gender*, 176–77, suggest that we might read 10:3–5 ironically, so that this passage is more about Solomon's need to "show off" than of any real superiority. But if Dtr1 wished to stress Solomon's superiority, the text is quite suitable (as Fewell and Gunn admit on p. 175). We need more evidence for the possibility that an ironic reading is intended, before suggesting that the meaning of this text is ambiguous.

80. Moore, 191–92.

the means for the growth of a foreign ruler, and his ability to answer all questions brought to him demonstrates his superiority to the queen.[81] W.J. Dumbrell argues that this passage has even greater significance, as it serves as the "virtual" endpoint of the Solomon story. All of Solomon's wealth, fame, and wisdom are displayed to the ruler of "perhaps the greatest trading empire of the time," and thus to the world (10:23–24), and "the world in the shape of the queen acknowledges the grandeur and the influence of the Solomonic court (1 Kgs 10:4–9)."[82]

In his encounters with specific foreign figures—Pharaoh, Hiram, and the Queen of Sheba—Solomon negotiates peace without compromising Israelite autonomy. Moore points out that this goes against the trend in the remainder of 1–2 Kgs, in which rulers of Israel and Judah are regularly compelled into disastrous treaty arrangements with foreigners.[83]

Finally, several texts generally reference Solomon's international stature. First Kings 5:10–14 tells us that Solomon's wisdom exceeded that of all the people of the east, that his fame spread throughout all the surrounding nations, and that people came "from all the kings of the earth" to hear Solomon's wisdom. We are then informed in 9:15 that Solomon gained wealth "from all the Kings of Arabia and the governors of the land." First Kings 10:23–24 summarizes this information, telling us he excelled all the kings of the earth in both riches and wisdom. The picture is that of a wise Iron Age monarch who successfully exploits Israel's position between Phoenicia and Arabia.[84] Dtr1 therefore goes to some lengths to provide both specific examples and general information highlighting Solomon's international acclaim.

Power—Building Activity

Dtr1 introduces the issue of forced labor under Solomon in 5:27–32. While some commentators object strongly to Solomon's "forced labor" here, Sweeney seems correct in reading this *corveé* as more a kind of taxation, than of the slavery reminiscent of Israel's experience in Egypt.[85]

81. Brueggemann, *Kings*, 131–32.
82. Dumbrell, *Covenant & Creation*, 155.
83. Moore, 188.
84. Master, "Trade," 508.
85. Sweeney, *Kings*, 103. Brueggemann, *Solomon*, 126–27, offers a particularly negative view of Solomon's actions in 5:13–18, objecting to an "opulent temple . . . built

The *corveé* here seems consistent within the purview of eighth-seventh century Judah: the rapid expansion of Jerusalem toward the end of the eighth century BCE required a substantial number of public workers.[86] In Solomon's case, *corveé* obligations are mitigated by the policy of "one month on, two months off" (5:28); furthermore, the strain on the population seems reasonable when we connect this passage to 2 Sam 24:9: a population of eight hundred thousand men in Israel, and three hundred thousand men in Judah, can easily support a workforce of thirty thousand lumberjacks.[87] The point of 5:27–28, therefore, is not to condemn Solomon for imposing a kind of slavery, but rather to again demonstrate his ability to corral and exercise power.[88]

The Dtr1 source document behind 9:15–23 perhaps gives us the origin of the tradition of Solomon's use of forced labor. Here, the "forced labor" (מַס־עֹבֵד) applies only to Canaanites living in Israel. The LXX here cites Solomon's construction of a wall to keep out the Canaanites; taken together, the LXX and MT suggest that the presence of Canaanite elements in Israel constituted a threat. Solomon thus achieves something by demonstrating his control over the Canaanites. Therefore, Dtr1 cites Solomon's institution of forced labor over Canaanites in order to register a credit to Solomon's reign.[89]

It is the act of building itself that begins to move the narrative in an ominous direction, beginning with 7:1–12a, which, as I suggested in my previous chapter, was moved forward to its current position by

---

on the backs of regimented peasants who had no voice in economic policy." He identifies the appointment of supervisors as reminding the reader of the "harsh, demanding role of supervisors" in Ex 5, calling the whole report "shameless in its economic arrangement."

86. Reich and Shukron, "Urban Development," 213–16.

87. Sweeney, *Kings*, 103–4, argues that the 800,000 figure includes the stonecutter and porters. But to get to his conclusion, one must find that the "one month on, two months off" policy applied to all the workers (not just the log men), an interpretation that seems doubtful from the text. Without significant time off, we would have to question whether an agrarian-based Israel would have sufficient farm workers to plant and harvest sufficiently to maintain a prosperous society.

88. Hurowitz suggests that Solomon sent 30,000 Israelites to Tyre in order to reduce the fees paid to Hiram. This supports Brueggemann's thesis that Solomon increased his wealth through exploitation of cheap labor, while also further demonstrating Solomon's ability to manage substantial building projects. Hurowitz, "Building the First Temple," 290.

89. See Knoppers, *Two Nations*, 1:125 for further response to the idea that 9:15–23 is intended to crticize Solomon.

Dtr2. The reader may well wonder why Solomon needs a new palace, since 2 Sam 5:11–2 and 7:2 have already reported David's palace of cedar ("cedar" being a measure of luxury). Again, Solomon exceeds David by constructing his own palace, instead of using that of his father. Solomon furthermore constructs other buildings: the House of the Forest of Lebanon, the Hall of Pillars, the Hall of the Throne, and the Hall of Judgment. By listing these buildings one after the other, the text creates a picture of a central government complex. Mulder portrays this as "unity of jurisdiction, unity of religion"—Solomon's efforts to centralize religion and government over the whole of Israel, going beyond the temple.[90]

To complete his building projects, Solomon apparently imports an enormous amount of lumber from Tyre. Other ANE texts attest to the high value placed on Phoenician timber throughout the region. Phoenician cedar region was known for its strength, durability, and pleasing fragrance, making it the construction timber of choice.[91] Solomon's acquisition of a large quantity of this prime building material must enhance his stature with readers familiar with the positive qualities of Phoenician cedar.

First Kings 7:9–12a impresses us with the finery of the materials, costly stones and cedar. A little later, 9:15–25 further suggests that Solomon's building activity exceeds what seems to be necessary, as per the reference in 9:19 to "whatever Solomon desired to build." Solomon enhances his power and stature through his building activity and creation of a permanent workforce, but the resulting construction appears to be excessive.

The "House of the Forest of Lebanon" ("HFL") is significant for another reason. First Kings 7:7 reads, "He (i.e., Solomon) made the Hall of the Throne *where he was to pronounce judgment*, the Hall of Justice, covered with cedar from floor to floor" (italics mine). Solomon thus builds the court complex with the intention of executing a juridical role. Dtr1 further implicitly criticizes this arrangement by giving the name of the complex: "House of the Forest of Lebanon." How does the complex come

---

90. Mulder, "Solomon's Temple," 53. Mulder goes on to discuss the Canaanite influences on the temple design. This is significant, however, only to the extent that Dtr1 and his audience were aware of Canaanite origins of aspects of the temple. If Dtr1 was not aware of historical Canaanite architecture, then he cannot be credited with making deliberate references to them.

91. Nam, 77.

to bear a non-Israelite name? The clearest answer is that the buildings were constructed with large quantities of lumber from Lebanon.

Power—Cult Leadership

Finally, Solomon takes on certain cultic responsibilities. John A. Davies notes that in 1 Kgs 8 the sole function of the priests is to transport the Ark and other temple furniture (8:1–11). The priests have no visible role in the sacrifices (verses 5, 14, 62; 63), and it is Solomon, not a priest, who blesses the congregation (verse 14, cf. Lev 9:22–23) and consecrates the temple court (verse 64, cf. Lev 21:23).[92] Cogan notes other examples in the DH of kings performing cultic ritual, including David (2 Sam 6:18), Jeroboam (1 Kgs 12:32), and Ahaz (2 Kgs 16:12–15).[93] We might add David's performance in 2 Sam 24:25 to this list. It is notable, however, that Cogan's latter two examples are those of kings who engage in acts in conflict against the Yahwistic cult: Jeroboam sacrifices to a false god in Bethel, and Ahaz builds an altar modeled on one from Aram. This suggests again that Dtr1 says that Solomon has gone too far in expanding his royal prerogatives. As Norman Habel puts it, "by claiming control over the temple as the sacred center of the empire, the monarch usurps the power of the priests as God's representatives chosen to rule God's people."[94]

Wiseman prefers to interpret 8:62–63 to mean Solomon, along with "all Israel," brought offerings that were then duly sacrificed by the priests. He reads 9:25, which specifies that "Solomon used to offer up burnt offerings and sacrifices," in the same way.[95] Seow suggests further that 9:25 fulfills Deut 16:16–17's stipulation that all male Israelites offer sacrifices at the three annual festivals.[96] Solomon certainly could not have sacrificed 120,000 sheep (8:63) all by himself, and so required logistical help,

---

92. Davies, "New Adam," 48. Römer, "1 Kings 8," 69, attributes vv. 63–64 to P, but does not comment on the statement that it is Solomon, and not the priests, who perform these "priestly" rituals.

93. Cogan, 289.

94. Habel, *Biblical Land Ideologies*, 24.

95. Wiseman, 123–24, 128.

96. Seow, 84; Mulder, *Kings,* 495–97. The concept of the king performing the "priestly" sacrificial function here seems related to 1 Kgs 12:33 and 2 Kgs 16:12–15, where other kings take similar action, although in negative contexts. Solomon thus acts as a king of power, meeting and exceeding the examples of his successors.

priests being the logical assistants. But Dtr1's specific naming of Solomon as the one making the offerings, without reference to the priests in these specific contexts, suggests that, for Dtr1, Solomon has ascended to a higher role than kings usually would or should take in such instances.

Cultic Syncretism

First Kings 7:12b–51 focuses on the construction of the temple and its furnishings, and at the same time highlights Solomon's tendency toward syncretistic behavior. In 7:14, Solomon employs one Hiram of Tyre, rather than an Israelite, to construct temple furniture, thus syncretizing the construction of the objects associated with temple worship. Montgomery and Gehman cite other ancient accounts in which artisans are summoned from foreign lands to work on state buildings;[97] this action by Solomon thus further enhances his international acclaim. The narrator does not make us privy to the names of anyone else involved in temple and furnishings construction and design, except for this Hiram.

Solomon further enhances his royal power through the arrangement of this furniture. While surveys by Elizabeth Bloch-Smith, C. Mark McCormick, and Victor Hurowitz note the absence of royal imagery in the temple and its surroundings,[98] Bloch-Smith shows how Dtr1 describes a building arrangement which demonstrates Yahweh's endorsement of the monarchy. The Bronze Sea of 7:23–26 most likely represents the chaotic forces of nature defeated by Yahweh, as memorialized in passages such as 2 Sam 22:8–16 and Ps 29. After his victory, Yahweh enters his temple, bestowing blessings on king and people which are recorded on the oversized pillars[99] *Jachin* and *Bo'az* (1 Kgs 7:15–22).[100]

---

97. Montgomery and Gehman, 167–68.

98. Bloch-Smith, "Solomon's Temple," 18–31; McCormick, *Palace and Temple*; Hurowitz, "Exalted House."

99. Mulder, *Kings*, 318–20, suggests that these pillars were known "pagan" symbols, indicating their adoption from Canaanite Phoenician use. If so, then they may serve as further examples of Solomon's willingness to syncretize Yahwistic religion.

100. Bloch-Smith, "Symbolism," 27. In support of R.B.Y. Scott's suggestion that these words indicated prophecies of blessings for the royal dynasty, Hurowitz cites an inscription that describes the pillars and their capitals of a new Assyrian temple, in which the pillars are said to bear an inscription commemorating the king's sacrifice. Scott, "Pillars," 143–49; Hurowitz, "Aspects," 83–84.

Dtr1 further stresses syncretism in chapter 10. First Kings 10:11–12 expands on 10:10, describing the foreign wealth and luxuries Solomon is able to acquire from his relationships with Hiram and the Queen of Sheba.[101] House and Walsh highlight the incomparability formulae of verses 10 and 12 to demonstrate that the queen's gifts are modest relative to Solomon's profits from his Red Sea trade of 9:28.[102] Solomon's immense wealth thus enhances his stature, yet at the same time we realize that this amount of wealth has required extensive trade activity with foreigners. First Kings 10:12 further highlights Solomon's willingness to incorporate foreign elements into Israelite worship, as a distinctive foreign wood is used to furnish the temple.

First Kings 10:14–29 summarizes Solomon's wealth and influence. Verse 14 draws together the section 9:10–10:12 in that the weight of Solomon's gold in this verse, 666 talents, approximates the total received by Solomon in 9:14, 9: 28, and 10:10 (660 talents). The remainder of the chapter then focuses on Solomon's wealth, in rather "international" terms: we do not see anything distinctively Israelite in this section. The section twice refers to the "House of the Forest of Lebanon" (10:17, 21), the building named for a foreign place, constructed with foreign materials, and housing the royal treasury of foreign gold.[103]

In chapter 11, Dtr1 ascribes Solomon's downfall solely to religious syncretism fostered by his numerous wives. Solomon's love for Yahweh in 3:3 turns into love for foreign women in 11:1. Solomon's great acclaim is still part of the picture: 700 wives and 300 concubines speak to his enormous power. Nevertheless, verses 1–2 demonstrate that Solomon's accumulation of wives results from his foreign relationships. It is these foreign connections, highlighted by his marriage to Pharaoh's daughter (11:1), which have fostered his downfall, as foreshadowed by the words of the "true mother" in 3:17–18.

The result of syncretism is a loss of power, demonstrated by the rivals who appear in verses 14–40. Edelman notes that Hadad (11:14) and Rezon (11:23, 25) are both introduced as a שָׂטָן, "adversary." Outside of its three uses here, in the DH שָׂטָן appears only in 1 Sam 29:4, 2 Sam 19:23,

---

101. Hens-Piazza, 100, suggests that vv. 11–12 here are meant to qualify the quantity of spices given to Solomon by the Queen.

102. Paul R. House, *Kings*, 162; Walsh, 127–28.

103. Jones, 175, refers to the HFL as an armory, based on the presence of "golden shields" in 10:17. But shields made of gold have more of an aesthetic than practical value, and 10:21 describes other luxury items stored in the HFL.

and 1 Kgs 5:18. In the last of these, Solomon, describing why he is ready to build the temple, states that he has "neither adversary (שָׂטָן) nor evil occurent" (AV). The שָׂטָן is not linked to the loss of land or kingdom, but only to the loss of power and influence.

The prophetic commission which had been given to Solomon at the start, "So Solomon sat on the throne of his father David; and his kingdom was firmly established," (2:12), is entirely undone in 11:11, explicated further in verses 37–38.[104] It is because of Solomon's idolatry that power moves from Solomon to Jeroboam.

De-Emphasizing the Cult

In 1 Kings 8, the temple, host of the Ark of the Covenant (itself nothing more than a box for storing the Torah), becomes the central place for worship in Israel. The temple's dedication stresses its function as a place of prayer. This follows a key idea of the DH as a whole, which de-emphasizes cultic issues and stresses prayer above sacrifice.[105] Other key speeches in the DH reflect this movement. For example, in 1 Sam 12:20–25, Samuel intercedes for Israel through prayer, rather than some other cultic activity, in order to remove the sin of the people. And in 2 Sam 7:19, David responds with prayer, rather than sacrifice, to Yahweh's declaration that he would establish David's line. As per Solomon in 1 Kgs 8, David orients himself toward the place of Yahweh's presence[106] in order to make his supplication.[107] The house of Yahweh is the location where Israel might hope to encounter him, but encounter is effected through prayer.

Dtr1 duly references sacrifices which he encounters in his sources: 3:4–5, 15; 8:5, 63–4; 9:25. And in 8:21, Solomon does cite the temple's function as the resting place of the Ark of the Covenant. Samuel E. Balentine draws attention to Dtr's distinctive theology of the sanctuary: instead of the Ark embodying the divine presence (as implied in the Priestly section 8:1–11), it is merely the name of Yahweh which is placed on the

---

104. McConville, *Earthly Power*, 157.

105. Noth, 89ff; A.D.H. Mayes, *Story of Israel*, 6–7.

106. Firth, *Samuel*, 390, identifes this place as the tent mentioned in 7:2.

107. McCarter Jr., *II Samuel* 209–31, in his discussion of 2 Sam 7, offers an analysis focusing on the permanent setting of the houses of both David and Yahweh. 2 Sam 7 shows that Yahweh will have neither "freedom" to move about, nor "freedom" to choose a new king. The permanent place of Yahweh in Jerusalem makes Jerusalem the place toward which prayers should be directed.

temple.¹⁰⁸ Thus, in Solomon's speech in chapter 8, Dtr1 concentrates on the temple as the focal point of prayer to Yahweh, going so far as to transform the altar from a place of sacrifice into a place of adjuration.¹⁰⁹

First Kings 8 develops this theology further in verses 27–30, beginning with Solomon's rhetorical question and reply, "Will God indeed dwell on earth? Even heaven and the highest heaven cannot contain you, much less this house that I have built!" This section reflects the idea that the attachment of Yahweh's name to the temple is merely symbolic, as Yahweh dwells beyond earthly realms (verse 30). In no sense does Yahweh dwell in the temple. Solomon instead hopes that Yahweh will look toward the temple as the focal point of the prayers of the Israelites (verses 29–30)¹¹⁰, thus reconciling the ideas of Yahweh's absolute transcendence with His dwelling on earth.¹¹¹

First Kings 8 also highlights notions of repentance and forgiveness (סלח, 8:30, 34, 36, 39, 50 (this last belongs to Dtr2)). סלח occurs relatively infrequently in the Hebrew Bible, compared to words that express similar concepts, including נשׂא, עבר, and כפר.¹¹² The paucity of appearances becomes more pronounced in light of the fact that, of its forty-six appearances, five are in 1 Kgs 8, and five more are in the parallel 2 Chr 6. The tendency of סלח to appear in exilic or post-exilic texts leads some commentators to take Solomon's prayer as an exilic or post-exilic composition¹¹³ (but see the previous chapter for my explanation as to why 8:31–40 should be regarded as pre-exilic).

Stamm proposes that the earliest text using סלח is 2 Kgs 5:18, in which Na'aman expresses to Elisha that Yahweh may "forgive" (סלח) him for bowing to another deity in the presence of Na'aman's superior. Na'aman uses סלח in order to communicate the wish that he may be forgiven, the same idea that Solomon puts forth in 1 Kgs 8. Virtually all scholars agree that this occurrence of סלח is part of a pre-exilic Elijah/Elisha cycle. If 2 Kgs 5:18 was part of Dtr1's source material, then Dtr1

---

108. Balentine, *Prayer*, 81–82.

109. Hurowitz, *I Have Built*, 289–90.

110. The only other Hebrew Bible text that refers to the temple as a house of prayer is Isaiah 56:7, usually thought to be post-exilic. Isa 56 of course also opens the temple to foreigners, as per 1Kgs 8:41–43, which I attributed to Dtr2 (see chapter 3). Trito-Isaiah thus draws from the ideas of both Dtr1 and Dtr2 here.

111. Cogan, 292.

112. "סלח", *TLOT*, 798.

113. "סלח", *TDOT* 10:258–65.

probably adopted the term סלח for use in Solomon's speech in 1 Kgs 8. Other passages in the HB which use this word then likely draw on the themes of 1 Kgs 8.

The concept of "forgiveness" as expressed in 1 Kgs 8 fits the progressive deuteronomistic theology of the DH. Dtr's theological expositions in Josh 1, 6, and 23 exhort the Israelites to devote themselves to Yahweh; repentance is not indicated, because Israel had not yet come to a place of rebellion. Judges 2, however, cites Israelite apostasy, and thus the need to repent. First Samuel 12 further develops this idea,[114] and 2 Sam 7:14–15 specifically applies the concept of Yahweh's forgiveness to David's line—especially significant given Dtr1's interest in demonstrating Yahweh's grace afforded to the line of David.[115] Yet it is only with the construction of the temple that Israel gains a fixed location where forgiveness is possible. First Kings 8 thus stresses forgiveness, intertwining this with the more familiar Dtr idea of שוב, "return," in 8:33, 34, 35, 47 (2x), and 48.[116]

Wisdom

As described in the previous chapter, Dtr1 has little to offer regarding Solomon's wisdom, beyond his transmission of older materials. Dtr1's reference to "all his wisdom" in 11:41 signals Dtr1's acceptance of a significant Solomon wisdom tradition, so that Dtr1 duly incorporates the relevant source materials into his work. These passages, including 3:4–15*, 4:29–34, 9:10–14, 10:1–10, and 10:23–25, teach that Solomon's wisdom leads to wealth and fame.[117] The only discernable deuteronomistic editing takes place in 3:4–15 and 10:1, 9, passages which do not challenge the idea that wisdom leads to tangible material benefits.[118]

First Kings 5:9–14 shows that Solomon's wisdom expanded from the legal skill implied in 3:4–15, and the administrative acumen suggested in

114. Wolff, "Kerygma," 87–88.

115. Mayes, *Story of Israel*, 110–11.

116. Wolff, 92.

117. Walsh, 77; Kang, 229–30. While *Elohim* grants wealth and wisdom in 3:12–13, long life depends explicitly on Solomon's obedience. This theological distinction marks 3:14 as Dtr1's addition.

118. Brettler "Structure," 87–97; Porten, "Structure," 97, 127–28. Brettler correctly emphasizes that the 10:1–10 focuses on Solomon's wealth, rather than his wisdom (*pace* Porten). But 10:1–10 also indicates that Solomon's wealth is a product of his wisdom.

4:1–19, to include, in the words of Donald J. Wiseman, "school wisdom of the east."[119] Wiseman notes the *surpassing* (verse 30), rather than simply "bypassing", nature of Solomon's wisdom which draws outside visitors, no doubt including the Queen of Sheba in chapter 10.[120] The phrases in 5:23, תְּבוּנָה הַרְבֵּה מְאֹד, "very great understanding," and רֹחַב לֵב, "largeness of heart," point to the comprehensive nature of Solomon's knowledge, as per the metaphor "as vast as the sand on the seashore."[121] This tradition does not suggest that Solomon created some new form of wisdom, but rather that his wisdom exceeded that of all others.

Dtr1's lack of regard for Solomon's wisdom can be seen in his segregation of the term "wisdom" from his use of the divine name. It is *Elohim* who receives the credit for Solomon's wisdom, not Yahweh.[122] Especially telling are "encomium" passages extolling Solomon's greatness, 5:9 and 10:24. In both cases, as in 3:11–12, *Elohim* grants wisdom to Solomon. This perhaps gives Solomon's wisdom an international flavor, rather than a more "Israelite-specific" wisdom which might be implied if credit went to Yahweh.[123]

Deuteronomistic Ideology

Dtr1 centers his Solomon story on Solomon's prayer of 1 Kgs 8. This becomes particularly apparent when we move 7:1–12 to its original setting after 1 Kgs 8, thus locating "construction" passages both before and after the theological highlight passage of Solomon's reign. The outer passages of 1 Kgs 4–5 and 9:10–10:29 duly describe Solomon's wisdom, wealth, and fame, as per Dtr1's sources. But these things lose their importance in light of the theological teaching regarding the presence of the name of Yahweh in the temple, and Yahweh's maintenance of His covenant with David's line (1 Kgs 8:20–21, 24–27).

Dtr1 begins Solomon's story with his marriage to an Egyptian princess, and ends it by detailing the aftermath of his cultic infidelity brought

---

119. Wiseman, 95.

120. Ibid., 96.

121. Mulder, 146.

122. LXX has κύριος, the usual rendering of יהוה, in 5:9, but the English translations are certainly correct in taking this to be harmonizing.

123. Clements, 33. This plays to the common ANE idea that, while ordinary people must think and observe to gain wisdom, kings are supernaturally endowed.

on by Solomon's marriage to foreigners. Cultic centralization, Yahwistic exclusivity, and the covenant with David are particular interests of Dtr.[124] Solomon's power, along with his wisdom and resulting wealth and fame, are not listed factors in his undoing, just as these things do not especially draw Dtr1's interest in other parts of the DH. Rather, it is apostasy brought on by interaction with foreigners which leads to disaster. As in other parts of the DH, Dtr1 weaves together source material to create a chapter of his monumental history, this one of the powerful, wise, wealthy monarch who manages to construct the temple. But as cultic infidelity had wrecked Israel in the past, the worship of foreign gods destroys Israel again, despite Solomon's unsurpassed wisdom and power.

Conclusions

First Kings 3 sets the stage for Dtr1's Solomon narrative. The *waw*-consecutive at 3:4 unifies 1 Kgs 3:1–15*, marking this entire section as the introduction to Solomon's story. The dream sequence at Gibeon then feeds into the rest of the Solomon narrative. Dtr1 faithfully conveys his received tradition identifying Solomon as the wisest of kings, enjoying the resulting wealth and fame (3:13). But the deuteronomistic features of 3:4–15* reveal Dtr1's desire to develop the narrative to show that Solomon's ultimate success depends on his obedience to law (3:14).

Dtr1 stresses Solomon's political strength, along with the latent dangers of syncretism. The warning against syncretism is a hallmark of deuteronomistic thought: the DH is concerned about a "holy people," in contrast to the priestly view of holy objects and/ or rituals.[125] The themes of power and syncretism are evident in each section of chapters 4–10, except for the absence of references to syncretism in chapter 8. Solomon consistently projects his power throughout these chapters and is always quite willing to work with foreigners. Solomon's wisdom and wealth are certainly present as well, but do not appear as consistently as his power and syncretism. Perhaps most telling, while Dtr1 chronicles challenges to Solomon's power in 1 Kgs 11, he does not mention Solomon's wisdom or wealth at all.

Dtr1's approval of the Davidic monarchy does not necessarily translate into approval of all of Solomon's behavior, even during Solomon's

---

124. Wolff, 87–90; Cross, 278–81; Sweeeny, 25–30.
125. Weinfeld, *Deuteronomic*, 227–32.

successful period in chapters 3–10. Dtr1 regularly cites instances of syncretistic behavior. As it is syncretism that leads to Solomon's downfall, Dtr1 thus foreshadows what will eventually happen. This fits Dtr1's overall message that Judah needs to eliminate its syncretistic elements before it's too late!

Dtr1 evidently inherited traditions about Solomon's wisdom, wealth, power, and perhaps certain syncretistic elements. Presuming that his audience was aware of these traditions, it seems likely that while Dtr1 felt compelled to include all of these in his work (noting in 11:41 that there is more "out there" on Solomon and his wisdom), he elected to profile Solomon's power above all. Thus, Dtr1 is willing to affirm the pre-exilic idea that wisdom leads to material benefits. But while Dtr1 upholds this tradition, his presentation of Solomon as a wise king is clearly subsidiary to his main presentation of Solomon as a king of unsurpassed royal power. Of course, power in itself also does not lead to ultimate success, as David is regularly presented as the standard of excellence to which Solomon must measure up. The David of Dtr1's 1 Kgs 3–11* is not the embattled king of the SN, but is rather the pinnacle of faithfulness among Israelite kings that we see in the remainder of 1–2 Kgs.

For Dtr1, the main danger to Solomon is not power or wealth, but religious syncretism. Solomon's power becomes dangerously great as he moves into the role of judge, and as he intensifies his building activity. These activities make him appear more like a typical ANE monarch and less adherent to Mosaic ideals. The welcoming of foreign elements into Israel is dangerous, and eventually leads to the downfall of Solomon and of the United Kingdom.

5

Themes of the Revolt Narrative

HAVING EXAMINED THE MAJOR ideological features of Dtr1's Solomon narrative, we will move on in chapter 6 to the ideology of Dtr2 as reflected in the Masoretic Text. But before we do so, we need to consider the place of the Solomon narrative within the Deuteronomistic History. Dtr1's Solomon story makes Solomon into the most powerful, most successful of kings. We easily appreciate the heights reached by Solomon and Israel—followed by their downfall. The contributions of Dtr2 are more subtle, however. He keeps the same central story but shifts things to make Solomon darker, and less accomplished. Throughout this book, I've referenced specific passages which work to criticize the monarch throughout 1 Kgs 3–11, mostly the work of Dtr1 and his sources. But to truly appreciate the ideology of Dtr2's Solomon narrative, we need to review the immediately preceding section, inserted only after Dtr1 had completed his work. The Solomon story is the story of Solomon as king. The preceding account, usually called the "Succession Narrative" (SN, usually identified as 2 Sam 9–20 and 1 Kgs 1–2), is also the story of a king, King David. This literary connection invites us to read King Solomon in light of King David. Therefore, to prepare for a new reading of 1 Kgs 3–11, we should identify some major ideas of the SN.

Dtr1's David is the archetype for rulers in Kings. From 1 Kgs 3 onward, David is remembered as the king who consistently obeys Yahweh.[1] His performance is the standard by which the book of Kings evaluates

---

1. First Kings 15:5 notes David's lifelong righteousness "except in the matter of Uriah the Hittite." Since this phrase is absent in the LXX and is without parallel in 1–2 Kgs, it is "universally" considered to be a post-Dtr expansion, as per Cogan, *1 Kings*, 393.

succeeding rulers of Judah. The "righteousness" of some kings of Judah may at times equal that of David, but no one exceeds him. Even Josiah, the greatest of the kings of Judah, who "walked in all the ways of David his father," does not exhibit greater righteousness than David.[2] Most importantly for the Solomon story, David sets the high standard of Torah obedience that Solomon is expected to meet (3:6, 14; 9:4; 11:6). Our evaluation of Solomon depends in part on our understanding of David as the king of unparalleled righteousness.

But the SN tends to portray David very differently. This David is more politically calculating than pious, wielding power in his own interest.[3] A particularly notorious failure occurs in 2 Sam 11, where David commits adultery with Bathsheba, and then has her husband Uriah murdered.[4] But David's poor behavior in the SN extends far beyond this episode. In 2 Sam 13 David proves unable to protect his daughter Tamar from Amnon, and explicitly does not punish Amnon for raping her (13:21). David's failure to maintain a central justice system then becomes the immediate cause of Absalom's revolt (15:2–6). And in the following chapters, David makes many decisions which seem questionable at best, clearly mistaken at worst. Leading up to the battle between the forces of David and those of Absalom, David in 18:1 at first seeks to personally lead his army, but in 18:4 allows himself to be easily dissuaded by "the people" from taking part in the battle. David nevertheless instructs his soldiers in 18:5 to "deal gently" with Absalom, effectively hamstringing the military operation.[5] As the SN proceeds, David appears weaker and weaker with respect to Joab. David's control of his general deteriorates to the point

---

2. 2 Kgs 23:25 describes an incomparable Josiah as follows: "Before him there was no king like him, who turned to the LORD with all his heart, with all his soul, and with all his might . . ." But Knoppers, "Incomparability," has shown that the key term in this verse is the word שׁוב, "he turned." Josiah's unique trait is not his righteousness, but his reforms.

3. Birch, "Samuel," 963; Campbell, 2 Samuel, 101.

4. This episode is the only negative chapter of David's life which finds mention after 1 Kgs 2. 1 Kgs 15:5 references David's sin "in the matter of Uriah the Hittite." Since this phrase uniquely remembers a shortcoming of David and is also absent LXX, commentators universally take it to be a post-Dtr gloss.

5. David appears as a sympathetic figure here, to the point where Campbell, 156–57 suggests that David's behavior may be seen as "pious." But the suggestion of Firth, Samuel, 476, that David's order is really about his personal feelings, seems more likely. Sympathy for David the man cannot overrule an evaluation of David the king, and, as emphasized by Cartledge, Samuel, 596, the instruction to "deal gently" with Absalom makes for a poor motivational speech.

where, in 20:8–23, Joab is able assassinate David's general, Amasa, then ascend to top post in the army himself, apparently with David's assent.[6] By the end of 2 Sam 20, Joab appears to be the de facto strongman of the kingdom, with David disappearing from the narrative entirely after 20:6.[7]

The inclusion of the SN in Dtr1's DH would therefore weaken a central tenet of Dtr1's message, that David's piety sets the standard against which succeeding kings are to be measured. Similar to the argument presented in chapter 3, the importance of David's model reign to the rest of Kings renders implausible that, absent extensive editing, Dtr1 would have permitted such negative portrayals of King David to remain in his work.[8]

The so-called "History of David's Rise" ("HDR", essentially comprising 1 Sam 16–2 Sam 8) of course also frequently places David in a negative light (detailed by Van Seters, building on the work of Halpern and McKenzie).[9] But the adventures of an up-and-coming leader are distinguishable from the acts of an established monarch. Römer notes two theological distinctions which point to Dtr1's utilization of the HDR in his work. First, the HDR repeatedly states that "Yahweh was with David" (1 Sam 16:18, 17:37, 18:12, 14, 28; 20:13; 2 Sam 5:10), so that the divine presence guarantees David's success. Second, by showing the Saulides' and others' frequent expression of submission and love (אָהֵב) to David, the HDR effectively calls the northern tribes to submit to the rule of the house of Judah.[10]

---

6. Halpern, *Demons*, 91 argues that David is responsible for Amasa's death, as this removes his humiliation at having been compelled to take the rebel general as his own. Halpern's interpretation depends on recognizing Joab as David's loyal servant, whereas most commentators view Joab more as a thorn in David's side.

7. Ishida, "Political," 184–85, gives a fuller analysis. Ishida punctuates his conclusions with the observation that the officials' list of 2 Sam 20:23–26, unlike its counterparts in 8:15–18 and 1 Kgs 4:1–6, does not begin with the king, thus suggesting that Joab, first on the list, had gained ruling power.

8. Römer, *So-Called*, 94 suggests that Dtr1 may have included a version of the SN lacking 2 Sam 11–12 and parts of chs. 15–17 and 19. But it is very problematic to find some basis of straining out parts of chs. 15–17 and 19, other than using "David's appearance" as a key. Fischer, *Von Hebron*, undertakes the effort, in doing so eliminating the concepts of a "Succession Narrative" separate from the "History of David's Rise" (roughly 1 Sam 16—2 Sam 5).

9. John Van Seters, *Saga*, 190–206.

10. Römer, 95–96, explains that אָהֵב here has a clearly political meaning, as in Assyrian treaties which refer to the loyalty of a vassal with his suzerain.

More likely, the SN was added to an established text, perhaps even to deliberately weaken the idea of David as the archetypical Israelite king. On these grounds John Van Seters and, more recently, Thomas Römer argue against a pre-exilic DH (roughly equivalent to my Dtr1) containing the SN.[11] Their logic is inescapable: the David of 2 Sam 9–20 and 1 Kgs 1–2 can hardly be reconciled with the royal model of obedience to Yahweh of 1–2 Kgs. Dtr1 could not reasonably have included this passage in his work. Therefore, it was added later, probably by a writer who had a less grand view of the monarchy.

The SN nevertheless retains several strong links to Dtr1's Solomon Narrative. First, the SN and the Solomon narrative are the only parts of Dtr1 which make extensive use of the word חָכְמָה, "wisdom," and deal extensively with the idea of wisdom. The SN has figures described as wise in chapters 13, 14, and 20, and also contains the debate between royal counselors in chapter 17. The Solomon story, of course, contains a number of references to and descriptions of Solomon's חָכְמָה, particularly in chapters 3, 4, 9, and 10.

Second, as Van Seters has shown, 2 Sam 17:5–14 almost certainly depends on 1 Kgs 12:1–20, which in turn depends on 1 Kgs 11. Van Seters demonstrates the similarities between the language and context of 1 Kgs 12:15 and those of 2 Sam 17:14b. Both passages refer to Yahweh thwarting the efforts of royal counselors, so that Yahweh can bring harm to the respective kings. Both kings seek advice from the counselors of their respective fathers, then incorrectly choose counsel based on flattery rather than sound judgment. The major difference between the two passages is in their presentation of "good" versus "bad" counsel. In 1 Kgs 12, the advice of the older men, rejected by Rehoboam, is good both morally and pragmatically. In 2 Sam 17, however, Ahithophel's counsel, rejected by Absalom, is "good" in the sense that his pragmatism is godlike (2 Sam 16:23), but morally reprehensible. Second Samuel 17 becomes a contest between two experienced counselors, with victory achieved through subversion of "good" (practical, though immoral) advice. It is very unlikely that the complex account in 2 Sam 17 was reduced to the much simpler form in 1 Kgs 12.[12]

---

11. Van Seters, "Conflicting;" Römer, 94–95 (for which see footnote 8).

12. Van Seters, 85–86. Van Seters also lists other cases of SN (which he calls the "Court History") dependency on Dtr1 passages, including 2 Sam 20:1 and 1 Kgs 12:16; 2 Sam 16:1–3 and 1 Sam 25:81; 2 Sam 18:19–32 and 1 Sam 4:12–18.

The SN and the Solomon story are also the only two extended accounts of sitting kings in the DH. The textual continuity of these sections, with Solomon immediately following the SN, invites comparison between the two models of kingship. Most noticeable is that Dtr1 presents Solomon above and beyond as a king of strength, whereas the SN exposes David's weaknesses. David in the SN regularly cannot control events around him. This distinction is particularly evident in the relationships between each king and the women in his reign. In chapter 4 I noted that Claudia Camp describes how Solomon "manages" the sexuality of women in his reign, not permitting his Egyptian wife or the Queen of Sheba to exercise undue influence over him. In contrast, David proves unable to prevent the rape of his daughter Tamar or the violation of ten of his concubines (2 Sam 16:21–22), while he is manipulated by the wise woman of Tekoa.

Succession Narrative: Issues

The Solomon story within the DH is easy to define: Solomon enters the picture in 1 Kgs 1, and leaves at his death and summary evaluation at 11:43. While some scholars occasionally advocate somewhat different boundaries,[13] the Masoretic text suggests that 1 Kgs 1–11 should be regarded as a distinct unit. This observation of course does not preclude the possibility that the Solomon narrative was composed in stages! But as it appears in the MT, the Solomon story begins with the intrigue leading to Solomon's ascension, and ends with Solomon's death.

The boundaries for the SN, however, are entirely theoretical. The text itself nowhere marks off the passages commonly assigned to it: 2 Sam 9–20, and 1 Kgs 1–2. It does not comprise the life of any particular individual: while King David is certainly the main character of this section, SN proponents routinely omit 2 Sam 7–8 and 21–24 from the SN, despite David's dominance of these chapters as well. The existence of a SN has nevertheless been accepted by almost all scholars since its proposal

---

13. LXX^{LUC} begins 3 Kgdms with MT 1 Kgs 2:12, at which point Solomon's reign begins. In 1907 H. St. J. Thackery delineated five different LXX translation units in LXX^{B}, including "ββ," which runs from 3 Kgdms 2:12–21:43. On this basis, some scholars prefer to begin their discussion of the Solomon story at 1 Kgs 2:12. However, as I explained in chapter 2, the LXX *Urtext* and the MT diverged early on, so that it is appropriate to study their transmission histories separately. Keulen, *Versions*, 1–20, offers an excellent review of the LXX sections.

by Julius Wellhausen and explication by Leonhard Rost.[14] Walter Dietrich puts it, "to this day, Rost's careful and impressive reasoning has granted his thesis almost canonical standing, at least within German Old Testament scholarship."[15] Nevertheless, there has recently been a good deal of debate about the limits and dating of the SN, and, consequently, its compositional purpose and theological relationship to the rest of the DH.

The remainder of this chapter has two parts. First, I discuss the limits of the SN: its beginning and end. I propose that the SN as generally accepted was actually composed in stages, with a pre-existing 2 Sam 9. Second Samuel 13–20 was composed first, with chapters 10–12 added later, and 1 Kgs 1–2 last. Since, as per Dietrich, the SN is still commonly understood to comprise 2 Sam 9–20 and 1 Kgs 1–2, I follow Marsha C. White in using the term "Revolt Narrative" (RN) to label the shorter portion 2 Sam 13–20.[16] The RN contains all of the above linking features with the Solomon Narrative. Second, I will discuss themes of the RN related to the Solomon narrative. The simple fact that the most extensive chronicles of individual kings of Israel occur in succession invites the reader to compare these two sections of the DH.

A Brief History of Scholarship

Modern study on the SN generally begins with Rost's 1926 work *Die Überlieferung von der Thronnachfolge Davids*, published in English as "The Succession to the Throne of David."[17] According to Rost, the purpose of 2 Sam 9–20 and 1 Kgs 1–2 was to explain how Solomon came to follow David as ruler of Israel. The narrative's key question, "Who shall sit on the throne of David?" find its answer in 1 Kgs 1:30, where David tells Bathsheba, "Your son Solomon shall succeed me as king." This re-

---

14. Wellhausen, *Prolegomena*, 262; Rost, *Succession*.

15. Dietrich, *Early Monarchy*, 232. Other recent proponents include Mayes, *Story of Israel*; Fokkelman, *Samuel* (4 vols.); Anderson (who also includes 2 Sam 1:1—5:10), *2 Samuel*; Mulder, *Kings*; Cartledge, *Samuel*; Sweeney, *Josiah*; Römer, *So-Called*; Sweeney, *Kings*; Wijk-Bos, *Samuel*. Carlson, *David*, offers an important dissent, arguing that 2 Sam gives the account of the reign of King David, with chs. 2–7 describing "David under the Blessing," and chs. 9–24 "David under the Curse." Ackroyd, "Succession Narrative," 383–96, develops Carlson's thesis. Also see Brueggemann, *Solomon*.

16. White, *Elijah*, 146, cited in McKenzie, "Succession Narrative," 124.

17. Rost's SN actually included 2 Sam 6:16, 20–23; 7:11b, 16 as well. See Rost, 87, and the discussion below.

sult is ratified in 2:46b, "so the kingdom was established in the hand of Solomon."[18] Aside from defining the limits and theme of the narrative, Rost drew much attention to its distinctive literary "style," including rich descriptions, heavy usage of metaphors, and a reliance on reported speech above plain narration.[19]

In an important 1944 article, Gerhard von Rad developed Rost's ideas by focusing on the SN's genre and theology. Von Rad accepted Rost's major views on theme and style, presenting the SN as the earliest "history writing" in Israel. Composed during the Solomonic "enlightenment," the SN moves away from ideas like supernatural events, cultic issues, and holy war. Yahweh becomes an unseen force, retreating from "main character" to background.[20] While von Rad argued that the SN was written prior to the composition of 1 Kgs 3–11 (following Roth, von Rad holds that the SN was written during Solomon's reign), he did not attempt to connect themes of the SN to the Solomon narrative. Instead, when von Rad took up 1 and 2 Kings in a 1947 article, he focused on deuteronomistic editing and the lack of it in 1 Kgs 1–2, arguing that deuteronomistic editing was unnecessary in the works dedicated to telling David's story.[21] Yet the concept of Yahweh as an unseen force, rather unconcerned with cultic issues, actually fits the Solomon narrative as well, and forms part of the theological message of 1 Kgs 8.[22]

---

18. Rost, 70. Noth, *1 Konige*, 9–11, suggests that this statement is effectively made in 1 Kgs 2:12, so that 2:13–46a were added by a later editor. The fact that LXX^{Luc} begins a new book here supports this idea. Also see Gray, *Kings*, 16; Mulder, 105–6; Cogan, 175.

19. Rost, 90–104. A notable weakness, however, is that Rost, like most Bible scholars of his time, did not consider the possibility of narrative irony, or that humans in the SN might mis-speak about God. See further Dietrich, 231–2.

20. Von Rad, "Beginnings," 176–204.

21. Von Rad, "Deuteronomic Theology," 216.

22. Von Rad's demonstration that these theological ideas distinguish the SN from the earlier Davidic material is not always appreciated by modern "literary" critics who work with Rost. For example, based solely on his evaluation of Rost's ideas concerning stylistic distinctions, Bar-Efrat, "Rost," 22, definitively concludes that "there is no Succession Narrative." Alter, *David*, xi, also cannot find stylistic distinctions.

Endpoint of the SN

In the 1960s and 70s several scholars questioned the inclusion of 1 Kgs 1–2 in the SN.[23] For example, J.W. Flanagan pointed out that problems in 1 Kgs 1–2 are resolved differently than they are in 2 Sam 9–20. In 2 Samuel, the narrative moves from Mephibosheth to the Bathsheba affair to Amnon to Absalom to Sheba, with plots and subplots often left hanging. While King David is the main character, things are usually resolved outside of the King's will and presence. By contrast, matters in 1 Kgs 1–2 are generally settled by royal edict.[24] Flanagan further notes that the SN compares Absalom not to Adonijah, but to Sheba (2 Sam 20:6), who is not a figure in the succession issue. The two rebellions in 2 Sam 9–20 have in common instead their threats to David, regardless of succession issues.[25]

In a 1981 article, followed by his 1984 commentary on 2 Samuel, P. Kyle McCarter firmly distinguishes the material in 1 Kgs 1–2 from that of 2 Sam 9–20. McCarter sees Solomon as the focus of 1 Kgs 1–2, while the material in 2 Sam 9–20 deals with issues pertinent to the time of David. First Kings 1–2 was composed as a "pro-Solomon description of Solomon's rise, using characters from "pro-David" sections of 1–2 Sam.[26] The author of 1 Kgs 1–2 then inserted into 2 Sam previously composed material which gave background information for key characters of 1 Kgs 1–2, including Joab, Shimei, and Barzillai.[27]

Even more importantly, Gilliam Keys shows in the 1996 publication of her dissertation that the style and structure of 1 Kgs 1–2 is so different from 2 Sam 10–20 that these chapters almost certainly were authored by a different hand than that of the original succession narrative.[28] Keys puts together an impressive list of stylistic arguments supporting her position. First, every action in 1 Kings 1–2 requires about 3–5 verses to describe, whereas the amount of text required for each action in 2 Sam 9–20 varies widely. Second Samuel 9–20 changes pace at key intervals to heighten

---

23. Mowinckel, "Historiography;" Liver, "Acts of Solomon;" Stoebe, "Geprägte;" Flanagan, "Court History;" Brueggemann, "2 Samuel 16:5–14."

24. Flanagan, 174.

25. Ibid., 175.

26. McCarter, "Plots," 355–67; McCarter, *2 Samuel*, 12–14. Also see Knoppers, *Two Nations*, 1:63–64, for ways in which 1 Kgs 1–2 depends on 2 Sam.

27. McCarter, "Plots," 362.

28. Keys, *Wages*, 72–80, argues that the SN actually begins with 2 Sam 10.

the drama: the use of this technique is particularly stunning in the delay between David's sins and his punishment, and the slow pace of David's flight from Jerusalem. Second Samuel 9–20 also features many examples of similes and metaphors, and uses direct speech to convey feelings and emotion. But none of these phenomena are found in 1 Kgs 1–2. Keys further points out that while Robert Alter and J.P. Fokkelman accept 1 Kgs 1–2 as part of the SN, they both unknowingly draw attention to stylistic differences between these chapters and the rest of the SN. Alter cites 1 Kgs 1–2 for containing good examples of the use of repetition;[29] this feature is lacking in 2 Sam 9–20. And while Fokkelman can break down 2 Sam 9–20 into short scenes of a few verses each, he is unable to do so for 1 Kgs 1; for him, the entire chapter is instead one long scene.[30] Fokkelman argues that since Solomon in 1 Kgs 1:1–51 appears consistently as the object rather than the subject of the narrative, this passage must be part of the "history" of David rather than the start of the Solomon story.[31] But Solomon's movement from object to subject in 1 Kgs 1–2 more logically makes these chapters a transitional passage, marking the end of one reign and the beginning of the next. David and Solomon are co-rulers in 1:39–52, but then the author effectively installs Solomon as the new king by transforming him from object to subject. First Kings 1–2 is certainly about Solomon's ascension, but 2 Sam 9–20 comprises drama surrounding the leaders of Israel.[32]

First Kings 1–2 also characterizes Nathan and Bathsheba differently than does 2 Sam 11–12. In 2 Sam 11–12, Bathsheba acts simply as an object, without voice save for two words in 11:5, הָרָה אָנֹכִי, "I'm pregnant." Nathan behaves as a prophet, clearly speaking for Yahweh, yet is called a prophet only once, in 12:25. In 1 Kgs 1–2, Bathsheba finds a significant voice, speaking to David and Solomon in order to persuade. She is approached by David in 2 Sam 11 only as a sexual object and a wife to be comforted. In 1 Kgs 1–2 she plays neither role, but instead appears as a "player" in royal politics, with an extensive speaking role. And while Nathan is referenced as a prophet only once in 2 Sam 12, he is called a

---

29. Alter, *Narrative*, 98–100.
30. Fokkelman, *David*, 345.
31. Ibid., 369.
32. Keys, 43–70, argues that the main theme of 2 Sam 9–20 (or, in her final analysis, 2 Sam 10–20), is the sin and punishment of David as a man. However, as a number of passages go beyond David, we are better off regarding this section as a leadership drama set during David's reign.

"prophet" eight times in 1 Kgs 1, even though he acts more like a royal advisor. Bathsheba and Nathan are certainly drawn from 2 Sam 11–12, but the author of 1 Kgs 1–2 has very different ideas of their roles and characteristics.

Blenkinsopp renews the older position of Wellhausen and Rost that the commonalities of 1 Kgs 1–2 with 2 Sam 11–20 point to their unity.[33] But Blenkinsopp does not consider whether 2 Sam 11–20 (or 2 Sam 13–20) might stand as a completed work on its own. One of the problems is that Blenkinsopp follows Rost's position that the SN first and foremost is the story of how Solomon came to succeed David on the throne of Israel.[34] The problem is that Solomon receives only the briefest of mentions in 2 Sam 12:25, then disappears until 1 Kgs. As per Blenkinsopp, 1 Kgs 1–2 certainly does continue the storyline of 2 Sam 11–20, taking up many of the subplots. But these observations alone do not prove that 2 Sam 11–20 and 1 Kgs 1–2 were composed as part of the same work.

Cogan describes the dependence of 1 Kgs on 2 Sam 9–20 as a "chimera," because it is not until 1 Kgs 1 that the concept of a *succession* narrative becomes apparent. Rost found the theme of his SN in Bathsheba's words if 1 Kgs 1:20, ". . . the eyes of all Israel are on you to tell them who shall sit on the throne of my lord the king after him."[35] 1 Kgs 1–2 certainly depends on characters developed within 2 Samuel and takes up some of its story lines.[36] But the reader will not get the idea that 2 Sam 9–20 is part of a larger "Succession Narrative" without the material of 1 Kgs 1–2.

Starting Point of the SN

The central issue for those who argue against beginning the SN at 2 Sam 9 has simply been the "unsatisfactory nature"[37] of chapter 9 as a starting point. Rost argues that 2 Sam 9 is needed to understand 2 Sam 16:1–4

---

33. Blenkinsopp, "Succession Narrative," 38. As per the title of his article, Blenkinsopp argues that the SN commences with 2 Sam 11.

34. Ibid., 44.

35. Cogan, *1 Kings*, 166.

36. This has been a key argument to those who include 1 Kgs 1–2 in the SN, including Whybray, 8–9, 23–24; Gunn, *David*, 133; Jones, *Kings, Vol. I*, 49; Jones, *Nathan*, 33. 1 Kgs 2 certainly shares thematic links with 2 Sam 9–20, but this observation in itself does not indicate that both were part of the same work. Chapter 6 shows that 1 Kgs 1–2 in fact draws from 2 Sam 11–20.

37. Keys, 74.

and 19:25–30, and given the close connections of the three passages, 2 Sam 9 therefore must be part of the SN.³⁸ Keys, however, points to thematic links between 2 Sam 9 and certain episodes of 1 Samuel, particularly referencing 1 Sam 18 and 20. David's desire to show חֶסֶד ("kindness") to a relative of Saul certainly draws on elements of earlier passages, and 1 Sam 18 and 20, like 2 Sam 9, make significant use of the terms אָכַל ("eat"), לֶחֶם ("bread"), and שֻׁלְחָן ("table").³⁹

However, thematic and linguistic elements of the SN often do tie into earlier aspects of the books of Samuel. For example, אָכַל and לֶחֶם continue to retain significance in 16:1–4, as Ziba appears with food for David's household to eat. The frequency of elements common to HDR and SN is often cited by scholars who deny the existence of a separate SN.⁴⁰ Rost's observations thus do not so much tie 2 Sam 9 to chapters 16 and 19 as demonstrate the latter chapters' reliance on 2 Sam 9.

Keys furthermore discusses the unsatisfactory nature of 9:1 as a beginning for the SN. 9:1 begins abruptly with וַיֹּאמֶר דָּוִד, "and David said," a *waw*-consecutive. She prefers the *waw*-conversive וַיְהִי אַחֲרֵי־כֵן, "and it happened after this," as a more grammatically consistent section beginning.⁴¹ However, Keys also notes the presence of two lists of David's officers ending 2 Sam 8 and 2 Sam 20. She recognizes that these could be structural markers, although she quickly dismisses this possibility on the grounds that these markers alone do not provide evidence for a once-separate work running from 2 Sam 9–20.⁴² Yet 2 Sam 9 constitutes something of a problem on its own: if it is not part of the SN, then it was either part of something earlier, or it was composed as an entirely separate piece.

Fokkelman suggests that the new unit begins at 8:15, as this verse is more strongly connected to verses 16–18 than to verse 14. The proclamation of David as king to administer justice and righteousness works

---

38. Rost, 66.

39. Keys, 78. Auld cites a number of further linguistic parallels between 1 Sam 20 and 2 Sam 9. Auld, *Samuel*, 435–36.

40. Von Rad, "Beginnings," 176–204; Bar-Efrat, "Rost Revisited," 22; Carlson, 50.

41. Keys, 79–80.

42. Keys, 79; Flanagan, 177; Hertzberg, 375. Following Hertzberg, Flanagan also sees the lists as begin and end markers, suggesting that by 20:23–26 the state of David's kingdom has essentially returned to where it was at 2 Sam 8:16–18. But Flanagan does not consider differences between the two lists.

nicely with 8:18b to frame David's officer list.[43] Fokkelman argues for a break between verses 14 and 15 on literary grounds, as the name "David" goes from direct object in verse 14 to subject in verse 15.[44] Fokkelman raises an interesting point, but we must consider the language before verse 14 as well. For example, 8:13a, וַיַּעַשׂ דָּוִד שֵׁם בְּשֻׁבוֹ, "and David made himself a name," and 15a וַיִּמְלֹךְ דָּוִד עַל־כָּל־יִשְׂרָאֵל, "and David reigned over all Israel," look similar. Thus, 15a can just as well be taken as the conclusion to the prior section. Verse 15b, however, begins וַיְהִי דָוִד עֹשֶׂה, "and it happened that David did...", thus beginning with a *wayehi* clause which often starts a new section in the DH.[45] Therefore, grammatically, 8:15b serves quite well as the start of the introduction to 2 Sam 9.

Second Samuel 8:15b continues עֹשֶׂה מִשְׁפָּט וּצְדָקָה, "doing righteousness and justice." This phrase appears twenty-five times in poetic texts, but only two other times in prose, Gen 18:19 and 1 Kgs 10:9.[46] In Jeremiah, this ideal becomes a standard by which kings are judged (Jer 22:3, 15; 23:5; 33:15).[47] In the DH the legendary David and Solomon are the only kings who manage to accomplish this ideal. David and Solomon are also the only kings for whom Dtr presents officers. As Na'aman notes, the officer lists certainly cannot be authentic[48], which highlights the question: what is their purpose? Following 2 Sam 8:15b, the list of 8:16–18 serves to explicate a clear delegation of authority, in line with earlier ideals expressed in Ex 18, Num 11, and Deut 1. These passages show that a leader does "justice and righteousness" by setting up a bureaucracy to supply local leaders.

A second way in which a ruler may seek to establish justice and righteousness is to show mercy and grace to one's defeated adversaries. This is what David does after establishing his bureaucracy: he searches for remaining descendants of Saul's family וְאֶעֱשֶׂה עִמּוֹ חֶסֶד "... that I may do good to him." While 2 Sam 9 has traditionally marked the start

---

43. Fokkelman, *Throne*, 262.

44. Ibid., 261.

45. Keys makes this general point in her discussion of 2 Sam 9 but does not test it against 2 Sam 8:15b. See Keys, 80. See also Waltke and O'Connor, who cite Wolfgang Schneider's contention that וַיְהִי often serves an "introductory and transitional" means of breaking up narrative. Schneider, *Grammatik*, 261, cited in Waltke and O'Connor, *Syntax*, 634.

46. Fokkelman, *Throne*, 262n.

47. Auld, *Samuel*, 431.

48. Na'aman, "Book of Kings," 131–32.

of the SN, David's reference to Jonathan at the end of 9:1 more closely connects this passage to David's friendship with Jonathan in the "History of David's Rise" ("HDR," usually thought to run from approximately 1 Sam 16—2 Sam 5[49]), particularly 1 Sam 18–20. Jonathan is not mentioned after 2 Sam 9; in 2 Sam 19:24 Mephibosheth is "grandson of Saul." Jonathan in 1 Sam 20:14–16 alludes to his own untimely death, compelling David to swear to maintain Jonathan's family name after David has become king. Second Samuel 9 reflects David's fulfillment of his promise, and thus belongs to the HDR.[50]

Furthermore, as von Rad, Keys, and others point out, the SN is very much about David's weakness.[51] The David of the SN is frequently indecisive, appearing unable to alter the course of events as they unfold about him. This is one factor in Keys' decision to begin the SN at 2 Sam 10, since in 10:1–5, David suffers insult but appears powerless to respond.[52] This presentation of David starkly contrasts with his depiction in 2 Sam 9, in which he is very much in control of events.[53]

Campbell reads 2 Sam 9:1—11:1 and 12:26–31 as a pair of "anticipatory appendices": the strong ties between 2 Sam 9 and 1 Sam 18–20, the difference in David's character between 2 Sam 9 and 2 Sam 11–20, and a shift in "literary style" between 2 Sam 9–11:1 and what follows, all point to a break between 11:1 and 11:2.[54] The narrative of 10:1–11:1 and 12:26–31 was apparently moved from its original position prior to 2 Sam 8:15, in order to give historical context to the story of David and Bathsheba.[55]

---

49. McCarter, *1 Samuel*, 26–30. McCater's HDR runs from 1 Sam 16:14—2 Sam 5:10.

50. Ackroyd, "Succession," 390; Van Seters, *Saga*, 280–82.

51. Von Rad, 182; Keys, 142.

52. Keys, 125, 143.

53. David is so much in control that commentators often attribute various nefarious motives to David's actions. For example, Gunn, 96–97, and Auld, 436–37, read 9:10 to say that Saul's estate pays for Mephibosheth's provisioning at David's table. But McCarter, *II Samuel*, 262, explains that the superior LXX clearly shows that it is David who pays for Mephibosheth's support, as per David's sentiments in 9:1, 3, and 7.

54. Campbell, 88–91.

55. As per Rost, 60–62, who argued that it was only 10:6b ("the sons of the Ammonites sent and hired . . .")–11:1 and 12:26–31 which were intended to form the David-Bathsheba backdrop. Rost argued that 10:1–6a was originally part of the pericope begun in 9:1. However, 2 Chr 19:1–6a follows 2 Sam 10:1–6a, without mention of David's encounter with Mephibosheth prior.

Second Samuel 11–12

The next issue to consider is the relationship of 2 Sam 11–12 to chapters 13–20. While Brueggemann, for example, plainly identifies chapters 11–12, 13–14, 15–20, and 1 Kgs 1–2 as different "sections" of the SN,[56] the links between 13–14 and 15–20 are much stronger than those between any of the others. Charles Conroy, seconded by McCarter, stresses Absalom's central role in chapters 13–14: the first scene in these chapters opens and closes with him (13:1, 22), and the three time-indications in chapters 13–14 (13:23, 38; 14:28) all relate to Absalom.[57]

Rost acknowledges a key thematic difference between chapters 13–20 and 11–12, in that chapters 13–20 serve as background to the succession, while chapters 11–12 describe a succession which actually took place.[58] Von Rad similarly points to a major break between chapters 12 and 13.[59] Whybray accepts the unity of chapters 11–20, but notes that the oracle of Nathan in 2 Sam 12, which appears from 12:1 to have been conveyed to David through cultic means, "is the one great exception to the general rule" in the SN that Yahweh does not work through the cult.[60] Charles Conroy goes so far as to simply declare that since 2 Sam 13–20 has a relatively independent narrative identity, it can be legitimately studied on its own.[61]

Commentators often follow Rost's idea that the Ammonite Wars of 2 Sam 10:1–11:1, 12:26–31 serve as the framework to the David and Bathsheba story.[62] But the Ammonite War story works quite well without the David and Bathsheba intrusion, as we see in the parallel 1 Chr 19:1–20:3.[63] Rost likely did not consider 1 Chr because he was work-

---

56. Brueggemann, "Trust and Freedom," 6.
57. Conroy, 92; McCarter, *II Samuel*, 327.
58. Rost, 73.
59. Von Rad, 181.
60. Whybray, 68–69.
61. Conroy, 6.
62. Rost, 73–74.
63. Some commentators point to 2 Chr 20:1, which parallels 2 Sam 11:1, ("in the spring of the year, the time when kings go out to battle, David sent Joab with his officers and all Israel with him; they ravaged the Ammonites, and besieged Rabbah. But David remained at Jerusalem), as evidence that Chronicles "edited out" the David and Bathsheba story. But McKenzie, "2 Samuel 11:1," argues that this verse is not at all negative toward David. It instead is an integral part of the Ammonite War account (although in 2 Sam 11:1, it certainly becomes part of the David & Bathsheba story as well).

ing under the then-widely-held idea that Chronicles was based on MT Samuel. However, most scholars today take the position that Chronicles was based on a Samuel *Urtext*, rather than the MT or LXX.[64]

Rost includes 2 Sam 11–12 in his SN for two reasons. First, he specifies a number of connections of characters and plot between 2 Sam 11–12 and 13–20.[65] However, Steven McKenzie argues that while chapters 13–20 feature strong connections to chapters 11–12, these connections are unidimensional: nothing in chapters 13–20 presupposes 2 Sam 11–12.[66] Second, Rost further delineates connections between 2 Sam 11–12 and 1 Kgs 1–2. But this argument is obviated by Keys' demonstration that 1 Kgs 1–2 was written subsequent to her SN.[67]

Rost and others highlight the SN's use of "numerous, striking images, which are scattered about like flowers on the meadows."[68] Rost lists a number of them, including some colorful hyperbolic metaphors. As Rost puts it,

> People are like water poured out on the earth which cannot be stopped from flowing away (14:14). David is like an angel of God (14:17, 20; 19:28). Ahithophel hopes to bring the people to Absalom like a bride to her husband (17:3).[69] His advice is as an oracle from God (16:23). David is as strong and angry as a wild bear robbed of its cubs (17:8). He is like 10,000 of his warriors (18:3). A brave soldier has the heart of a lion (17:11). Israel is as numerous as the sand by the sea (17:11).[70]

Notably, none of these images come from chapters 10–12. Rost's only example from these chapters is 11:21, where the author compares the death of Uriah to that of Abimelech ben Jerubaal.[71] But this is more historical comparison than hyperbolic metaphor. Given the elements

---

64. Klein, *1 Chronicles*, 26–44. Klein offers a thorough analysis of the specific issues leading to this assessment.

65. Rost, 76–77.

66. McKenzie, "Succession Narrative," 133–34, actually holds that 2 Sam 11–12 postdates 1 Kgs 1–2 as well.

67. Keys, 70.

68. Rost, 92.

69. This metaphor appears in LXX, not MT, and the LXX is doubtful, as Ahithophel's speech is otherwise devoid of such metaphors. See Caquot and Robert, *Samuel*, 537.

70. Rost, 92.

71. Ibid.

of the David-Bathsheba episode, including adultery, intrigue, murder, exposure, retribution, and repentance, the author certainly had opportunity to construct hyperbolic metaphors for this account. But he does not do so. This stylistic difference suggests that the author of 11:2—12:25 is different from that of 13–20.[72]

McKenzie compiles a list of instances in 1–2 Samuel in which the author defends David from wrongdoing in connection to unfortunate episodes which occurred with David nearby. Where other commentators, including McCarter, have shown that the HDR serves this "political" purpose, McKenzie extends this aim to the SN as well.[73] Among other episodes, McKenzie includes the convenient deaths of Nabal, Saul, Abner, and Ishbaal.[74] This list renders unique 2 Sam 11:2–12:25, which unambiguously charges David with willful adultery and premeditated murder. The narrator's treatment of David's actions in this section is so different from that of the rest of the SN and 1–2 Sam in general that it points to a different author altogether.

McKenzie argues that 2 Sam 11–12 was written later than 1 Kgs 1–11. He observes that the characterizations in 1 Kgs 1–2 of Bathsheba and Nathan do not presuppose their presence as described in 2 Sam 10–12, citing Bathsheba's introduction as "Solomon's mother" in 1 Kgs 1:11. However, once we've concluded that 1 Kgs 1–2 was written after 2 Sam 13–20, we see that its major characters—David, Adonijah, Nathan, Benaiah, Joab, Abiathar, and Shimei—are drawn from 2 Sam. The only exception is Abishag, who gets a thorough introduction in verses 1–4. Even more, the author of 1 Kgs 1–2 draws on prior relationships, developing rivalries between Abiathar and Zadok, and between Benaiah and Joab. Thus, conversations between Nathan and Bathsheba seem more plausible if the reader understands that the two have a prior history. If 1 Kgs 1–2 pre-dates 2 Sam 10–12, then Bathsheba becomes a brand new character, brought in without introduction, contrary to the

---

72. In arguing vs. the existence of a succession narrative, Bar-Efrat, "Rost," 16, notes that since most of the above metaphors occur in the speeches of the wise woman of Tekoa and Hushai the Arkite, this type of metaphor should be viewed as a characteristic of two particularly persuasive speakers, rather than characteristic of the author's style. Bar-Efrat then goes on to list other examples of metaphor in 1 Sam 25, to show that this style is not necessarily uncommon. But 2 Sam 16:23 and 19:28 also contain this type of metaphor, which is entirely absent in 11:2–12:25.

73. Van Seters, *History*, 268; McCarter, *I Samuel*, 27–30.

74. McKenzie, "So-Called," 127–28. See also Halpern, *Demons*, 73–93, and Heym's classic novel *David*.

general approach of the author of 1 Kgs 1–2. Therefore, 1 Kgs 1–2 was most likely composed after 2 Sam 11–12, rather than before.

Revolt Narrative Themes

This leaves us the single unit 2 Sam 13–20, the "Revolt Narrative" (RN). Several key themes of the RN impact the way 1 Kgs 1–11 is to be read. The first of these themes, "David's inability to manage women," draws a direct contrast with Solomon and is especially apparent in the episodes in which the two monarchs relate to women. The contrast between David and Solomon becomes particularly apparent in 1 Kgs 1–2. The second theme is the idea of wisdom as persuasion, focusing on the adjective חָכָם ("wise") and the noun עֵצָה ("counsel"). This "wisdom" of the RN is distinct from the wisdom associated with Solomon, in which knowledge leads to wealth and acclaim. This new (to the DH) concept of wisdom finds voice in ironic usages in 1 Kgs 1–2, and Dtr2's version of the DH. The third and fourth themes, "the king as poor judge" and "the folly of the people" also become effective ideas for Dtr2's version of 1 Kgs 1–11.

RN Theme 1: King David's Poor Management of Women

As I explained in the previous chapter, each section of the Solomon narrative presents Solomon as a strong, effective leader, who consistently accomplishes his will. Solomon's goodness and fidelity to Yahweh may at times be questionable, but there is never a question about Solomon's control of his kingdom. In contrast, the David of the RN often cannot manage events around him. The central plots, Absalom's rebellion followed by that of Sheba, point to a kingdom which is dysfunctional at its core. But even beyond the specific unfolding of the revolt, David acts weakly.

We can appreciate the contrast between Solomon and David most directly by looking at the relationship of the two kings toward women. The RN and Solomon narratives (during Solomon's period of success, 1 Kgs 3–10) each contain three examples of the king's interaction with women. Solomon manages the movements of his Egyptian wife (especially in 1 Kgs 3:1 and 9:24), marries off two "daughters" to district governors (4:11, 15), and displays superior wisdom over the Queen of Sheba during her visit (10:1–10). In the RN, David instructs Tamar to visit her brother Amnon, finds himself deceived by the wise woman of Tekoa, and directs ten of his concubines to remain behind in danger when he flees Jerusalem at Absalom's revolt. In the Solomonic narratives, Solomon maintains his position of authority and influence, while David displays an inability to deal well with the women in his life.

David's initial RN interaction with women appears in 13:7, when he instructs Tamar to go to her brother Amnon's residence to give him food. David here is responding to Amnon's request that Tamar prepare (תְלַבֵּב) two hearty-dumplings (לְבִבוֹת), a request with seductive undertones. David, however, fails to realize the danger of Amnon's request, and simply grants it, only changing the words to the non-sexually-charged עֲשִׂי־לֹו הַבִּרְיָה (prepare food for him) in 13:7. David in fact chooses the same noun and verb used by Jonadab in verse 5, giving no apparent attention to the implications of Amnon's words. While commentators generally describe David as "unwitting," it is clear that David was presented with signs of Amnon's intentions, and ignored them.[75] Furthermore, when David hears of Amnon's crime, he takes no action whatsoever, public or private, another mark of indecision.[76] Perhaps worse, David does nothing for his daughter Tamar, who remains "desolate" in her brother Absalom's house (13:20).

David next encounters a woman in the RN when he hears the plea of the wise woman of Tekoa. David proves to be an inadequate judge. He is entirely unable to see through the woman's ruse, only sensing Joab's involvement after the woman has revealed the meaning of her story. David is fooled by the Tekoa woman, manipulated into giving orders which cannot be carried out.

David's third interaction with women in the RN occurs in the broken story of 2 Sam 15:16, 16:21–22, and 20:3. In 15:16 David leaves ten of his concubines in his palace when he flees Jerusalem, and in 16:21–22, Absalom, on the advice of Ahithophel, has sexual relations with these women.[77] The presence of הַבַּיִת in each of these passages underscores David's loss of control of his private affairs. As Ken Stone puts it, "as all Israel can see, David has been unable to maintain control over sexual access to

---

75. Conroy, 18; Gunn, 9; Rosenberg, 146; Alter, 267. Reis, 179, assesses David's behavior even more negatively.

76. Rosenberg, 146–47, draws attention to David's unusual form of anger (13:21) which evidences itself neither publicly *nor* privately.

77. Carlson observes that David left the concubines to keep "the house" (הַבַּיִת), which he takes to be a deuteronomistic fulfillment of Deut 28:30.

the women of his house, and so has failed with regard to what is, in many cultures, a critical criterion for the assessment of manhood."[78]

David's troubles here stand in contrast to Solomon, who successfully manages his household until his fall in 1 Kgs 11. Solomon's marriage to Pharaoh's daughter in 1 Kgs 3:1 represents a disturbing threat to his fidelity to Yahweh, but the author of the Solomon story carefully controls the queen's movements in 3:1, 7:9, and 9:24. Solomon further remains in command during his encounter with the Queen of Sheba in 1 Kgs 10:1–10.[79] And while David is unable to protect his daughter, the "incarnation of the status of his household,"[80] Solomon effective utilizes his "daughters"[81] to help him to manage his empire by marrying them to regional governors. This distinction highlights Solomon's power and David's relative weakness.

RN Theme 2: Wisdom as Persuasion

The adjective חָכָם, "wise," appears five times in the SN/ RN: 2 Sam 13:3, 14:2, 14:20, 20:16, and 20:22. The noun form חָכְמַת also appears in 14:20. In 14:2 and 20:16, חָכָם describes anonymous women who negotiate with powerful figures in order to preserve life. In 20:22 חָכָם describes a plan which saves the city of Abel Beth Maacah. Its use by the wise woman of Tekoa in 14:20, מַלְאַךְ כְּחָכְמַת חָכָם וַאדֹנִי, "and my Lord is wise, like the wisdom of the angel of God," appears to be a strategic description of King David, in which the king certainly does not appear to be wise. And חָכָם first appears in the RN in 13:3, where it is applied to Jonadab, David's nephew and the רֵעַ, "friend" of the crown prince Amnon.[82]

The presence of wisdom is also apparent in passages in 2 Sam 15–17 which feature the royal counselors Ahithophel and Hushai. While these men and their words are never described with the word חָכָם or its

---

78. Ken Stone, *Sex*, 121.

79. As demonstrated in the previous chapter.

80. Matthews and Benjamin, *Social World*, 181.

81. While the term in 4:11, 15, בַּת שְׁלֹמֹה "daughter of Solomon," is likely a political term (as discussed in chapter 3), the notion of these women as representatives of Solomon's household, as in Matthews and Benjamin, still seems valid.

82. Nili Sacher Fox questions whether רֵעַ represents a court position in this context. רֵעַ is nevertheless an official position in 1 Kgs 4:5, and the fact that Jonadab appears to play the role of court official later in the chapter suggests that he had a court function, perhaps originally as attendant to the crown prince. Fox, *Service*, 122.

derivatives, these chapters focus squarely on the issue of good counsel. Ahithophel and Hushai are invited to give their opinions precisely because their recommendations are presumed to be wise.

The Solomon Narrative attributes several different types of wisdom to King Solomon, including the ability to do justice, administrative and business acumen, composition of wise sayings, and knowledge of the natural universe. The RN, however, describes a particular category of wisdom, which, paradoxically, is distinct from the types of wisdom attributed to Solomon. Wisdom in the RN indicates the ability to do what is called for to achieve a short-term objective. The RN is particularly interested in the use of language to persuade. The RN consists of a mere eight chapters, yet no fewer than five of its characters are either described as חָכָם, "wise," or can fairly be said to be wise. All of these demonstrate mastery in the art of persuasive language.

Jonadab

In 2 Samuel 13:3, Amnon's רֵעַ, "friend," Jonadab, is introduced with the adjective חָכָם. While the text is not explicit, Amnon as oldest son is the presumed crown prince.[83] English translations render the other RN instances of ⊠akam as "wise" yet regularly look to some other word to describe Jonadab. Thus, we have "crafty" (NRSV, ESV), "subtil/subtle" (AV, JPS), or "shrewd" (NAS, NIV). These translations apparently look ahead to the story, where Jonadab's words lead to Amnon's rape of David's daughter Tamar. They may be looking backwards as well to Gen 3:1, in which the serpent is described as *arum*, a word which tends to match the translation of ⊠akam here: crafty in the NRSV, subtle in the KJV/JPS. Also in 13:3 Jonadab's wisdom takes the modifier מְאֹד, "very", which usually functions as an intensifier, but really cannot be said to alter the fundamental meaning of the word with which it is paired.[84] So it is most consistent to describe Jonadab as "very wise."[85]

---

83. Matthews and Benjamin, 181, suggest that Amnon's rape was a political maneuver, symbolizing his control over the household of his rival Absalom (who is expressly identified in 13:1, 4). While events of the chapter do not explicitly rule out this possibility, David's anger in 13:21 suggests that Amnon hurt his case for succeeding David more than he helped it.

84. Waltke and O'Connor, *Syntax*, 268n, note that the range of meaning goes beyond "very," but in this case, intensification seems appropriate.

85. So McCarter, 314; Alter, 266; Auld, 473.

Second Samuel 13:1–22 gives the account of Amnon, who is in love with his half-sister Tamar. Because Tamar is also the daughter of King David, Amnon cannot romance her, and so "makes himself ill" (13:2). Jonadab advises Amnon to appear sick before King David, then ask the king to instruct Tamar to prepare food for Amnon in Amnon's home. David does so, giving Amnon the opportunity to have his way with Tamar.

Commentators often condemn Jonadab for his advice to Amnon in 13:5, in which he persuades Amnon to "feign" sickness.[86] But Jonadab's advice is actually quite plain and open. He instructs Amnon to lie on his bed and הִתְחָל, the *hithpa'el* form of חָלָה, "become weak, tired." Waltke and O'Connor identify the use of the *hithpa'el* in verse 5 as an example of an "estimative-declarative reflexive," denoting "esteeming or presenting oneself . . . without regard to the question of truthfulness."[87] Yet Jonadab cannot logically be suggesting that Amnon *feign* illness, as Amnon had already "made himself ill" (לְהִתְחַלּוֹת) in verse 2. Amnon is "lovesick," but he is nevertheless ill: indeed, it is Amnon's sickly (דַּל) appearance in verse 4 which has drawn Jonadab's attention in the first place.

Appearing to be sick may not seem like a good idea to Amnon.[88] First and Second Samuel portrays kings and potential kings (Saul, David, Absalom) in glowing physical terms. And the RN proceeds after chapter 14 as if Absalom is a potential heir to the throne, even though 2 Sam 3:3 mentions a son ahead of Absalom, Chileab (כִּלְאָב, "sickly"). Chileab does not appear in the text after 3:3; instead, Absalom, and later, Adonijah, appear to be next in line for the throne after Amnon.[89]

Jonadab's position as Amnon's רֵעַ gives Jonadab the means to understand the truth of Amnon's condition. Jonadab's advice in verse 5, then, is simply that Amnon reveal to his father David that he is ill, but in a private setting, away from court. In that context Amnon can ask his father to send Tamar to visit him and prepare food for him. The *hithpa'el* of חָלָה in

86. See also Anderson, 174; Fokkelman, *David*, 104; Rosenberg, *King and Kin*, 140-2; Gordon, "Divided," 97; Cartledge, *Samuel*, 535.

87. Waltke and O'Connor, 430-1.

88. Rosenberg, 140-43, develops the idea that if Amnon was merely a candidate for the throne, rather than crown prince, then he likely faced heightened pressure to present himself as healthy and emotionally stable.

89. Names based on roots indicating poor health also occur in Ruth 1:2, where Elimelech's sons מַחְלוֹן, "Mahlon" and כִּלְיוֹן, "Chilion," suggest respectively "pining away" and "sickly." The similarity between "Chlion" of Ruth 1:2 and "Chileab" of 2 Sam further suggests that giving the name "Chileab" to David's second son in 2 Sam is done to indicate an untimely passing, rendering Absalom next in line to the throne after Amnon.

verse 2 clearly does not indicate deception, so the same stem of the same word in 13:5 also should not be taken to indicate deception. Instead, the "estimative-declarative" sense of הִתְחָל has Amnon presenting his true condition, no longer hiding the illness evident in verses 2 and 4.[90]

Jonadab thus recommends words which will affect Amnon's immediate goal, a private encounter with Tamar. Jonadab's advice does not work out in the long run, however, as it leads to disaster for all. An act of rape certainly cannot help Amnon beyond immediate gratification, so Jonadab's plan ultimately harms his patron. Jonadab's wisdom, therefore, is not part of the big picture but rather is confined to an immediate episode.

Jonadab's short-view wisdom is further apparent in his only other appearance in the Hebrew Bible, later in 2 Sam 13. Two years after Tamar's rape, Absalom assassinates Amnon in the presence of all the king's sons (13:23-29). A report then comes to David and his court that all of the king's sons had been killed (13:30). Jonadab, however, realizes that Absalom has taken his revenge against Amnon only, drawing attention to the fact that this was the result of Amnon's rape of Tamar. Jonadab reassures the king that his other sons are alive and well, preventing a general panic (verses 32-35).[91] Absalom's actions do not constitute the beginnings of a larger conflict; Jonadab explains that Absalom's action simply represents one man's revenge on another. Jonadab thus gives sound, helpful advice, carefully choosing the words which will serve the immediate interests of his patron (here, David).

Wise Women

The other characters of the RN who are explicitly described as "wise" are anonymous women, the woman of Tekoa (2 Sam 14:2-20) and the woman of Abel Beth Maacah (20:16-22). The narrator never spells out

---

90. Campbell, 128, agrees that since the NRSV does not use "pretend" in v. 2, it should avoid that connotation in vv. 5-6. Conroy, 29; Fokkelman, *David*, 104; and Alter, *The David Story*, 265-66, pick up on the fact that vv. 2 and 5 feature the same term for being ill, but nevertheless insist that Jonadab advises Amnon to make a pretense.

91. Weeks, *Wisdom*, 77, following ideas of Whybray, *Intellectual*, 90, distinguishes between the "non-professional and ultimately disastrous" advice Jonadab gives in 13:5, and the "sensible and perceptive" counsel he renders in vv. 32-33. Only the former is associated with his "wisdom." But why should the reader associate his characteristic of wisdom with the advice of v. 5 only, rather than with the individual throughout his appearance in this chapter?

exactly what makes these women wise. The contexts of the two passages, however, show that both are able to negotiate effectively: the woman of Tekoa gains protection for her (fictitious) son and in reality restores Absalom to David's court, while the woman of Beth Maacah prevents the destruction of her city.

Claudia Camp portrays these women as emblematic of an early female leadership figure in Israel, which existed perhaps through the reign of David, but no later.[92] Camp reasons that the wisdom of these women comes from village and tribe, since the (minimal) descriptions afforded these women suggests that they would have had little contact with the king's court.[93] Yet the contexts suggest otherwise. The wise woman of Tekoa is somehow known to Joab, which indicates in itself that she was a person of some importance. The fact that Joab has selected her for the purpose of persuading the king to take a particular course of action indicates that he had reason to believe that she would be capable within a royal court setting. Her task is challenging, yet she exhibits sufficient court skills to get the job done.[94]

The wise woman of Abel Beth Maacah also displays more than tribal or village wisdom. She appears to have been designated spokesperson for the village: she clearly has influence, as she is able to convince her city to execute a person who had been granted refuge.[95] 2 Sam 20:17 particularly demonstrates her diplomatic mastery: by publically verifying Joab's identity and exhorting him to listen to her, the wise woman draws the soldiers' attention away from their siege works to her presentation of the appropriateness of Joab's actions.[96] After she makes her case, it will be difficult for Joab to persuade his men to take action which they may regard as unjust (cf. 18:12 and 20:12).

Geyer highlights the particular aptness of the wise woman's response and action in verses 21b–22. Joab orders the city of Abel Beth Maacah

---

92. Camp, "Wise Women," 195.

93. Ibid., 197.

94. Auld, 496.

95. Geyer, "2 Samuel 20:13–22," 34, suggests the designation "wise" here serves as a title for a leadership position.

96. Aschkenasy, *Window*, 98–99, argues that something about this woman, perhaps some distinctive clothing, must have drawn Joab close to the wall, particularly in light of Joab's imagined exchange with David in 2 Sam 11:21. This would testify to the status of the wise woman in Ancient Israel. But Darr, "Abel," 107, points out that overall evidence for this idea is lacking.

to surrender Sheba; but the wise woman instead says that she will have him killed in Abel. The distinction defines the relationship of Abel (and, by extension, Israel) to David's kingdom. Joab's terms would make Abel a conquered people: they will have surrendered to Joab's demands. But by executing Sheba directly, Abel repudiates the northern secession by demonstrating that they have denied Sheba refuge. As per the wise advice of Ahithophel in 17:2b-3, civil war may be avoided through the death of a single individual—David in chapter 17, Sheba here.⁹⁷

The accounts of the wise women of the RN share further similarities which distinguish them from the mother of 1 Kgs 3. Each of them appeals to a wise saying to make their point. In 2 Sam 14:14, the wise woman of Tekoa tells David, "We must all die; we are like water spilled on the ground, which cannot be gathered up. But God will not take away a life; he will devise plans so as not to keep an outcast banished forever from his presence."⁹⁸ Similarly, 2 Sam 20:18 says of the wise woman of Abel Beth Maacah, "Then she said, 'They used to say in the old days, "Let them inquire at Abel"; and so they would settle a matter.'" The women use language to appeal to higher ideals in order to make their respective cases.

חָכְמָה in Dtr1's Solomon narrative is a means toward wealth and fame. Dtr1 associates חָכְמָה with Solomon's success, so making it appear positive. The moral value of חָכְמָה is less clear in the RN, however. James L. Crenshaw goes so far as to argue that these three chapters, 13, 14, and 20, present a "negative" attitude toward wisdom: Crenshaw characterizes Jonadab's words as "scheming," states that the wise woman of Tekoa instigates a "clever ruse," and describes the behavior of the wise woman of Abel as "traitorous."⁹⁹

But in each case, the morality of the counsel in question is much less clear. Jonadab helps Amnon to obtain a private moment with Tamar, but the text nowhere indicates that Jonadab was aware of a more sinister intent of Amnon. The presence of Tamar in Amnon's residence does not attract Jonadab's concern, any more than it attracts the concern of David, or of Tamar herself.¹⁰⁰ And Jonadab's wisdom later in the chapter

---

97. Geyer, 39-40.

98. The text here is very difficult, with significant differences between MT and LT. The NRSV tends to follow 4QSamc. See McCarter, *2 Samuel*, 340-1, and Auld, *Samuel*, 492-3, for discussions of the textual issues.

99. Crenshaw, "Method," 317. See also his comments on 322.

100. Reis, "Cupidity," 173, goes so far as to argue that Tamar herself actively

works to the benefit of David and Israel. In 2 Sam 13, Jonadab is simply trying to aid his friend. This is consistent with Jonadab's advice later in the chapter, when his cool evaluation forestalls an over-reaction to the news of Amnon's assassination.[101] The wise woman of Tekoa is deceptive, but to a positive end, and she certainly is no more deceptive than Nathan in 2 Sam 12:1–4. Finally the wise woman of Abel Beth Maacah can be considered "traitorous" only with respect to a man described as a "scoundrel." In fact, her actions save her city from destruction.

"Wise" Tamar?

Phyllis Trible suggests that Tamar is another RN wise woman, highlighting her words in verses 12, 13, and 15. Trible suggests that Tamar slows the action through her speech, giving Amnon sound reasons not to proceed, along with the viable alternative of requesting permission for a proper marriage.[102] Interestingly, in verses 12–18 Tamar seems to lose some of her identity, gaining reference only through pronouns. Nevertheless, as Reis points out, Tamar has already set herself up as a woman who, at a minimum, proves unable to anticipate the danger in visiting Amnon in his personal residence. Tamar does slow things down, but this is clearly a case of "too little, too late."

Royal Counselors

The RN also features the term עֵצָה, "counsel," which is often associated with wisdom. Nili Shupak describes עֵצָה as "the official form of expression for the wise man," citing Jer 18:18 to show that it corresponds to "the law of the priest" and "the word of the prophet."[103] But Shupak also notes that while some scholars have identified the "wise man" with the king's counselor, we cannot automatically deduce that a royal counselor

---

engineers the sexual encounter, which Reis find to be consensual. Tamar's food has erotic connotations, and she is willing to enter Amnon's chamber and remain with him alone even after the servants have left, believing that a sexual act will be concomitant with marriage.

101. Weeks, 77.
102. Trible, *Terror*, 45–46.
103. Shupak, *Wisdom*, 44.

is emblematic of wisdom.[104] The frequent appearance of עֵצָה in a royal court context (at least 38 times by Whybray's count) points to its use as a technical political term.[105] But since the root (verbal form יָעַץ) occurs 175 times in the OT, and only 29 in the wisdom literature (Job and Proverbs; no occurrences in Qoheleth),[106] Whybray's suggestion that it generally meant "advice" seems accurate.[107]

עֵצָה is repeatedly used to describe the contest of advice between Ahithophel and Hushai, which takes place in 15:31–37; 16:15–23; and 17:1–14, 23. עֵצָה occurs only rarely in the DH, used here and in 1 Kgs 12, the account of the newly-installed Rehoboam as he ponders his response to protestors from the north. (עֵצָה appears also in Deut 32:28; Judg 20:7; and 2 Kgs 18:20).

Second Samuel 16:23 states Ahithophel's intellectual acumen directly: "Now in those days the counsel that Ahithophel gave was as if one consulted the oracle of God; so all the counsel of Ahithophel was esteemed, both by David and by Absalom." This description gives us the reason that David in 15:34 sees the need to send Hushai to Absalom's court, in order to subvert Ahithophel's advice. David's instruction sets up a battle of wits between the two counselors. Commentators often conclude that Ahithophel's advice really is wise, although the advice is never specifically characterized as such by the author. Ahithophel's initial advice in 16:21, that Absalom lay with David's concubines, aims to severely reduce the possibility of reconciliation between Absalom and David,[108] but it is hard to say how this helps Absalom while David is still a factor. Ahithophel's further advice, that he be permitted to lead a small strike force designed to quickly kill David, might have led to a quick victory, but it seems unclear that this would have resulted in a longer-term peace.

The author focuses the succeeding narrative not on the value of the counsel of Ahithophel and Hushai, but rather on the words they use to promote it. Both Ahithophel and Hushai display success in convincing others to take their advice. Second Samuel 17:1–14 displays their mastery of this type of dialog. Similar to the speech of the wise women, Ahithophel and Hushai use colorful metaphors to draw vivid pictures to illustrate

---

104. Ibid., 43.
105. Whybray, *Intellectual*, 132.
106. יָעַץ *yā ʿaṣ*, *TDOT*.
107. Whybray, *Intellectual*, 133.
108. Hertzberg, 350; Bodner, *Observed*, 128.

their points. Ahithophel uses the striking image in 17:3a, "I will bring all the people back to you as a bride comes home to her husband." Hushai then exceeds his rival in the use of vivid language in 17:8–13. David and his men are "like a bear robbed of her cubs in the field." The "valiant warrior, whose heart is like the heart of a lion, will utterly melt with fear." All Israel should be summoned to Absalom, "like the sand by the sea for multitude," and will attack David "as the dew falls on the ground. And if he escapes into a city, then all Israel will bring ropes to that city, and we shall drag it into the valley, until not even a pebble is to be found there."

The contest between Ahithophel and Hushai is not so much about evaluating facts to demonstrate the strengths and weaknesses of a plan (although these are factors), as it is about "wowing" their audiences with rich metaphorical language. Hushai does not carry the day with better argumentation. His primary tool in his victory of counsel over Ahithophel is the use of language to capture the attention and imagination of his audience. It is the art of persuasion which the narrator emphasizes in order to illustrate the "wisdom" of these two men.

Again, the RN presentation of counsel differs substantially from Dtr1's idea of wisdom as presented in the Solomon narrative. Dtr1 accepts the proposal that the pursuit and application of wisdom results in wealth and fame. There are limitations to what wisdom can achieve, however: life results from obedience, rather than wisdom, so that Solomon's wisdom cannot ultimately preclude or prevent his downfall. But while Dtr1 may not be over-enamored with wisdom, he does not portray wisdom as something which can be used for subversive purposes.

RN Theme 3: King as Inappropriate Judge

Three times in 2 Sam 13–20 the king or potential king takes on a judicial role (14:1–24; 15:1–6; 19:24–30). The king's function of "judge of last resort" follows the usual ANE practice, in which monarchs maintained the prestigious role of forestalling the oppression of those who lacked power.[109] This occurs, for example, in the Kirta epic in which Yatzib objects to his father Kirta's failure to behave like a king by neglecting to hear the cases of widows and orphans, and in the famous claim of Hammurabi of Babylon, that he was appointed "that the strong might not oppress the oppress the weak." Hammurabi thus is endowed by the sun god with special abil-

---

109. Levinson, "Conception," 76.

ity to understand principles of justice. We see this in Israelite literature in Ps 72:1, "Give the King your justice, O God, and your righteousness to a king's son."[110] Dtr1's Solomon story refers as well to the king's role as judge of last resort. Solomon requests wisdom in 1 Kgs 3:9 so that he may "judge" the people, then finds himself in that role in 3:16–28.

In each of these three instances, the king proves to be less than up to the task. The first occurs in 2 Sam 14, which features a plaintiff in the form of the wise woman of Tekoa. David is quick to pass judgment; he does not realize that the Tekoa woman is acting deceitfully, in order to bring home a lesson about him. The wise woman tells the king that one of her two sons had killed the other in the midst of a dispute, and that her fellow townspeople now wanted to hold the living son accountable by executing him. This would have the unfortunate consequence of leaving the sons' dead father without a male heir (and, by extensions, leave the woman without family and means of support). David declares that, in these circumstances, the living son must be allowed to survive.

The wise woman must explain the parable in order to get David to understand what her "case" is really about: she has actually been talking of the king. David had banished his son Absalom for killing another son, Amnon. Therefore, as David prescribes forgiveness for the wise woman's son, he should do the same for his own.

David, however, must have this explained to him in detail. One of the great ironies here is the wise woman's words in 14:20, "But my lord has wisdom like the wisdom of the angel[111] of God to know all things that are on the earth." This comment draws on what Joseph Blenkinsopp calls "the beauty and divine wisdom of the king," which he links to the "Yahwist Paradise recital" of Gen 2.[112] Yet David hardly displays wisdom here. Second Samuel 14:20 alludes to two other passages in which individuals compare David to an "angel of God." The Philistine ruler Achish uses this simile in 1 Sam 29:9, and Mephibosheth makes the same comparison in 2 Sam 19:27. The contexts of both of these occurrences show David to be acting questionably: he deceives Achish and mishandles Mephibosheth's

---

110. Ibid.

111. While virtually all English versions of 2 Samuel translate מַלְאַךְ here as "angel," Polzin, *2 Samuel*, 140–3, prefers "messenger" in order to clarify the relationship between this "messenger" and others in 2 Sam. "Messengers" include the speaker, the wise woman of Tekoa, who herself acts as a messenger of Joab.

112. Blenkinsopp, "Theme and Motif," 50.

case.¹¹³ Therefore, instead of imagining that David figures out that this is a "wise" woman pretending to be a mourner, it is more realistic to read the king as one who imagines that this woman is a genuine plaintiff who has been coached by Joab.¹¹⁴

Iain Provan points out that two of the three "wise" figures, the wise woman of Tekoa and Jonadab, demonstrate their wisdom to be greater than that of King David. As discussed earlier, in 2 Sam 13 Jonadab twice manages to manipulate David, first by giving Amnon a strategy for gaining access to Tamar, then later correcting a report that David's sons had been killed. This is followed in chapter 14 by the ruse of the wise woman of Tekoa. "The main point, however, is this: that David knows nowhere near as much in these stories as the other wise people around him."¹¹⁵

The second RN instance of a king acting in a judicial capacity occurs in 2 Sam 15:1–6, when Absalom takes on the role of judge of last resort. Absalom clearly indicates his willingness to pervert justice by simply siding with potential petitioners. He reveals that his "justice" is easily corruptible. While the immediate effect of Absalom's statements here denigrates this usurper, the author of the RN also points to a potential problem of a king taking on a juridical role. Aside from pursuing justice, kings also need to maintain their political power, creating a temptation to pervert justice for political gain.

Absalom's comment in 15:3 וְשֹׁמֵעַ אֵין־לְךָ מֵאֵת הַמֶּלֶךְ, "but there is no one from the king to hear you" hearkens to Deut 1:16b, where Moses charges his appointed judges to שָׁמֹעַ בֵּין־אֲחֵיכֶם "hear between your brothers," and to Solomon's request for a לֵב שֹׁמֵעַ לִשְׁפֹּט אֶת־עַמְּךָ a "hearing heart to judge your people." Absalom's apparent regular use of this refrain over the space of four years suggests that King David did not adequately provide judges to hear cases. Deut 17:8–9 teaches that "the place where Yahweh your god will choose" should host a judge to hear cases which are too difficult for regional jurists to handle. It seems that, rather than appoint a chief judge, David was expecting to perform this duty himself, as in 2 Sam 14.

David takes on the role of judge once again in 2 Sam 19: 24–30 in his final encounter with the lame Mephibosheth. Mephibosheth had

---

113. Polzin, 141.

114. Pyper, *2 Samuel 12:1–15*, 125.

115. Provan, "Seeing," 168. The third "wise" figure of 2 Sam 13–20, the wise woman of Abel Beth Maacah (20:16–22), also appears wiser than her counterpart Joab, who at this juncture can be said to be "standing in" for David.

failed to accompany David on the king's flight from Jerusalem. In 16:1–4, Mephibosheth's servant Ziba had met David with provisions, explaining that Mephibosheth had declined to follow David. David had rewarded Ziba by giving him Mephibosheth's property. In 19:25–28, however, Mephibosheth explains that Ziba had in fact abandoned him, leaving him unable to accompany David. Mephibosheth's claim is buttressed by narration which informs us in verse 24 that "he had not taken care of his feet, or trimmed his beard, or washed his clothes, from the day the king left until the day he came back in safety."

Many scholars have debated the validity of Mephibosheth's claims. Most agree that Mephibosheth was truly loyal to the king, but some argue that his disheveled appearance reminds us of the Gibeonite deception in Joshua 9 and thus points to deception on his part.[116] Rosenberg goes so far as to argue that it is essential to the story that neither David nor the reader know the truth, highlighting David's disinterest in reaching a considered decision.[117] Rather than take on the intricacies of Mephibosheth's case, David adjudicates it quickly in verse 29, "why do you speak more about your matters? I say: you and Ziba divide the land." Instead of the hard work of justice, David opts for quick disposal.

It is clear that David's solution cannot be the most just option. But, again, the king is curiously anonymous in this passage. The author's failure to name David suggests that he is not merely disapproving of David's behavior, but that he frowns upon the general concept of king as judge.[118]

RN Theme 4: Folly of the People

Just as the RN questions the efficacy of kings who act as judges, it also highlights the faulty judgment of the people. In 2 Sam 14:6, it is through the promise of positive royal judicial action that Absalom "stole the hearts

---

116. Scholars who argue that Mephibosheth is telling the truth in 2 Sam 19 include Whybray, *Succession*, 44; Hertzberg, *Samuel*, 356; Gunn, 138n; Fokkelman, *David*, 32; Gordon, *Samuel*, 291; Damrosch, *Transformations*, 247; Sternberg, *Poetics*, 380; Alter, 316; Cartledge, 616; Van Seters, *Saga*, 285. Scholars who question Mephibosheth's honesty include Budde, *Samuel*, 270; Gressman, *Geschichtsschreibung*, 170-83; Ackroyd, *Second*, 181. For more on the various viewpoints, see the excellent discussion in Schipper, *Mephibosheth*, 49-60.

117. Rosenberg, 161–62.

118. We cannot make too much of the narrator's failure to use the name "David" in this passage, however, since the next section, 19:31–40, which relates David's conversation with Barzillai, also refers to "the king" exclusively without naming David.

of the people of Israel." We see more on this in 2 Sam 17. At this juncture, Absalom's coup is in full swing. The rebels have gained control of Jerusalem, forcing King David to flee the capital. Absalom is now plotting his next move with the aid of his chief counselor, Ahithophel, whose advice is thought to be equivalent to the message of "an oracle of God" (16:23). David himself specifically cites Ahithophel's defection to Absalom as a central cause of alarm (15:31–34). Present as well at this meeting are כָּל־זִקְנֵי יִשְׂרָאֵל, "all the elders of Israel," who have joined Absalom's revolt.

2 Sam 17 opens with Ahithophel's proposal that he, Ahithophel, lead a small, quickly formed strike force to attack the fleeing David, so that the King might be captured before he can organize his troops. Once David has been killed, David's army will have little reason to resist: Absalom, David's oldest son, is, after all, the natural heir to the throne. Absalom himself will not face danger if he is not part of the strike force. The elders duly endorse this plan in 17:4.

Absalom nevertheless seeks a second opinion, and so summons Hushai to ask his advice. Hushai, wishing to delay action so as to give David time to organize his troops, declares to Absalom that Ahithophel's plan will not work, due to David's tremendous resourcefulness in battle.[119] Hushai argues that David will surely hide himself, and that since the king is an expert in guerilla warfare, Absalom is much better off raising a large army before pursuing his foe. Absalom thus should build up his troops, drawing forces from the whole of the kingdom, then lead the army himself in pursuit of David (17:7–13).

This time, it is כָּל־אִישׁ יִשְׂרָאֵל, "all the men of Israel" who, with Absalom, decide that Hushai's advice is superior to that of Ahithophel (2 Sam 17:14). We do not have any indication that Hushai has persuaded the elders; instead, it seems more likely that he is successful because he has gotten the "men" involved. As a result, Absalom delays his attack, giving David time to organize his troops and crush the rebellion. Once again, the judgment of the people proves to be faulty. Thus, in 1–2 Sam, when the people make an evaluation of leadership, it is the wrong one.

---

119. Firth 467–68, cites Hushai's skill in navigating a delicate path, as the note that he is summoned in 17:5 indicates that he is not yet part of Absalom's "inner circle."

Second Samuel 11–12

As we saw earlier in this chapter, 2 Sam 11:2[120]–12:25 looks to have been composed separately from the RN. The language and themes are considerably different from chapters 13–20, as ae the characters. Bathsheba, Uriah, Nathan, and Solomon do not appear in the RN, although these chapters do retain Joab.[121]

Although the differences between 2 Sam 11–12 and 13–20 argue for different authors, the two sections do share common elements. David is revealed to be weak and often sinful, although his sin in chapter 11 is much more serious than anything he does in the RN. David's weakness, however, is less clear with Bathsheba than it is with the women of the RN. David is able to both control and protect Bathsheba. The price of David's control may appear high, as Bathsheba loses her husband and the child she has conceived with David. But the author never reveals anything of Bathsheba's feelings,[122] in notable contrast to the RN's Tamar (13:19–20). Second Samuel 11–12 instead focuses on David's control of events. David does lose control of the situation when Nathan dramatically reveals his sin, but he always manages Bathsheba's action and movements. This distinguishes the David of 2 Sam 11–12 from the David of the RN.

Second Samuel 12:1–6 also contains a judgment scene reminiscent of David's encounter with the wise woman of Tekoa in chapter 14. In 2 Sam 12, David is again portrayed as an inadequate judge: as per his encounter in chapter 14, David does not realize that the case is about him. But while David is unnamed throughout 2 Sam 14, the narrator takes the exact opposite approach in chapters 10–12. Only in 11:8–9 does the narrator use the term הַמֶּלֶךְ, "the king," with respect to David, and even here, the reference to David specifically is unclear.[123] One possibility is that the

---

120. I noted earlier in this chapter that 2 Sam 11:1 is repeated in 1 Chr 20:1 as part of the seamless narrative 20:1–3 (cf. 2 Sam 12:26–31). Therefore, 2 Sam 11:1 likely belongs to a literary strata which pre-dates 2 Sam 11:2–12:25.

121. Eschelbach, *Joab*. Eschelbach argues that Joab is David's consistent "foil" throughout 2 Sam and 1 Kgs 1–2, pushing for justice, fidelity to Yahweh, and David's place as King of Israel. Joab's open willingness to participate in Uriah's murder here, however, suggests that the author of 2 Sam 11–12 is willing to give Joab some negative attributes.

122. Exum, "Bathsheba," 50. Exum argues that the failure to reveal anything of Bathsheba's point of view is central to this account.

123. in these verses occurs as part of noun phrases: בֵּית הַמֶּלֶךְ, "the house of the king," and מַשְׂאַת הַמֶּלֶךְ, "a portion from the king." The first of these expressions may simply be an idiom for "the palace," while the second likely refers to "a

author of 2 Sam 10–12 is deliberately attacking the fact of David's kingship, perhaps to criticize the institution of the monarchy itself.[124]

Conclusions

The Revolt Narrative of 2 Sam 13–20 contains clear allusions to Dtr1's Solomon narrative. These are the only two sections of the DH that extensively address wisdom themes, and that repeatedly use the word חָכְמָה and its derivatives. However, the concept behind wisdom is different: while Dtr1 characterizes the general notion of חָכְמָה in various forms as a means to wealth and fame, the RN simply portrays חָכְמָה as the ability to discern what needs to be done to achieve a short-term goal. חָכְמָה in the RN generally involves using clever words to persuade.

The RN further addresses the concept of the king as judge. In three passages in which the king takes on judicial responsibilities, the king is found to be less than capable. The RN thus argues that, contrary to the ANE ideal, kings should not act as judges!

Finally, the RN presents David as unable to properly manage women in his life. David has three notable interactions with women: his daughter, Tamar; the "wise woman" of Tekoa; and his ten concubines. In each of these relationships, he proves unable to control or protect the women involved. The David of the RN stands in stark contrast with the Solomon of Dtr1's 1 Kgs 3–10, who demonstrates control over his Egyptian wife, his "daughters," and the Queen of Sheba.

While commentators have tended historically to define the SN of 2 Sam 9–20 and 1 Kgs 1–2 as a unified composition, it is much more likely that 2 Sam 10–12 and 1 Kgs 1–2 were composed subsequent to the "Revolt Narrative" (RN) of 2 Sam 13–20. Second Samuel 10–12 maintains thematic links to the RN, presenting an additional example of King David's inability to function as a competent judge (although David is named in 2 Sam 12, while anonymous in 2 Sam 14 and 19). Second Samuel 10–12 nevertheless treats the female character of this section, Bathsheba, as someone who does fall under David's control, in contrast to women of the RN.

---

characteristic gift for a guest or dignitary" as in Gen 43:34. The MT of the end of 11:8 is in question in any case, with McCarter arguing for deletion of הַמֶּלֶךְ at the end of this verse. McCarter, *II Samuel*, 280; Auld, 451.

124. So McKenzie, "Succession Narrative."

And what of 1 Kgs 1–2? This falls between the RN and the "final form" of the Solomon story. If it was written subsequent to the composition of Dtr1's Solomon story, with the idea that it would serve as introduction to Solomon's reign, then we should expect it to demonstrate links to 1 Kgs 3–11. And, obviously, as it has long been thought to serve as the conclusion to the SN, 1 Kgs 1–2 has strong connections to the RN. We are now ready to examine connections between these chapters and what comes before and after.

6

From David to Solomon

HUMAN BEINGS ARE FASCINATED by powerful leaders; this drives interest in David and Solomon. So the idea of examining David and Solomon as *leaders* captures our imagination. One example comes from the work of the popular historian Garry Wills, who, relying on ideas from Max Weber, distinguishes the charismatic David from the bureaucratic Solomon. For Wills, the Revolt Narrative illustrates a central difficulty with charismatic rule, in that conquest, the charismatic leader's forte, must eventually give way to consolidation. While David in the RN retains the benefits of "his privileged position with God," he ultimately fails in his efforts to create an enduring state.[1] Wills notes the particular problem of succession for the charismatic leader: "personal magic" does not transfer easily from one leader to another. Therefore, the end of the united monarchy after Solomon's death was the inevitable fate of a kingdom which had been created through charismatic leadership.[2]

Wills is perhaps harder than necessary on the idea of bureaucracy; history is replete with examples of empires which were created through conquest, then endured through effective bureaucracy. But he is correct in concluding that Solomon in no way inherited his father's charisma. The movement from David to Solomon is not merely a transition of kings, but it is a transition of leadership style. First Kings 1–2 gives not only the account of Solomon's ascension; it creatively describes the different ruling styles of David and Solomon.

---

1. Wills, *Trumpets*, 102.
2. Ibid., 111.

First Kings 1–2 in the Deuteronomistic History

First Kings 1–2 introduces Solomon and describes his ascension to the throne, thus influencing our reading of the succeeding Solomon narrative of 1 Kgs 3–11. Yet, with the exception of Abishag, 1 Kgs 1–2 draws all of its named characters from 2 Sam 10–20, and the storyline and narrative are more closely related to these chapters than to the material of 1 Kgs 3–11. Furthermore, except for Solomon, all of the characters from 1 Kgs 1–2 (Abishag, Nathan, and Bathsheba) drop out entirely after this narrative, with the exception of three men who appear solely in the officers list of 1 Kgs 4:1–6 (Benaiah, Zadok, and, curiously, Zadok's rival Abiathar). The key to these chapters is their portrayal of Solomon as a king who acts decisively to unilaterally control Israel's institutions. Solomon is "wise" in 1 Kgs 1–2, but the wisdom he exhibits consists of political acumen that helps him to establish power, nothing more. His wisdom here is the same sort of wisdom found in the RN: ability to accomplish a short term objective.

First Kings 1–2 demonstrates the differences between Kings David and Solomon through use of their interaction with SN individuals. In these chapters, each king is approached by Bathsheba with a petition initiated by another high ranking Israelite, Nathan in 1 Kgs 1 and Adonijah in 1 Kgs 2. Nathan and Adonijah each expect that his petition will be granted because it is Bathsheba (David's wife, Solomon's mother) making the request. But while Nathan is successful, Adonijah is not. David can be swayed by a woman; Solomon will not be convinced.

The two kings also differ in their relationships to their highest ranking generals. One of David's problems in the RN is his inability to control his leading commander Joab, who repeatedly acts contrary to David's orders. Joab continues to behave independently in 1 Kgs 1, taking part in Adonijah's gathering without David's knowledge. Solomon's general Benaiah, however, is loyal to a fault, never once questioning his king but faithfully carrying out Solomon's orders (usually having to do with questionable executions). Thus, it is through the development of Bathsheba and Joab/ Benaiah that the author of 1 Kgs 1–2 reveals to us differences in the administrative abilities of Kings David and Solomon.

Women and Power

In chapters 4 and 5 I explained how the RN and the Solomon story use women to reveal David's weakness and Solomon's strength. Until his downfall in 1 Kgs 11, Solomon successfully manages the women around him: his Egyptian wife, his "daughters" from 1 Kgs 4, and the Queen of Sheba. His relationships with these women hold potential for mishap or embarrassment, but Solomon successfully works these relationships to his benefit. By way of contrast, David's relationships with Tamar, the wise woman of Tekoa, and his ten concubines lead to his disgrace, as he is deceived by the wise woman and is unable to protect his daughter and concubines from sexual defilement. First Kgs 1–2 heightens this contrast through use of its principal female characters, Abishag and Bathsheba.

Abishag appears several times in chapters 1–2, but the author never permits her to speak or take any action on her own. Her sole literary function is to reveal characteristics of those around her: David, Bathsheba, Adonijah, Solomon. Abishag becomes David's companion, apparently with David's approval, as by 1:15 she appears to be his attendant of choice. Several commentators stress that Bathsheba must have felt that she has been replaced by Abishag as the object of David's desire.[3] Yet, more important to the story is that Bathsheba is no longer under David's control. She appears here in order to make a request of David, but with less than complete honesty: Bathsheba "reminds" David of a promise that he had never made, to designate Solomon as his heir.[4]

Commentators often draw out the contrast between Bathsheba's portrayal in 2 Sam 11–12 and her actions and words in 1 Kgs 1–2. In 2 Sam 11–12, the author permits Bathsheba only one short phrase: הָרָה אָנֹכִי, "I'm pregnant" (11:5). Her movements to and from David's house in 2 Sam 11–12 are entirely controlled by David. In 1 Kgs 1–2, however, Bathsheba appears more independent, initiating petitions from David and Solomon.[5]

---

3. Berlin, *Poetics*, 27–28, 74; Klein, "Bathsheba," 59.

4 Steussy, *David*, 92, and Jacobs, "Mothering," 78–79, among others, hold that David possibly did make such a promise, of which the narrator has elected not to inform us directly. Yet the fact that the text does not tell us that such a commitment was made, combined with Nathan's elaborate planning, suggests that this is simply another instance, as with fake petitions in 2 Sam 11–20, in which David falls for a ruse.

5. Jacobs, "Mothering," 67–84, further discusses Bathsheba's motivations and strategies.

Sara M. Koenig states that in her speech to King David in 1:17–21 Bathsheba "is neither (Nathan's) puppet nor his parrot, but acts with her own initiative and intelligence."[6] Koenig goes on to list seven differences between Nathan's instructions and Bathsheba's speech. However, the differences are confined to expansions upon, rather than deviations from, Nathan's instructions. For example, Bathsheba tells David that he does not know that Adonijah has taken the throne (verse 18), and that the eyes of all Israel are upon David to hear who will succeed him (verse 20), and that Bathsheba "and (her) son Solomon" will be counted as offenders should Adonijah become king (verse 21).[7] Bathsheba adapts Nathan's general instructions in order to create a stronger speech, going even further than instructed in bowing to David and wishing him long life in verse 31. But she is clearly doing Nathan's bidding.

In her speech, Bathsheba displays a number of intriguing similarities to another woman who had fooled King David long ago, the wise woman of Tekoa, whose encounter is described in 2 Sam 14:1–20. Both women are sent to the king by a high-ranking official who has an agenda. Each woman then uses her ingenuity to achieve the result desired by the man sending her. Their common strategy is to present a petition that is not quite what it seems. The focus of each petition is to preserve the life of the woman's son (the implication of 1 Kgs 1:21). In the background, another son has already died (recalling in Bathsheba's case her infant son by David who dies in 2 Sam 12), so that the remaining son is all that the petitioning woman will have left. As a nice narrative touch, the king in 1 Kgs 1:15–21, like the king in 2 Sam 14, is unnamed, and referenced repeatedly as "the king." And as the wise woman of Tekoa finds success, Bathsheba also convinces David that he had promised to make Solomon king.

While the relationship between these episodes is vague enough that both may simply be drawing upon the same type scene,[8] the fact

---

6. Koenig, *Bathsheba?*, 92. A number of other commentators similarly laud Bathsheba's political acumen, including Fokkelman, *David*, 357–58; Walsh, *1 Kings*, 12–13; Klein, 60–61; Moore, *Faith*, 30–31.

7. Ibid., 92–94. Walsh, 13, sees these expansions of Nathan's "script" as evidence of Bathsheba's "strong character." But since Hebrew narrative often features repetition with difference, we should look for more substantial evidence that deviation of word choice points to independence of character. Another way to understand this passage is that, instead of a "script," Nathan gives guidelines, upon which Bathsheba should improvise as seems best to her.

8. See Alter, *Narrative*, 47–62, for a discussion of "type scenes."

that 1 Kgs 1–2 draws on the RN in other ways suggests that the author of 1 Kgs 1:15–21 had 2 Sam 14 in mind. Yet the two episodes have one immediately noticeable difference that perhaps accounts for the fact that the relationship between the two women usually goes unnoticed: the narrator of 2 Sam 14 specifically calls the woman of Tekoa "wise," whereas 1 Kgs 1 does not use any wisdom vocabulary to describe Bathsheba, her words, or her actions.

While 1 Kgs 1:15–21 appears to draw on 2 Sam 14:1–20, certain elements of 1 Kgs 1 and 2 suggest that Bathsheba does not belong to the class of "wise women" described in the RN. First, when we compare Bathsheba's words and actions to those of the one who approaches her in the first place, her ally Nathan, we see that "wisdom" in 1 Kgs 1 comes from Nathan, not Bathsheba. Keith Bodner alludes to this wrinkle in his comparison of Bathsheba in 1 Kgs 1 to Rebekah in Gen 27. According to Bodner, the privileges of both Esau and Adonijah "are being subverted in favor of a younger son by means of the wiles and skills of an assertive and innovative mother."[9] Bodner nevertheless runs into a problem with Nathan the prophet, whose presence and activity renders the comparison to Gen 27 (which lacks a figure analogous to Nathan) less cogent.[10] Nathan's presence presents a real difficulty for Bodner's thesis, since, if anyone can be said to demonstrate "wiles and skills" in 1 Kgs 1, it is the prophet. Nathan is the one who hits upon the idea of using Bathsheba to get Solomon named as King: Nathan approaches Bathsheba in 1:11, not the other way around. Nathan is also the one who introduces the word pair יֵשֵׁב ... יִמְלֹךְ ("he will rule ... he will sit") in 1:13, repeated by Bathsheba in verse 17, Nathan himself in verse 24, and a number of others through chapters 1–2. The joining of these words and repetition of the phrase help to fix in David's mind the idea that David had promised to have Solomon succeed him as king.[11] Bathsheba does follow in the ancient tradition of women who use deception to get what they want,[12] but here Bathsheba is simply the tool: at no point does she speak or act contrary to the requests of Nathan (or, in chapter 2, Adonijah). Mishael

---

9 8 Bodner, *Observed*, 147.

10. Ibid.

11. Gray, *Kings*, 77; De Vries, *1 Kings*, 15. In his critique of Gray, De Vries posits that "such subtle psychologizing has to be beyond the naïve art of the narrator; however much of it may possibly have motivated the historical Nathan and Bathsheba." Was the narrator really less sophisticated than the "historical" Nathan?

12. Moore, "1 Kings 1:11–31," 342.

Maswari Caspi and Rachel S. Haverlock compare Nathan and Bathsheba to Naomi and Ruth in Ruth 3: Naomi and Nathan send Ruth and Bathsheba to powerful men, uninvited, to ask for provision for their welfare. Yet, as Caspi and Haverlock point out, Nathan shows far less confidence in Bathsheba's abilities than does Naomi with Ruth, going so far as to place the specific words in Bathsheba's mouth (1:13-14).[13]

Bathsheba's next (and last!) appearance in 1 Kgs, 2:13-25 further helps us to understand the characters of Solomon and David, particularly when we consider this episode in light of 1 Kgs 1. As in 1:11-21, Bathsheba is approached by a high official (the king's brother Adonijah) who asks her to make a request of the sitting king (Solomon). As she had done in the earlier episode, Bathsheba approaches the king, editing Adonijah's words in order to strengthen her request. But she is now approaching Solomon, not David, and so the plot takes a different turn.

Solomon provides a decidedly more pleasing reception for Bathsheba in 1 Kgs 2 than had David in 1 Kgs 1. In 1 Kgs 1, Bathsheba appears as a supplicant, remaining in that position through the story in question. This state of affairs holds also to similar scenes in the RN and the Solomon story. The wise woman of Tekoa stands in a subordinate position throughout 2 Sam 14:1-21. In 2 Sam 20:16-22, the wise woman of Abel Beth Maacah in a sense approaches Joab, appearing on the city wall as Joab is organizing his assault. She maintains her position as supplicant through the episode. And the story of Solomon and the Two Prostitutes of 1 Kgs 3:16-28 presents the true mother in a subordinate position as supplicant throughout.[14] These women all remain standing as they present their petitions; all find success.

By way of contrast, 1 Kgs 2:19 delays the conversation in order to allow Solomon to receive his mother. Verse 19b, וַיָּקָם הַמֶּלֶךְ לִקְרָאתָהּ וַיִּשְׁתַּחוּ לָהּ, "and the king rose to meet her, and he bowed himself to her," does not spare words to describe Solomon's actions, even before he orders a throne brought for her. Particularly noteworthy is Solomon's positioning of Bathsheba's throne at his right. While other ANE texts depict kings showing deep respect for their mothers, this location of the king-mother in this place of honor (as in Ps 45:10 and 110:1) appears to be unique.[15] Commentators occasionally discuss Bathsheba's role as גְּבִרָה,

---

13. Caspi and Haverlock, *Women*, 111-12.

14. Garsiel, "Revealing." As noted in chapter two, Garsiel draws attention to her physical demeanor as an indication that she is the true mother.

15. Marsman, *Women*, 345-70, contains an exhaustive summary.

"queen mother" to Solomon, citing extensive discussion of this position in Egyptian literature.[16] But her new status in 1 Kgs 2 does not change her function in the story from what it was in chapter 1. Instead, it is Solomon's treatment of Bathsheba, particularly in contrast to the treatment rendered by David in 1:15–21, that makes this occasion remarkable.[17]

The conversation between Solomon and Bathsheba bears this out. Adonijah's request for Abishag in 2:13–17 puzzles commentators: why does not Adonijah realize that Solomon will interpret his request as a move for the throne? Ernst Würthwein and others argue that Bathsheba changes the wording of Adonijah's request in order to manipulate Solomon into executing Adonijah,[18] but most commentators agree that the changes seem minor, more designed to communicate effectively, than to influence Solomon toward execution.[19] Some commentators further assert that while Adonijah may have been unaware that his request would be seen in a bad light by Solomon, Bathsheba was not.[20] The text offers no support for this position, however. Claudia Camp proposes that Adonijah is effectively seeking to make a deal: Abishag, in exchange for surrendering all future claims to the throne.[21] Again, this seems to over-read the text. David Gunn makes perhaps the most compelling argument, that despite appearances to most modern readers, Adonijah and Bathsheba simply did not view Adonijah's request for Abishag as a threat to Solomon's throne. Solomon's response has more to do with his own desire to eliminate possible threats to his rule than with a legitimate threat.[22]

Unless we can show that Bathsheba has a different understanding of the significance of Adonijah's than Adonijah himself has, the text just does not support the idea that Bathsheba was trying to accomplish anything more than simply trying to help Adonijah get what he wanted. As she had

---

16. Ahlström, *Syncretism*; Andreasen, "Queen Mother."

17. Sweeney, *Kings*, 68, sees this contrast as pointing to something "amiss" in 2:19–22. Walsh, 52, also notes contrasting behaviors of David and Solomon vis-à-vis Bathsheba.

18. Würthwein, *Könige Kaptiel 1–16*, 22; Klein, *Sexual*, 69–70; Jacobs, "Mothering," 81; Willis, Pleffer, and Llewelyn, "Conversation," 142.

19. Walsh, 52–53; Koenig, 101–3.

20. Robinson, *First Kings*, 41–42; Alter, *David*, 378; Brueggemann, *Kings*, 31–32; Seibert, *Subversive*, 138–40.

21. Camp, "Kings," 106.

22. Gunn, *David*, 137n, writes that any other explanation would render Adonijah and Bathsheba "imbeciles." See Fritz, 28–29, for a similar opinion.

done with Nathan's request in 1:17–21, Bathsheba changes the words of Adonijah's expressed desire, perhaps the better to see it fulfilled. She nevertheless again does what a man instructs her to do or say, appearing only in accordance with others' concerns.[23] Bathsheba certainly acts with intelligence, but, contra Koenig, we do not see initiative or independence.

Even though 1 Kgs 1–2 develops Bathsheba's character more than does 2 Sam 11–12, her function remains constricted. She and Abishag appear here in order to demonstrate differences between the main characters, Solomon and David. This explains the distinctions between the royal treatment of Bathsheba in 1:15–17 and 2:19. Solomon affords Bathsheba great respect and honor, while David does not. Just as in 2 Sam 14, David shows no deference to the woman who comes to see him, yet he immediately grants her request. In contrast, Solomon physically and verbally demonstrates considerable respect while retaining the ability to deny the woman's request.

2 Sam 14:1–20, 1 Kgs 1:15–21, and 1 Kgs 3:16–28 share elements with two other passages in the DH in which the king must choose between two parties, 2 Sam 19:24–30 and 2 Kgs 6:26–31.[24] All of these accounts feature an unnamed king who exhibits difficulty in rendering a just decision. In her examination of anonymous characters in the Hebrew Bible, Adele Reinhartz asserts that narrators assign names to distinguish characters from each other.[25] An important corollary of this thesis is that characters left anonymous may "converge" into each other, thus fleshing out a broad character type.[26] In these instances of kings who must make judgments, the technique of leaving the kings nameless invites the reader to develop a strong idea of a court type-scene, where a supplicant approaches a king who lacks sufficient perspicacity to comprehend what is really happening.[27]

---

23. Sackenfeld, *Wives?*, 77.

24. Lyke, *Tekoa*, 102n. Lyke holds that 2 Sam 14:1–20 and 1 Kgs 3:16–27 "in many ways adumbrate" David's encounter with Bathsheba in 1 Kgs 1. In all three cases, a woman comes to the king to save the life of a surviving son. However, in his formal comparison of 2 Sam 14 (pp. 100–7), Lyke does not further consider 1 Kgs 1, looking only at 1 Kgs 3:16–28; 2 Kgs 6:26–31; and Est 7, even though 1 Kgs 1 seems to share Lyke's four common themes: a woman comes to the king for justice, the life of her remaining son is at stake, the mother and king are expected to save the son's life, and the royal figure is depicted in contrast to the ideal.

25. Reinhartz, *Anonymity*, 8.

26. Ibid., 139–53.

27. The exception to this pattern is, of course, 2 Sam 12:1–7, which unambiguously

The implication that an anonymous king will prove to be an incapable judge allows the narrator to employ a neat trick in 2:19–22. This episode between Bathsheba and Solomon begins much the same way as the passages featuring anonymous kings: in 1 Kgs 2:19b–21, the king is unnamed. The narrator gives no clue of what is about to happen, patterning verses 20–21 on Bathsheba's peaceful conversation with Adonijah in verses 16–17.[28] Suddenly, the name "Solomon" appears (וַיַּעַן הַמֶּלֶךְ שְׁלֹמֹה "and King Solomon answered") at the start of verse 22, breaking the pattern and shifting the mood.[29] The narrator thus reveals a king who does not simply grant cleverly-worded requests from women. Anonymous kings have proved to be poor judges throughout 2 Samuel into 1 Kings. This account begins this way, with an anonymous king about to be persuaded into a bad arrange. But in an instant, the king takes on a name, "Solomon," and finds the capacity to deny his supplicant's request. Solomon suddenly shows that he can ably manage a woman under his authority.

This episode recalls numerous prior incidents in 1–2 Samuel regarding claimants to the throne and their women. While in Saul's service, David had been promised Saul's elder daughter Mara, but for unclear reasons, she was given to another man. David then married Saul's younger daughter Michal, but when David's relationship with Saul soured, David fled, and Michal also was given to another. After the death of the rival Judahite chief Nabal, David married the dead man's wife, presumably taking his property and position in the tribe, paving the way toward his ascension to the throne of Judah. David also marries Ahinoam (1 Sam 25:43), who may have been Saul's wife, the mother of Jonathan (1 Sam 14:50, see 1 Sam 20:30). Later, Ishbaal accuses Abner of

---

names David as King. As at other times, the supplicant, Nathan, comes with a problem of which David misses the significance. The type-scene involving an anonymous king probably relates to its unique function as a direct condemnation of the king, combined with the likelihood of unique authorship (as I argued in chapter 5).

28. Fokkelman, 395; Walsh, 52–53; Jones, *Kings*, 112. Jones also draws attention to similarities between the words of Adonijah and Bathsheba, noting that "repetition with slight variation is characteristic of Hebrew narrative." Sweeney, 68–69, judges elements of 2:19–21 to be ominous, reading with suspicion Solomon's lavish treatment of his mother, her request for a small favor (which turns out to be large), and Solomon's promise to fulfill her request (a promise he does not keep). Most readers see all of this as innocuous, simply setting us up for Solomon's surprising response in v. 22. See also Hens-Piazza, *Kings*, 28.

29. Walsh, 53 especially highlights this shift in tone.

sleeping with his concubine, and Absalom publicly sleeps with David's concubines. In all these instances, copulation with the king's women is perceived as an element in the struggle for the throne, perhaps part of a play for the throne. In each case, the king's inability to control the sexual activity of women in his charge weakens the king's appearance.

Adonijah's request also draws attention to the influence that women have over Solomon's father and perhaps might be expected to have over Solomon himself. The story seems headed in this direction in 2:20b, where Solomon declares, "Make your request, my mother; for I will not refuse you." King David often gives in to the requests of women, including Abigail (1 Sam 25:23–34), the wise woman of Tekoa, Saul's concubine Rizpah daughter of Aiah (by implication, 2 Sam 21:10–12), and, in 1 Kgs 1, Bathsheba. Perhaps David's empathy toward women gives Nathan the idea of enlisting Bathsheba in his move to steer the throne toward Solomon. As Nathan was successful, we can begin to understand why Adonijah would approach Bathsheba with his request. David had repeatedly granted requests of female supplicants. Why would David's son Solomon not give in to his own mother? But Solomon does refuse, and in doing so, prevents his rival's access to the royal harem.

Steven McKenzie points out that, in terms of the account of Adonijah asking for Abishag, Bathsheba's role really is unnecessary. The storyline distills into an account of Adonijah's request and Solomon's violent reaction.[30] McKenzie takes the position that Bathsheba appears in this account because in actuality she was the catalyst for Adonijah's request: otherwise, for McKenzie, there is no other reason for her mention at this juncture.[31] But since the text itself does not portray Bathsheba as the instigator, it is more logical to understand Bathsheba in terms of how the major characters relate to her. As per the RN, in 1 Kgs 1 David does what she asks; as per 1 Kgs 3–10, Solomon takes his own course.

Solomon's willingness and ability to deal ably with the women in his charge is one of the features of his reign that exceeds that of King David. Solomon continues to exhibit this mastery in his dealings with his Egyptian wife and with the Queen of Sheba, neither of whom is highlighted as a negative influence (until, perhaps, 1 Kgs 11). First Kings 2 thus introduces Solomon's successful management of the women in his life, a feature of his reign that becomes especially important in the account of his

---

30 McKenzie, *David*, 181.

31 Ibid., 181–2.

downfall in 1 Kgs 11, when the management of his women disintegrates along with his legacy.

Wisdom

One of the strongest connections between the RN and the Solomon story is the clear presence of wisdom in both. As explained in chapter 4, these are the only parts of the DH that feature the repeated use of חָכְמָה, and in which wisdom clear plays a significant role in the narrative. Yet I've also demonstrated that the wisdom of the RN is of a different type than that of Solomon. First Kings 1–2 bridges these two "wisdom" sections by applying the RN-style practical wisdom to Solomon. The wisdom of 1 Kgs 1–2 begins, however, with the עֵצָה, "counsel," of Nathan, which reminds us of the עֵצָה of David's earlier advisers, Ahithophel and Hushai.

First Kings 1: Wisdom of Nathan

As I noted earlier, Nathan the prophet is certainly the "wisest" character of 1 Kgs 1. The narrator does not use any wisdom vocabulary in his description of Nathan's words and endeavors, but Nathan behaves wisely as he develops and executes his plan to put Solomon on the throne. Nathan realizes that if he can make David angry at Adonijah, he may be able to motivate David to act. So to influence David, he manipulates Bathsheba in two ways. In 1:11 Nathan references Adonijah as "son of Haggith," thus suggesting that the title of "queen mother" may be up for grabs. He then suggests in 1:12 that Bathsheba and her son will be in danger if Adonijah becomes king. Nathan thus recognizes both David's weakness and Bathsheba's vulnerability, using both to his advantage.[32]

In 1 Kings 1:13, Nathan introduces the idea that David had promised to make Solomon his successor. This is the first time the DH mentions this promise, causing many readers to ask whether this promise was invented by Nathan. Some commentators hold that the author simply does not give us enough information to judge the veracity of Nathan's claim, with Walsh going so far as to state that the reader is *meant* to wonder whether David actually made such a promise.[33]

32. Hens-Piazza, 15.

33. Fokkelman, 354n; House, *Kings*, 90; Mulder, *Kings*, 54; Cogan, *1 Kings*, 166; Walsh, 12. Fokkelman also celebrates this "literary obtruseness."

But the narrative supplies definitive clues that David had never made such a commitment. Nathan in 1:13 speaks in the context of giving counsel, עֵצָה, to Bathsheba, as he plots to save her life.[34] He tells her to tell David that David had promised to *her* to make Solomon king. Bathsheba speaks to David not in court, but in his private chamber (NAS offers "bedroom"), and when Nathan appears later, he makes no mention of this promise. This suggests that the "promise" was not public, but was rather a private matter between King and Queen.[35] If so, then how would Nathan know of it? And if he knew through private communication with Bathsheba and/or David, then why not mention it when he arrived? The most likely explanation is that Nathan simply suggests to Bathsheba to join him in deception.

Nathan is quite clever as he deals with David. He tells Bathsheba what to say, then waits for her to complete her private audience with the king. Nathan then adapts his own advice, and plays off of Bathsheba's words in his speech to David in verses 22–27.[36] He does not merely "confirm" her words, as she had suggested in 1:14, but expands upon them to achieve his objective.[37] Nathan then carefully shifts the focus away from Adonijah onto David himself, asking whether David was supporting Adonijah's moves. This puts David on the defensive, so that he will appear weak if he does not take action.[38] Nathan thus fosters David's desire to act again as the man in charge, and so make Solomon king.[39]

As mentioned earlier, a remarkable feature of 1 Kgs 1 is that the narrator refers to Nathan as "Nathan the prophet" eight (!) times. As there is no other Nathan in this chapter,[40] we might wonder why the narrator finds it necessary to repeatedly remind us that he is "the prophet." This point is especially noteworthy when we compare the other episodes

---

34. Ishida, "Succession," 185.

35. Long, *I Kings*, 37; cf. Seow, "Kings," 19, who suggests "pillow talk."

36. Cazeaux, *Royauté*, 291–93; Koenig, 94–95.

37 Virtually all major English versions, including NRSV, JPS, NASB, NIV, and ESV, follow the AV by rendering מִלֵּאתִי, which usually has the sense of "filling" or "making complete, as "I will confirm." Mulder, 55, "I will complete," and Alter, *David*, 366, "I shall fill in" reflect a truer sense of this word.

38. Moore, *Faith*, 210.

39. Kalimi, "Rise," 15–18, gives more on the "wisdom" of Nathan in 1 Kgs 1.

40. 2 Sam 5:14 names sons born to David in Jerusalem, including one "Nathan," listed right before Solomon. Sweeney, 55, suggests that Nathan the prophet may have been this son of David, but offers no supporting evidence for this position.

in which Nathan appears: he is introduced as "Nathan the prophet" in 2 Sam 7:2, then is never again called a prophet in 2 Sam 7 or 2 Sam 12, except in 12:25.

Würthwein compares Nathan's role as kingmaker to that of another prophet, Samuel, in 1 Sam 10:1–13, with the important distinction that Nathan never claims to be speaking for Yahweh in 1 Kgs 1.[41] Nathan takes part in Solomon's coronation in 1:38[42] but otherwise does not act in the role of prophet. He speaks more like a counselor, arguing through reason rather than appealing to the authority of Yahweh (as in his other appearances in 2 Sam 7:4–17 and 12:7–12) to persuade David.[43] The designation "prophet," therefore, does not describe Nathan's role in 1 Kgs 1 but rather explains the source of his influence, in a manner similar to that of the RN. The RN tells us that Ahithophel's words are highly regarded due to his reputation as someone whose words are "as the oracle of God" (2 Sam 16:23), and Absalom listens to Hushai because he was known as David's "friend" (2 Sam 16:17). The author of 1 Kgs 1–2 now wishes to explain the source of Nathan's reputability and so repeatedly reminds us of Nathan's identity as a prophet.[44]

Iain W. Provan further shows how Nathan's function alludes to Jonadab's role in 2 Sam 13:30–36. In that chapter, Jonadab, described as חָכָם מְאֹד, "very wise," in 13:2, displays more knowledge of the actions of the king's sons than does King David. David's ignorance of Adonijah's feast

---

41. Würthwein, 14; Jones, 93. Nevertheless, there are significant differences between Nathan and Samuel. Nathan is called a prophet, but does not act in that role; Samuel in 1 Sam 10 acts as a prophet, but is not called a prophet!

42. While Nathan is present for the coronation, in 1:39 the anointing is performed by Zadok the priest alone (despite David's instructions in 1:34 that both take part in the anointing; De Vries, 17, reads 1:34 to specify Zadok alone). In 1:43, Abiathar's son Jonathan reports to Adonijah that Solomon had been anointed by both Zadok *and* Nathan (some manuscripts omit Nathan from Solomon's anointing, but the MT is preferable as the *lecto dificilor*). De Vries, 17, suggests simply that Jonathan's report is "garbled," but what purpose could the narrator have in reporting such a "garbling"? Another possibility is that Jonathan is trying to strengthen the veracity of his report by including Nathan; a report pointing to Zadok only could be seen as a simple reflection of the implied conflict between the families of Abiathar and Zadok. Jonathan's reporting clearly alludes to the report of Zadok's son Ahimaaz in 2 Sam 18:19–29.

43. Hens-Piazza, 15, extends Nathan's "scheming" to include manipulation of Bathsheba, as in 1:13 he provides her the "motive that will prompt her to cooperate." This seems like reaching, however, as Bathsheba could be expected to wish to promote her son's prospects in any case.

44. Walsh, 10 especially stresses the narrator's repeated designation while Nathan "is embroiled in a sordid palace intrigue with no apparent divine mandate."

and overall play for the throne in 1 Kgs 1 brings to mind his ignorance about the doings at Absalom's feast in 2 Sam 13. Both times David's lack of knowledge threatens to lead to a course of action (or non-action) that will be disastrous (1 Kgs 1, of course, presents a disaster from Nathan's point of view).[45] Thus, as in 2 Sam 13, a court counselor must take action in order to engender the best result.

Antti Laato reconciles Nathan's characters in 2 Sam 7 and 1 Kgs 1 by arguing that in both instances Nathan shrewdly tries to guide Israel away from disastrous internal struggles, such as those involving Absalom and Sheba, during the time of transition from a tribal-based society to a centralized monarchy.[46] But this observation speaks only to Nathan's ideology—which in fact may explain the reason that the author of 1 Kgs 1 assigns Nathan to orchestrate Solomon's ascension. Nathan's political outlook may be similar in 2 Sam 7 and 1 Kgs 1, but his role is different, changing from prophet to counselor.

First Kings 2: Wisdom of Solomon

While Nathan is the first figure in 1 Kgs who can be said to display "wisdom," pride of place in this area obviously belongs to Solomon. Unlike the case in the SN, Solomon is the only person designated "wise" in 1 Kgs. First Kgs 2:5–9 first applies this description to Solomon: David instructs him to use his "wisdom" in 2:6, because in 2:9 Solomon is "wise." The narrator thus credits David himself with recognizing that Solomon will exceed David in this area.[47]

King David centers his instructions of 1 Kgs 2:5–9 around his command in 2:7 to demonstrate חֶסֶד, "faithfulness," to the heirs of Barzillai in return for Barzillai's similar treatment of David as David was fleeing from Absalom.[48] This directive is obviously distinguished from the others in

---

45. Provan, "Seeing," 168.

46. Laato, "Second Samuel 7."

47. James S. Ackerman, "Knowing Good and Evil: A Literary Analysis of the Court History in 2 Samuel 9–20 and 1 Kings 1–2," *JBL* 109 (1990): 41–60, argues that David's failing with Mephibosheth in 2 Sam 19 serves as a strong precursor of his inability to avoid manipulation by Bathsheba in 1 Kgs 1, as the 2 Sam 19 passage shows that Daivd can no longer distinguish right from wrong.

48. The NRSV and ESV render תַּעֲשֶׂה־חֶסֶד in 2:7a as "deal loyally," certainly a fine translation. They then unfortunately suggest that the term is repeated in parallel by specficying "such loyalty" in 2:7b. The MT here simply has כִּי־כֵן, "for

that David here wants Solomon to reward someone for positive behavior, rather than to find a way to kill someone. Solomon's efforts to carry this command out, or not, are not reported. Some commentators read this as an implied criticism of Solomon, as 1 Kgs 2 does tell us how Solomon goes about the executions of Joab and Shimei. But it is also possible that 1 Kgs 2 does not tell us more about Solomon and the sons of Barzillai because there is not much more to tell. Second Samuel 19:31–38 describes how David had already pledged to reward Barzillai going forward, so that 1 Kgs 2:7 simply reiterates David's commitment to do חֶסֶד on an ongoing basis. Therefore the reason that 1 Kgs 2 says nothing about Barzillai's progeny after 2:7 is that Solomon is simply continuing a policy established by David.[49] Matters involving Joab and Shimei, however, require new strategies and means.

First Kings 2:5–9 noticeably separates the concepts of חָכְמָה and חֶסֶד. Just prior to the SN, David had twice displayed the same idea that he advocates here, showing חֶסֶד to a son because of the loyalty displayed by the father.[50] In 2 Sam 9:7, David determines to show kindness to Jonathan's son (חֶסֶד אֶעֱשֶׂה עִמְּךָ, "I will do kindness to you") for the sake of Jonathan, and David decides to show חֶסֶד (אֶעֱשֶׂה־חֶסֶד, "I will do kindness") to the son of Nahash the Ammonite in 2 Sam 10:2 because of Nahash's prior kindness to David. The parallel between Barzillai and Jonathan is particularly acute because in these cases, חֶסֶד involves a seat at the king's table. Doing חֶסֶד apparently does not require חָכְמָה. It is rather with regard to the disposal of internal threats where Solomon will need חָכְמָה.[51]

If חָכְמָה is not required to deal with the sons of Barzillai, the implications of חֶסֶד may nevertheless serve to unite 2:5–9. Citing the "covenantal undertones" of חֶסֶד Jones stresses the obligation, rather than grace, that David may have felt toward Barzillai.[52] Similarly, David's instructions regarding Joab and Shimei also suggest a degree of obligation. In 2:5,

---

thus," a less emphatic construction.

49. Jones, 109, argues that the "distinct covenantal undertones" of חֶסֶד suggest David's obligation to reward Barzillai for his earlier assistance.

50. See Glueck, *Ḥesed*, and Cogan, 186, for the reciprocal nature of *Ḥesed* in the Hebrew Bible.

51. House, 97, remarks that David's advice regarding the heirs of Barzilllai represents "wise political counsel." While this is certainly true, it misses the point of the idea of "wisdom" in 2:5–9. David is not telling Solomon, "here are some wise things to do." David is saying instead, "you will need wisdom in order to accomplish certain objectives."

52. Jones, 109.

David states that Joab had יָשֶׂם דְּמֵי־מִלְחָמָה בְּשָׁלֹם, "shed the blood of war in peace" thus violating a community ideal. And in 2:8, David recalls that Shimei had קִלְלַנִי קְלָלָה נִמְרֶצֶת, "cursed me with a grievous curse." The nature of this curse arguably was so heinous that David could not properly simply forgive.

In other ways, David's directions concerning Joab and Shimei are very similar to each other. David briefly recounts each man's "evil deeds," then instructs Solomon to use his wisdom to arrange a violent death.[53] David gives pragmatic advice here: as long as Joab and Shimei are alive, they will constitute latent threats to Solomon's throne.[54]

Walsh stresses David's words "to me" in 2:5a, which translate the independent Hebrew construction לִי. Walsh reads this as David's sense of personal hurt at Joab's assassinations, above and beyond the immorality of killing two innocent men.[55] But while we can certainly see that Job's actions may have offended David's personal feelings, more important here is the potential injury in each case to David's throne, which is more the subject of David's final speech as a whole. This supports the idea that, in 1 Kgs 2:2–9, wisdom is not about justice or righteousness; it is instead about the establishment and maintenance of power.

Solomon's "wisdom" in disposing of potential threats has much to do with his working around the concept of the oath. Keith Bodner has recently written about the extensive use and misuse of oaths in 1 Kgs 1–2, which points to a key aspect of Solomon's political acumen: in these chapters Solomon several times manipulates the use of the oath toward his advantage. Solomon's ascension to the throne in 1 Kgs 1 and his securing of it in 1 Kgs 2 are accomplished through "creative and dubious" uses of

---

53. Provan, "Barzillai," argues that Joab and Shimei respectively represent the rivals and allies of Solomon: Joab, having attended Adonijah's (premature) ascension celebration, is a perceived opponent, whereas Shimei apparently supports Solomon (2 Kgs 1:8, cf. 2:8). Wisdom, therefore, involves being aware of the latent threats from both enemies and friends. However, while Sweeeny, 55, agrees that the Shiemei of 1 Kgs 1:8 is the same as that of 1 Kgs 2, almost all other commentators (including De Vries, 14, and Cogan, 158) disagree. Buis, 41, identifies the Shimei of 1:8 with the Benjamite governor of 4:18 (Walsh, 8n, and Mulder, 47 also report this possibility). Since both of these Shimeis support Solomon, the suggestion that they are one and the same seems as reasonable as any, although Cogan, 158, regards this as unlikely.

54. Koopmans, "Testament," 447. Koopmans suggests that David done much the same early in his own reign in 2 Sam 1:13–16, 4:9–12, where he carries out executions in order to enhance regard for the throne, and gains the respect of the people as a result.

55. Walsh, 41.

oaths.⁵⁶ Given Solomon's reputation for wisdom, it is fitting that he is able to work creatively with oaths.

The first issue that Solomon must address as king is Adonijah, who, in 1:50, grasps the horns of the altar, in fear for his life. Solomon receives a report in 1:51 that Adonijah has said, "Let King Solomon swear to me first that he will not kill his servant with the sword." Adonijah insists on an oath, but Solomon does not grant it, instead simply declaring that Adonijah's fate will depend solely on his behavior.⁵⁷ But Solomon's condition is nebulous, without real security: what exactly does Adonijah need to do to prove himself a בֶּן־חַיִל, "worthy man"?⁵⁸ Solomon's words perhaps cause Solomon to appear just before his audience, yet at the same time his lack of an oath puts Solomon into a less awkward position should he decide later that it is necessary to have Adonijah executed. The problem with the oath becomes clearer in 2:8, where David expresses regret for an oath he had made that now prevents him from killing Shimei. Solomon avoids this dilemma simply by neglecting to make a promise.

Solomon's words nevertheless give us two causes for concern. First, while Solomon implies that the behavior of a בֶּן־חַיִל, should be sufficient for Adonijah to be secure, the reality is that this designation has not been adequate in the recent past. Adonijah uses the similar term אִישׁ חַיִל, "worthy man,"⁵⁹ to identify Jonathan in 1:42, concluding as a result that Jonathan's message must be good.⁶⁰ From Adonijah's point of view, Jonathan's message turns out to be anything but,⁶¹ so that being a אִישׁ חַיִל did not help. Second, Hens-Piazza points out the similarity between the phrase in 1:52b לֹא־יִפֹּל מִשַּׂעֲרָתוֹ אָרְצָה, "not a single hair will fall to the ground," and the words used by David in 2 Sam 14:11b, referring to Absalom (although David does not know at this time that he is talking

---

56. Bodner, 153.

57. Jones, 105, credits the narrator with skillfully "preparing the way" for Adonijah's downfall by placing responsibility on Adonijah himself. It seems that the narrator is doubly skilled, as Solomon gets the credit for assigning responsibility to Adonijah!

58. See Walsh, 32, for further discussion.

59. Mulder, 75 points out that while אִישׁ חַיִל usually carries a military connotation, the word חַיִל, "might," sometimes connotates metaphorical strength, as in notable wealth, sincerity, or valiance.

60. Reading w in the final phrase וְטוֹב תְּבַשֵּׂר to indicate a result clause.

61. The meaning of אֲבָל, "truly" or possibly "on the contrary, no" (as in Gen 17:19) is uncertain here: while AV and JPS translate this "verily," NRSV, NASB, and ESV prefer "No" (NASB is emphatic). Mulder, 75–76, has "You bet!," for which some credit should probably go to Mulder's translator, John Vriend.

about Absalom). Ironically, it is through his hair that Absalom dies in 2 Sam 18:9.[62] Perhaps in 1 Kgs 1:52 Solomon is alluding to the inevitable execution of Adonijah?

As an added touch, Solomon refuses to permit Adonijah to "do obeisance" in 1:53. The conversation between David and court attendants Bathsheba, Nathan, and Benaiah in 1:15–37 contains several wishes for blessings and health on those involved. This suggests that a meeting between Adonijah and Solomon may lead to a situation in which Solomon might be expected by court custom to make commitment to preserve Adonijah's welfare. Solomon avoids this by simply instructing Adonijah to go to his home.

First Kings 2 furnishes a second instance in which Solomon "wisely" avoids making an oath. Bathsheba asks her son for one "small" wish in 2:20, without naming it. Solomon agrees to grant it without promising to do so. As a result, he faces little awkwardness when he refuses his mother's request.[63]

Solomon's cleverness with respect to oaths is most apparent in his dealing with Shimei in 2:36–45. Again, while David regarded Shimei as a threat, the latter found protection in David's public oath of 2 Sam 19:23.[64] It is in connection with this oath that David uses the adjective חָכָם to describe Solomon in 2:9. Shimei deserves death by David's reckoning, but because of David's promise, Solomon will need "wisdom" in order to know what to do.[65]

---

62. Hens-Piazza, 20–21.

63. Sweeney, 69, asserts that Solomon's reversal here suggests that he "lacks credibility." But the absence of an oath here suggests that his advance promise to grant Bathsheba's request was a commitment understood as part of the formal court protocol, not to be executed in the case of an inappropriate request.

64. Anderson, *2 Samuel*, 237, lists several reasons for David's oath: general amnesty linked to re-taking the crown, the presence of 1,000 Benjamite witnesses (2 Sam 19:17); a boon to the "house of Israel" to win support. David therefore may not have wanted to extend mercy, but circumstances gave him little choice.

65. Walsh, 42–43, suggests that David himself introduces the creative use of oaths in 2:8. In 2 Sam 19 David says to Shimei, "you shall not die," a promise which is "without loopholes." But in 1 Kgs 2:8b David "remembers" saying אִם-אֲמִיתְךָ בֶּחָרֶב, almost universally rendered, "I will not put you to death with the sword," which, Walsh contends, permits someone other than David to kill Shimei. Walsh probably overreads here in two ways. First, if David were stressing to Solomon that it was only he himself that could not kill Shimei, then we would expect to see him stress this through the utilization of the first person pronoun, rather than his simple use of the first person verbal form. Second, the verb is hiph'il, which might better be translated, "I will not

Solomon cannot violate David's oath, but he can still treat Shimei as a potential threat. He therefore speaks to Shimei in language similar to that he had used with Adonijah in 1:52, stipulating in 2:37 that Shimei's life or death will depend on Shimei's own proper behavior. The author does not mention any oath during Solomon's conversation with Shimei in 2:36–38.[66] Shimei eventually travels from Jerusalem to Gath in order to retrieve runaway slaves—thus motivated by economics, rather than rebellion.[67] When Solomon confronts Shimei, Solomon nevertheless stresses that Shimei had sworn to Yahweh not to travel outside of Jerusalem. Violation of an oath sworn to Yahweh is apparently cause for death on its own.[68] Ironically, as Bodner points out, Solomon's wisdom here involves the circumvention of David's oath by means of another oath![69]

The wisdom of Solomon in 1 Kgs 2 thus involves manipulation of words in order to secure the throne.[70] Like Nathan's cleverness in 1 Kgs 1:11–14, Solomon's wisdom is subversive. Nathan uses wisdom to deceive; Solomon uses wisdom to justify murder. Solomon's wisdom is not something that will stop him from killing people who have not earned it.

The General Kept in Line

Bathsheba's literary function in 1 Kgs 1–2 is to highlight the different relationships that David and Solomon have with women. While the narrator develops Bathsheba in a way that reminds us of other women in the RN, she does not become a major character in her own right, but serves

---

cause you to be killed," thus indicating something broader than "I will not kill you myself." David's words in 1 Kgs 2:8 thus reflect the same idea as his words in 2 Sam 19:23.

66. Alter, 383, nevertheless reads Solomon's words in 2:36–37 as constituting an oath, suggesting that 2:38 may point to Shimei's implied oath.

67. Brueggemann, *Kings,* 36 stresses the "compelling force of economic risk" here.

68. Rosenberg, *Allegory,* 187, suggests that Solomon was even more devious. Rosenberg contends that the text implies that anonymous informants led Shimei out of Jerusalem to Gath, where old allies of David could report his presence to Solomon.

69. Bodner, 172.

70. Provan, "Seeing," 170. Provan connects Solomon's wisdom of 1 Kgs 2 to the wisdom of the wise woman of Abel Beth-Maacah in 2 Sam 20, who, like David, advocates killing in order to achieve security. The circumstances between the two narratives are so different, however, that a different type of wisdom is likely in vogue. Justification for the executions of Joab and Shimei are questionable at best, while 2 Sam 20:1 identifies Sheba as a אִישׁ בְּלִיַּעַל, "man of worthlessness," certainly deserving his ultimate fate.

only as a vehicle for understanding others. The narrator takes a similar approach with a second character drawn from the RN, Benaiah son of Jehoida.

Prior to 1 Kings, Benaiah appears only in lists of officials in 2 Sam 8:18 and 20:23 and in a short episode among the tales of David's mighty men in 23:20-22. Like Bathsheba, Benaiah has not been given much of a personality prior to 1 Kgs 1. But just as the character Bathsheba highlights differences between the susceptibility of David and Solomon to suggestion (particularly suggestions from women!), Benaiah's activity in 1 Kgs 1-2 serves to demonstrate Solomon's superior grip on authority.

In the RN, and even earlier, Joab represents a problem for David, often coming into conflict with the king. Joab is loyal in that he supports what he perceives to be in David's best interest. Joab nevertheless acts at different times at cross purposes to David's explicit commands: he kills Absalom, despite David's instructions to the contrary (2 Sam 18:5, 14); he rebukes David for mourning on a day of victory (19:1-7); and he assassinates David's appointed general Amasa (19:13; 20:10). In each instance, Joab's loyalty to David seems clear, but he clearly has no qualms about acting contrary to David's expressed instructions. Joab's repeated disobedience thus draws attention to David's weakness as a leader in the RN.

Dtr1 tells us in 1 Kgs 4:4 that Benaiah leads Solomon's army, replacing Joab from David's officer list. Benaiah therefore has become Solomon what Joab was to David. Yet while Joab often displays behavior that clearly moves beyond David's wishes, in 1 Kgs 1-2 Benaiah acts entirely in accordance with the instructions of his king; first David, then Solomon.

The first opportunity for comparison between Benaiah and Joab occurs in 1 Kgs 1:7-10. Joab supports Adonijah's move to become king, while Benaiah does not. The text does not state that Benaiah necessarily opposes Adonijah, but says only that Benaiah (along with Nathan the prophet, Shimei, and the otherwise unmentioned Rei) was not "with" him. Verse 10 nevertheless suggests that Benaiah is part of a "pro-Solomon" faction whose members were not invited to Adonijah's celebration. Although the text does not say that he is anything more than neutral,[71] most readers identify him and the הַגִּבּוֹרִים, "the warriors" (likely referring to the "Cherethites and Pelethites" of 1:38, led by Benaiah in 2 Sam 8:18

---

71. Mulder, 46-47, gives some personal considerations which may have precluded certain individuals from joining with Adonijah.

and 20:23), as members of Solomon's party.⁷² The text does not give reasons for Benaiah's failure to support Adonijah or for Adonijah's decision not to invite Benaiah to his sacrificial celebration.⁷³ Joab, however, is in the opposite camp, explicitly conferring with Adonijah in 1:7.

Joab's interaction with Adonijah in 1:7 seems consistent with his independent behavior in the RN. The text gives us no indication that Joab's behavior is in any way disloyal: to this point, the text does not suggest in any way that David might favor someone other than his eldest son as his successor. Verse 6 supports the logic of this conclusion: Adonijah had never displeased his father, and, in the tradition of kings thus far, is טוֹב־תֹּאַר מְאֹד, "very handsome" (compare David in 1 Sam 16:12, and Saul in 1 Sam 9:2).⁷⁴ These attributes remind us of Absalom, who had been described in many of the same terms; thus, the narrator is signaling that Adonijah's celebration is premature.⁷⁵ Joab nevertheless aligns himself with the presumed crown prince, rendering tacit approval of Adonijah's actions.⁷⁶

But Benaiah takes no action and is not involved in the palace intrigue to place Solomon on the throne. The planning and execution of the plan to put Solomon on the throne are the work of Nathan, aided

---

72. Seow, 18; Brueggemann, 12; Fritz, 16–17; Walsh, 8–10.

73. Sweeeney, 55, follows in the line of commentators who portray pro- and anti-Adonijah factions in terms of their association with David before and after he became King in Jerusalem. Joab and Abiathar were with David prior to his ascension to the throne, and Adonijah was born to Haggith while David reigned in Hebron (2 Sam 3:4). Benaiah is not otherwise clearly associated with Jerusalem, however. Sweeney suggests that he was associated with David in the latter's "pre-Jerusalem" days, although he gives no evidence. Benaiah is listed among David's heroes in 2 Sam 23:20–23, but this passage does not suggest that Benaiah was associated with David prior to Jerusalem.

74. Long, 38, contrasts Adonijah, who is (like Absalom and David) "aggressive, self-assured, handsome, powerful successful," with Solomon, who is introduced as merely the passive object of the actions of others. This may be an early indication of Solomon's bureaucratic style, juxtaposed with David's charisma.

75. Coogan, 156–57; Sweeeny, 54–55.

76. Tomoo Ishida, "Political," 185, argues that by this point Joab had become *de facto* ruler of Israel. If Adonijah had become king, he would have been Joab's puppet, just as Ishbaal was the puppet of Abner in 2 Sam 2:8–9. This interpretation supports the need for quick and decisive action on the part of Solomon's party. First Kings 1:41 supports this idea: it is Joab, not Adonijah, who expresses concern over the loud celebration of Solomon's coronation. However, overall evidence is very scanty for the idea that Joab, not Adonijah, was really in charge. The narrator seems more interested in likening Adonijah to Absalom than to Ishbaal, even though Joab's presence with Adonijah certainly heightens the severity of the situation.

by Bathsheba. Benaiah is absent from 1:10 until he is summoned by King David in 1:32, after the King has determined to appoint Solomon as successor. When David gives his instructions regarding Solomon's coronation, Benaiah speaks his first words in 1 Kings, beginning with אָמֵן ("amen/let it be so"). This is the word that defines Benaiah's character in 1 Kgs 1–2: Benaiah is completely loyal and obedient to his king.

In accordance with David's wishes, the remainder of Benaiah's speech in 1 Kgs 1:36–37 simply expresses the hope that David's ruling will be fulfilled, and pronounces blessings on Solomon's reign. Benaiah then becomes part of the group that coronates Solomon but remains silent and takes no further action until after Solomon takes the throne as sole ruler in 1 Kgs 2.

Benaiah's next appearance is simple and straightforward: in 2:25 Solomon sends Benaiah to kill Adonijah, and he does so. It is significant, however, that the narrator identifies Benaiah by name here. Per his style thus far, the narrator is not required to name Adonijah's executioner. In 1 Kgs 1:50–53, for example, when Adonijah grasps the horns of the altar, Solomon "sends" in order to communicate to Adonijah and to give instructions regarding his fate. The text does not tell us who it was that Solomon sent at that juncture. The fact that the narrator now gives us this information in 2:25 is a signal that Benaiah is gaining an identity as Solomon's loyal "hatchet man."

This becomes important in the handling of the problematic Joab situation. In 1 Kgs 2:28 Joab flees to the tent of Yahweh in order to grasp the horns of the altar, the action taken by Adonijah in order to preserve his own life in 1:50. First Kings 2:28 nevertheless specifies that while Joab had supported Adonijah, he had not supported Absalom, who, unlike Adonijah, had represented a clear threat to David.[77] More immediately, the text does not say that Joab was part of any sort of coup, and there is no indication that he was involved in any way with Adonijah's request for Abishag. Yet Solomon has just executed Adonijah and now apparently seeks to destroy all powerful individuals who had supported him.

Joab's flight to the tent of Yahweh hearkens to a tradition recorded in Ex 21:12–14 that stipulates a "place of safety" where someone accused of murder may find refuge. This precept appears to compel legal authorities to stage some sort of trial, to demonstrate to the community the crime for

---

77. First Kings 1–2 gives no direct indication that Adonijah intended to usurp David. We see only that he was trying to succeed him.

which an accused person is to die.⁷⁸ Benaiah's hesitation here is quite appropriate: Benaiah has been instructed to kill Joab, but Joab has claimed sanctuary at a sacred site. The tent seems to carry an air of the sacred: for example, in 1:39 Zadok anoints Solomon with oil from "the tent."⁷⁹ Furthermore, as just mentioned, Solomon apparently respects the right of sanctuary in this location in the past, giving credence to the idea of a trial with the words, "if he proves to be a worthy man, not one of his hairs shall fall to the ground; but if wickedness is found in him, he shall die" (1 Kgs 1:52). Solomon's intent with respect to Joab therefore requires clarification.

Benaiah will not decide on his own and so seeks the instruction of his king. A trial will not fit Solomon's interest, given the nebulous immediate charges. Therefore, in 2:31 the king immediately decides that Joab must be killed where he stands by the altar. Some Israelites may have at least raised a question about the propriety of executing a man in this place, given that Ex 21:14 stipulates that a guilty party is to be removed *from* the altar for execution. The act of removal will lead to questions and possibly even objections from the community. Solomon's selection of Benaiah as executioner thus proves to be prescient: Benaiah does not hesitate when Solomon directs Benaiah to kill Joab where he stands. Immediately after this display of unflinching loyalty, Solomon appoints Benaiah as general (2:35).⁸⁰

This situation reminds us of several instances in the RN in which Joab is confronted with an awkward situation, including the episodes in which Absalom is found trapped in 2 Sam 18:9–13, and in which Amasa is slow to organize the troops in 2 Sam 20:5–10. Both instances feature complex dilemmas in which the king's instructions require clarification. It therefore appears proper each time for Joab to report to David in order to learn the monarch's will. Joab instead takes direct action on his own, killing Absalom and Amasa. In each case, Joab can demonstrate

---

78. Sarna, *Exodus*, 122, and Childs, *Exodus*, 470, explain the community effort to exercise social control over the tenacity of the blood feud.

79. Hens-Piazza, 19, offers a discussion of the significance of oil from "the tent."

80. While of course Joab's death necessitates a new general, Solomon certainly is not obligated to appoint one right away. Neither is the narrator required to tell us who succeeded Joab: we know this because the identities of new generals are not revealed until some time after the deaths of Abner and Amasa in 2 Sam. The fact that the narrator immediately informs us that Benaiah was appointed to succeed Joab suggests a connection between Benaiah's act of killing Joab, and his promotion to leader of the army.

some justification for killing these men: Absalom's death effectively ends his rebellion, and Amasa's death effectively transfers control of the army to personnel who can organize the needed military action.[81] Yet David clearly is unhappy with Joab's action each time, and certainly would have preferred that Joab confer with him before taking action.

But while Joab had often acted on his own and frequently contrarily to David's wishes, Benaiah only does Solomon's bidding. David could not control his army commander, but Solomon is the master of his. This foreshadows a rule in 1 Kgs 3–10 that contains no hint of insubordination whatsoever. The security of Solomon's throne is an important element in the depiction of his power. Even as Solomon re-districts Israel in 4:7–19 and sets up forced labor in chapters 5 and 9, we see no word of objection from the populace. The text instead offers indications of great contentment: for example, the narrator's evaluation in 4:20, "Judah and Israel were as numerous as the sand by the sea; they ate and drank and were happy,"[82] and the observation of the Queen of Sheba, "Happy are your wives! Happy are these your servants, who continually attend you and hear your wisdom!" (1 Kgs 10:8).

Controlling the Cult

In 1 Kgs 1, David acts on the counsel of a prophet. Nathan had advised David twice in 2 Sam, in his reply to David's request to build a temple in 2 Sam 7, and in his rebuke of David's adultery and murder in 2 Sam 12. David had also consulted the prophet Gad in 1 Sam 22:5 and 2 Sam 24:13–18, and at other points in his career had utilized the services of unnamed prophets, including incidents reported in 1 Sam 23:1–4 and 2 Sam 21:1. David's willingness to submit to the word of prophets is a mark of his submission to Yahweh, particularly in light of the stormy relationship of David's predecessor Saul with the prophet Samuel. Solomon, however,

---

81. Whybray, *Succession*, 41, and Eschelbach, *Joab*, argue that Joab's executions are wholly justified. Joab kills Abner at a moment when Abner appears to pose a threat to David, approaching Hebron with an armed contingent. Later, Amasa's slow action had threatened to make Sheba's rebellion a success, again prompting Joab to action. However, Joab's deceptive means used in his killings (2 Sam 3:27; 20:9) puts him in a bad light.

82. While some readings interpret this comment ironically, we must permit the possibility that the author really means to say that no one objected. Absent compelling evidence for a post-modern interpretation, we should follow the plain meaning.

does not work with prophets but makes decisions unaided. Even Nathan, who had been so instrumental in Solomon's ascension, disappears after taking part in Solomon's consecration in 1 Kgs 1:38–39. This foreshadows the complete absence of references to prophets in Solomon's reign (as discussed in chapter 3).

Richard Nelson has shown that Dtr uses priests for three main purposes: to support the prophecy-fulfillment schema, to drive home ideological truths, and to guarantee legitimacy.[83] David and Saul are unable to control the office of priest, but the priests become subject to Solomon. Solomon effectively exiles Abiathar from Jerusalem, installing the line of Zadok in his place. The author of 1 Kgs 1–2 directly cites Abiathar's removal from the priesthood as a fulfillment of the prophecy given to Eli in 1 Sam 2–3. But the identity of the King removing the priest is also important to the author's purpose: it is not the righteous David, but Solomon who exercises the necessary power.

We see Solomon further exercising control over the cult in his reaction to Joab's flight to the altar in a desperate attempt to preserve his life (1 Kgs 2:28). Joab had reason to expect that his proximity to the altar might lead to a stay of execution: this was apparently the means by which Adonijah had survived in 1 Kgs 1:50. Joab's immediate behavior had certainly been no worse than that of Adonijah: if Adonijah, in seeking the throne, was permitted to live, then why not his supporter Joab? But Joab's move fails because Solomon acts decisively.

Solomon's control of cultic matters carries into his reign. He decides to build the temple, making his announcement in 1 Kgs 5:19, without consulting an adviser, or even Yahweh. Solomon instead simply gives his own interpretation of Nathan's oracle from 2 Sam 7:12–13, not incidentally stressing that the son of David who had been chosen by Yahweh should build Yahweh's temple.

This last point carries ominous undertones, coming as it does after the events of 1 Kgs 2. In that chapter, Solomon reiterates the concept of his secure throne each time he gives an execution order: Adonijah (2:24), Joab (2:33), Shimei (2:45). Dtr1 had reported that Solomon's throne was "established" (תִּכֹּן) in 2:12. Dtr2 develops this idea, showing what action is necessary to "establish" the kingdom. The establishment of Solomon's kingdom in 1 Kgs 2:46b, which expressly fulfills the dynastic promise of 2 Sam 7:13, takes on a different meaning when considering the executions

---

83. Nelson, "Priesthood," 191.

of Adonijah, Joab, and Shimei.[84] The security of Solomon as heir to the line of David justifies all.

This attitude contrasts remarkably with that of David in the History of David's rise (HDR). David never seems interested in his own legacy. Compare, for example, the way David approaches the question of the temple in 2 Sam 7:1–2, where he simply remarks on the inappropriateness of the Ark resting in a tent while the king lives in a palace. In the HDR, David uses his power for the well-being of the cult; Solomon uses the cult to secure his own kingdom and legacy.

Solomon's role as David's favored son becomes a major theme in Solomon's dedication of and prayer for the Temple 1 Kgs 8. As in 1 Kgs 5, Solomon refers to himself as Yahweh's chosen son (1 Kgs 8:17–20). In the prayer following, Solomon refers to the Temple numerous times as "the house which I have built," and he noticeably places his own needs ahead of those of the people in 8:52, 59.[85] Self-absorption thus becomes a major factor of his character.

Conclusions

While the RN and the Solomon narrative appear to have been composed separately, 1 Kgs 1–2 is clearly related to both. These chapters conclude the SN by introducing Solomon as a king who brings security to the throne after the chaos of the later years of David's rule. At the same time, these chapters introduce us to some of Solomon's major character traits, particularly his controlling nature, which rightly affects the reader's interpretation of the Solomon narrative to follow. First Kings 1–2 thus looks backwards and forwards, transitioning from David's ignorance and weakness to Solomon's wisdom and strength.

As in the RN and the Solomon story, the author of 1 Kgs 1–2 uses female characters to describe differences in the characters of David and Solomon. David poorly manages the women with whom he comes into contact. He (unwittingly) enables the rape of his daughter Tamar; he is fooled by the wise woman of Tekoa; his concubines are forced into public sexual relations with his usurper. Solomon, however, effectively manages the women around him, controlling the movements of his Egyptian wife,

---

84. McConville, *Political*, 152.
85. Walsh, 115.

marrying off two "daughters" to district governors, and displaying mastery over the Queen of Sheba during her visit.

The RN and Solomon story further illustrate the two rulers' control of their respective administrations. Joab acts independently by hiring the wise woman of Tekoa in 2 Sam 14:1, and by killing Absalom in 18:14 and Amasa in 20:10, but never receives more than mild verbal chastisement from David. Solomon, however, always appears in complete control of his administration, just as Benaiah follows Solomon's orders without question in 1 Kgs 2.

Yet Solomon's strength and wisdom have more to do with pragmatic control than righteous rule. First Kings 1–2 show that Solomon is able to "play the game" better than his illustrious predecessor. These chapters thus serve to explain how it is that Solomon achieves his political greatness and yet ultimately falls far short of Yahweh's standards.

Excursus: Abishag in 1 Kings 1:1–4

Abishag, introduced at the start of 1 Kgs 1, appears several times in chapters 1–2, but the author never permits her to speak or take any action on her own. Her sole literary function is to reveal characteristics of those around her: David, Bathsheba, Adonijah, Solomon. Commentators often understand that Abishag is appointed as royal concubine in 1:3 to test David's sexual virility, noting particularly that David לֹא יְדָעָהּ, "did not know her" in 1:4.[86] However, as demonstrated by Richard S. Hess, there is no biblical or other ANE data which points to sexual ability as a test of royal acumen.[87] Instead, the inability of the young Shunammite virgin Abishag to give warmth (חֹם, perhaps alluding to the חֹם transmitted by Elisha to the son of the Shunammite widow in 2 Kgs 4:34) to the king points to David's irreversible decline, and the decline of his ability to rule along with it.[88]

---

86. Buis, *Rois*, 39; Mulder, 35; Brueggemann, 12; Fritz, 14.

87. Hess, "Purpose," 434n. Gray, 77, cites an example from Ugarit of a king's illness disqualifying him from rule, but the "illness" here is not specified as sexual impotence. Sweeney, 53, points to a Sumerian/ Babylonian akitu festival where the king has relations with the high priestess, but this text also does not specifically link sexual potency to ability to rule.

88. Hess, 436–37, makes the most complete argument for this interpretation. Others who affirm this reading include House, 87–88; Walsh, 5; Alter, 364; Seow, 14; Cogan, 156; Hens-Piazza, 13.

First Kings 1:1 begins very simply and directly: וְהַמֶּלֶךְ דָּוִד זָקֵן בָּא בַּיָּמִים, "Now King David was old and advanced in years." David's advanced age serves as a metaphor for his style of charismatic leadership, which no longer meets the needs of the nation. Adonijah also represents the old order: he tries to gain attention through an exercise of power, summoning many of David's subjects to a pre-coronation event. The new king, however, gains attention not through popular acclaim, but rather through the word of the king. Adonijah's celebration in 1:5–10, following the note on David's age and unstoppable decay, enhances the idea that Israel needs a new kind of king who relies on more than just personal charisma.[89]

---

89. Caspi and Haverlock, *Women*, 110–11.

7

Solomon in Light of the Succession Narrative

Thus far, I've laid out principal themes of Dtr1's Solomon story, the Succession Narrative/ Revolt Narrative, and 1 Kgs 1–2, and I've described a number of the inter-relationships between these three parts of the Deuteronomistic History. We are now ready to put this information together in order to facilitate a sound reading of MT 1 Kgs 3–11.

There are two parts to this chapter. First, I will discuss the work of Dtr2 in 1 Kgs 3–11. The most extensive part of Dtr2's work here belongs to the story of Solomon and the Two Prostitutes in 1 Kgs 3:16–28, which, as explained in chapter 2, appear to be an extensive re-write of a story originating from outside Israel. Second, I will discuss ways in which the Revolt Narrative and 1 Kgs 1–2 impact the presentation of 1 Kgs 3–11. The difference between the Solomon Narrative of Dtr1 and the Masoretic Text of 1 Kgs 3–11 is not simply the specific additions made by Dtr2 and succeeding editors. First Kings 3–11 also has a revised literary context, which means that its meaning must be re-evaluated based on the contents of 2 Sam 11–20 and 1 Kgs 1–2.

The Work of Dtr2, Including 1 Kings 3:16–28

Dtr2's most substantial contribution to the DH is the story of "Solomon and the Two Prostitutes." This passage has generally been understood to be an example of Solomon's great wisdom, in which he settles a life-and-death dispute between two prostitutes.¹ In fact, this passage is really the account of Solomon's conversation with a single woman, the "true mother," who brings a petition to the king. As in the David/wise woman of Tekoa episode of 2 Sam 14 and the David/Bathsheba episode of 1 Kgs 1, both plaintiff and king are unnamed in 1 Kgs 3, and the issue has to do with a woman trying to preserve the life of her son. Unlike the prior passages, Solomon is not fooled by a ruse. But the King does render a poor judgment, and, as in 2 Sam 14, the words of the female plaintiff contain more than surface meaning.

Most commentators agree that Dtr adopted a folktale to provide an example of the juridical wisdom granted to Solomon by Yahweh: a difficult case requires extraordinary wisdom to execute justice.² But the folkloric origins of this passage do not indicate that it was placed in 1 Kgs 3 in order to demonstrate Solomon's wisdom.³ The king in this account simply does not display juridical acumen in presiding over this case. Despite several holes in her testimony⁴, the king does not bother to cross examine the first woman, and his decision to cut the living child in half seems unreasonably dangerous.⁵

---

1. Subheadings of English translations of the Old Testament tend to reflect the notion that Solomon acts wisely. The NIV titles this section, "A Wise Ruling;" NKJV has "Solomon's Wise Judgment;" ESV has "Solomon's Wisdom;" NASB, "Solomon Wisely Judges;" NRSV, "Solomon's Wisdom in Judgement." GNT has a strikingly difficult approach, "Solomon Judges a Difficult Case," which is closest to the intepretation proposed here.

2. Montgomery and Gehman, *Kings*, 110; Gray, *Kings*, 127; Würthwein, *Könige*, 36–37; Buis, *Rois*, 55–56; Mulder, *Kings*, 154; Cogan, *Kings*, 196; Fritz, *Kings*, 41–42; Sweeney, *Kings*, 82.

3. Gressman, *Geschichtsschreibung*, 198, cited in Gray, 127, documented 22 versions of this story from various parts of the world, suggesting that the original is from India. Conroy, *Samuel*, 148, points to the anonymity of the king as evidence for Israelite adaptation of a folkloric story.

4. The first woman claims to know exactly what happened while she was asleep, including the cause of death, and she does not recognize that the dead child is her son until morning light, after she had been awake for some time. For further discussion see Lasine, 67–68.

5. Weitzman, *Solomon*, 59–61. Weitzman references a 1920's child custody case presided over by former congressman Judge Vincent Brennan. Brennan ordered that the child be placed in an orphanage, then secretly videotaped the private reactions of the birth mother and foster mother, awarding custody to the woman who showed more outward biological reaction (crying, sobbing, etc.) Weitzman reports that even at the time, this was widely regarded as a shameless publicity stunt.

To get a sense of Dtr's editing and use of this story in the DH, it is helpful to examine the closest parallel version extant,[6] a Jaina story from southern India:

> A certain merchant had two wives; one of them had a son and the other had not. But the childless wife also took good care of the other's child, and the child was not able to distinguish, "this is my mother, that is not." After a time the merchant, with his wives and son, went to another country, and just after his arrival there he died. Then the two wives fell to quarrelling. One of them said, "Mine is the child," and the other said just the same. One said, "It is I who am the mistress of the house," and the other said, "It is I." At last they carried the dispute before a royal court of justice. The presiding minister of justice gave an order to his men, "First divide the whole property, then saw the child in two with a saw, and give one part to the one woman and the other part to the other." But when the mother heard the minister's sentence, it was as if a thunderbolt, enveloped in a thousand flames, had fallen on her head, and with her heart all trembling as if it had been pierced by a crooked dart, she contrived with difficulty to speak. "Ah, sire! Great minister!" she said, "It is not mine, this child! The money is of no use to me! Let the child be the son of that woman, and let her be the mistress of the house. As for me, it is no matter if I drag out an indigent life in strange houses; though it be from a distance, yet shall I see that child living, and so shall I attain the object of my life. Whereas, without my son, even now the whole living world is dead to me." But the other woman uttered never a word. Then the minister, beholding the distress of the former woman, said, "To her belongs the child, but not to that one." And he made the mother the mistress of the house, but the other woman he rebuked.[7]

Two aspects of this story are important for our understanding of the place of 1 Kgs 3:16–28 in its current context. First, the focus of the story clearly is not the "wisdom" of the minister. Rather, the story concentrates on the true mother's feelings and actions to preserve the life of her son. Second, this story relies on narration, rather than an explanation by the true mother, to explain how these women found themselves in such a difficult position.[8]

---

6. Gray, 127. Frazier, *Folklore*, 570, notes three similar versions from the same time and place as the account which I give here.

7. Tessitiori, "Two Jaina Versions," 149, cited in Frazier, *Folklore*, 570–71.

8. In 1 Kgs 3:16-28, the "other woman" has only two short lines, in 22a, "No, the

Given the MT of 1 Kgs 3:16–28, where all of the facts of the case are transmitted through the first woman (the plaintiff), we do better to look for significance in the words of the first woman. The narration affords her five verses to tell her story, certainly more than needed, so we should at least consider whether this woman's testimony itself has a deeper significance.[9] The form of this story is similar to that of the account of the wise woman of Tekoa in 2 Sam 14:1–20. In both stories, the kings and plaintiffs are unnamed throughout, although contexts make each king's identity clear. Dialog is essentially limited to the king and the plaintiff. There is one dead son, and a living son whose welfare is seriously threatened (according to 3:19, the "other woman's" son died because she lay on him, thus demonstrating her inability to properly care for her son). And, ironically, both stories feature assessments of the king's wisdom (2 Sam 14:20; 1 Kgs 3:28) which, given the circumstances, seem unwarranted.

Many readers are troubled by certain of the king's actions in this tale. The first woman's lengthy story raises many questions, yet the king does not probe her testimony, or even respond to it.[10] The second woman does not testify at all. Furthermore, while the king's response turns out well, for a few moments the innocent child appears to be in mortal danger.[11] The king's reasoning itself is open to question. As George E. Mendenhall observes, "one could just as easily argue ... that the true mother would rather see her child killed than give him up to an unscrupulous bitch."[12] Is the king's wisdom mixed with recklessness?

At the same time, the content and placement of this story cannot help but to shape the reader's conception of the Solomonic narrative and

---

living son is mine, and the dead son is yours," and 26b, "It shall be neither mine nor yours; divide it." These lines render her a stick figure, in contrast to the more revealing emotions of the first woman. While a number of commentators have questioned the identity of the true mother, Garsiel, "Revealing," demonstrates that textual indicators mark the first prostitute as the true mother. She speaks first each time, thus gaining the readers' sympathy; the term for the other woman, הָאִשָּׁה הָאַחֶרֶת, always represents an outsider who has borne illegitimate children; the first woman and true mother maintain proper decorum, whereas the second woman and false mother demonstrate none. On the methodology of consistency of characterization, see Brichto, *Poetics*, 52.

9. W. A. M. Beuken, "No Wise King," 3; Walsh, 142. Beuken and Walsh represent the tendency of commentators to avoid analyzing the details of 3:17–21. Both give verse-by-verse breakdowns of the structure, except for vv. 17–21, which they consider as one unit within the structure.

10. Walsh, *Kings*, 81 and Sweeney, *Kings*, 82, offer good discussions on this point.

11. Fontaine, "Response," 164.

12. Mendenhall, "Shady," 324.

the book of Kings. For example, Claudia Camp argues that 3:16–28 contributes to the larger Solomonic story by initiating a new unit in which Solomon redeems many of the failures of his father David.[13] Camp bases her thesis in part on the work of Carole Fontaine, who argues that 1 Kgs 3 features many of the same elements as 2 Sam 11–12: a king makes a choice; the choice has consequences; consequences are followed by a courtroom scene in which the life of a child is at stake.[14] According to Camp, Solomon's decision to choose wisdom in 3:9 transforms him into someone who engenders life in 3:16–28. Contrarily, David's infant son had died as a result of the Bathsheba incident, and chaos had come to Israel. But Solomon's wise choice allows him to save the life of a child, and bring order to a chaotic situation.[15]

David Jobling suggests that 1 Kgs 3–11 negatively correlates sexuality with wisdom.[16] Camp prefers to view this material as featuring *managed* sexuality—in his wisdom, Solomon is not against sex, but only 'wrong' sex. The prostitute, like the foreign Queen of Sheba in 1 Kgs 10, threatens the social patriarchal fabric through her (presumed) uncontrolled sexuality. But Solomon transforms the two prostitutes here into women who live, at least metaphorically, according to the norms of social order.[17]

The difficulty with this thesis is that while Camp draws on the broad social understanding of prostitute as social threat, not under the authority of a man, the narrator seems to have another idea in mind. The sexuality of the women does not come into play in 3:16–28. The dispute pertains not to sex, but to a definitive determination of motherhood of a specific child. Camp's argument would be stronger if the idea of prostitute as social threat was prominent in the Deuteronomistic History. But

---

13. Camp, *Strange Woman*, 165–69.

14. Fontaine, "Bearing," 146.

15. Camp, 166. On this point, Reinhartz argues that Solomon also metaphorically rehabilitates the "true mother" from prostitution as well. See Reinhartz, "Anonymous Women," 54.

16. Jobling, "Value," 481, argues that 1 Kgs 3–4 deals with Solomon's wisdom without considering sexuality, while 1 Kgs 11 (Solomon's fall) refers to his sexual shortcomings without mentioning wisdom. Jobling also sees wisdom taking the place of sexuality in Solomon's interaction with the two women of this story, and the Queen of Sheba account in ch. 10. While the issue of wisdom vs. sexuality is important to chapters 10 and 11, it is difficult to discern sexual overtones in the king's relationship with the women in 3:16–28.

17. Camp, 168.

while the concept of prostitution as a reference to "wrong sex" is fairly common in the Hebrew Bible as a whole, the term זֹנָה and its cognates occur in only one other place in Kings (a passing reference in 1 Kgs 22:38) and not at all in Samuel.[18] More likely, in 3:16ff Dtr2 wants us to picture women who are, as Fontaine puts it, "functional widows." They have no men (husband, father, brother, etc.) to protect them, and not even a name indicating a larger family attachment. They apparently are women who have taken up the profession out of economic necessity, living on the margins of society, with little hope of achieving justice.[19]

Phyllis Trible and Gina Hens-Piazza view the term "prostitute" in 3:16 as an identification, rather than as a judgment.[20] Avaren Ipsen goes farther, arguing that the women's *identification* as "prostitute" (as opposed to their *function*) is the crucial point. A modern Los Angeles prostitute pointed out to Ipsen that the fact that the women are prostitutes is *integral* to the setting, since the only way that a woman in ancient Israel could bring a matter before the king was if she did not have a man to otherwise speak for her. A woman living under the protection of father, husband, brother, or other male relative would have a male figure available to bring the case to the royal court.[21] Since the crux of the story depends on the true mother's deep compassion from her womb, the plaintiffs must be women who do not have the protection of men, and thus are cast as prostitutes.

First Kings 3:16–27: Structure[22]

Dtr2's arrangement of this story falls into two distinct parts.[23] Verses 16 through 22 give the facts of the case, stressing the first woman's testimony. The narrated discourse of 22b provides relief from the tension of

---

18. Here Camp draws on Bird, "Inquiry." But Bird's article offers little about the DH's use of this metaphor, concentrating more on Hosea and Genesis 38.

19. Fontaine, 155.

20. Trible, *Sexuality*, 31; Hens-Piazza, *Sociorhetorical*, 133.

21. Ipsen, "Solomon," 142.

22. Würthwein, 36–38; Mulder, *Kings*, 160; Fritz, 43. Most commentators read 1 Kgs 3:28 as a summary evaluation, separate from the story proper.

23. BHS divides this section after verse 23, in which the king essentially repeats the first part of verse 22, but it seems more logical to read the king's reiteration as the beginning of the second half of the story.

the first person speeches.[24] In verses 23 through 27, the king has most of the lines and directs the action, but the true mother also plays a crucial role. Each of the two parts fits neatly into its own distinct chiasm, with the key theme of each placed at the center.[25] As we shall see, the manner by which the two parts relate to each other gives us the necessary clues to apply this story to Solomon.

Part 1: 3:16–22

A   Women come before the king (16)
  B   Setting: conflict foreshadowed (17–18)
    C   Second woman's actions (19–20)
    C'   First woman's actions (21)
  B'   Setting: conflict actualized (22a)
A'   Women stand before the king (22b)

Part 1 begins and ends simply, with the two women standing before the king. In section A, they come to lay their case out before him; in section A', they wait to hear what he will say, and what decision he will make.

Section B, consisting of verses 17 and 18, features the first woman's description of the scene before her counterpart allegedly committed her crime. These verses not only set the foundation for this story's plot, but also hint at a major issue in Solomon's story through the fourfold use of the word בְּבַיִת, "in the house." The conflict takes place in part because the two women, whose characters turn out to be quite different, live in the same house. Nothing can be attributed to anyone outside of the house: "there was no stranger with us in the house" (18b).[26]

The focus of part one comes in sections C and C'. Section C describes the second woman's actions. In verse 19, her son dies. The cause of death is clear. It comes not through illness or disease or accident, or from what we know today as "sudden infant death syndrome." The child instead is killed by its mother, through her negligence. The picture of a mother inadvertently smothering the baby which sleeps by her side

---

24. Hens-Piazza, *Sociorhetorical,* 141.

25. While various outlines have been proposed, virtually all commentators recognize a major break between verses 22 and 23, or 23 and 24.

26. Garsiel, 236, points out that the assertion that this brothel was at this point devoid of clients is entirely plausible, given their late stage of pregnancy.

marks her as incapable on a fundamental level of providing care sufficient to nurture life. This woman's response to the tragedy further unveils her character. She acts in the dark: she kills in the night, then rises in the night to perform an act of deception, switching the two babies. Having caused a death, she now seeks control of another life which she will inevitably be unable to protect.

In arguing against the veracity of this tale, along with its dependence on older Indian accounts, Hermann Gunkel argued that the narrator overlooked the fact that a prostitute had no reason to value a child which was not born to her. In his estimation, there is no logical explanation for why she should burden herself with the duty of bringing up another's child. By way of contrast, Indian versions often bring larger familial rights into play, as with two wives surviving a single husband.[27]

Gunkel's objection is pertinent. Even if we stipulate that the second woman suffers from a sense of loss, or from some desire for a child to aid her own sense of self-value, we are still faced with her words in 3:26c, "It shall be neither mine nor yours; divide it."[28] While most readers contend that the true mother reveals herself through her willingness to surrender her child rather than see him killed, this does not satisfactorily explain the words of the second woman. The second woman is not merely willing to see the child die; she verbalizes her assent at his execution.

Dtr2 thus marks the second woman not merely as one of two women claiming a child, but as a force of evil.[29] If she gains possession of this child, it will certainly die, as this woman does not have the capacity to care for it. And if she cannot possess this child, she will call for its death, rather than allow it to be restored to its true mother. The child's mother, however, has the ability to nurture life, and so rises up to nurse her son. She acts not at night, but in the light of morning. Tragedy confronts her: the child is dead. But she examines (בין) him—again, in the morning, discovering that this child is not hers. The woman of evil deceives, but the first woman takes care to uncover truth. The actions of the two women reveal strong contrasts: one smothers and deceives at night; the other

---

27. Gunkel, *Folktale*, 156.

28. I will give evidence below to demonstrate that the first woman of 3:17–22 is the true mother of the living child.

29. The earliest known commentator to go in this direction is Flavius Josephus, who adds to 1 Kgs 3:27, "(The king) condemned the vileness of the other one, who, having killed her own child, was quite ready to countenance the loss of her friend as well" (*Ant.* 8:33).

nurtures and uncovers truth in the morning.³⁰ This contrast is the main point of verses 19 through 21.

Section B', verse 22, has the two women arguing back and forth over the child. The tense undercurrents of the living situation, introduced in section B, now surface, transformed into naked hostility. Justice now seems impossible to achieve; the court proceeding has devolved into a verbal free-for-all. At this point, the character of the first woman recedes into the background. She is no longer distinguished from her rival: the two women now use the same words to express the same sentiments: the living child is mine, the dead child is yours. Part 1 begins and ends in the same way: the two women sharing the same house, on seemingly equal footing before the king.

Part 1 features a tragic death, but Dtr2 does not mention it again after its occurrence because to bring it up again would abet the reader's empathy with the dead child's mother. Dtr2 instead concentrates solely on the fate of the living child. The struggle in this house is a struggle for influence over life. The dispassionate onlooker may view the living situation of section B without anticipating the difficulty which is to come. Indeed, the fact that they are prostitutes may make their living arrangement practical on a number of levels. But the characters of the two women are so different that they cannot for long co-exist in the home. One woman nurtures, and one destroys, but both hope to influence, and so will always struggle to control that which is alive.³¹

---

30. Wolde, "Who Guides Whom?," 627, and Hens-Piazza, 138–39, offers more on this contrast.

31. Women in Gen—2 Kgs are understood to attain personal value through their position as mothers. See Shargent, "Liminality," 34.

Part 2: 3:23–27

A   King states the problem (23)
  B   King orders action: Bring to me (a sword) (24)
    C   "Cut him up!" (King's words of division) (25)
      D   *watomer* (and she said), followed by true mother's feelings of love (26a)
      D'   *watomer*, followed by true mother's words of love (26b)
    C'   "Cut him up!" (Other woman's words) (26c)
  B'   King orders action: Give to her (the child) (27a)
A'   King states the solution (27b)

Part 2 revolves around the words and actions of the king, but the true mother claims the climax of this part of the story. As in part 1, the second woman is a mere caricature, speaking but a single sentence, here showing only her endorsement of the development of the plot as it pertains to her.

The king had been silent throughout the first part of this story. Now, in section A verse 23, he begins by summarizing his view of the problem, essentially repeating the words of verse 22. His observation matches his observation of A', which consists of two words, הִיא אִמּוֹ ("she is his mother"), again stating his assessment of the situation at hand. Part II belongs to the king; it is his words which begin and end it.

B and B' feature the king's orders for action. His first words of verse 24, "bring to me," correspond to those of verse 27, תְּנוּ־לָהּ, "give to her." The bringing of the sword and the giving of the child to the true mother are the high dramatic actions of this story.

The word גְּזֹרוּ, "cut (him) in pieces," links C and C'. This word opens the king's initial judgment in verse 25, and in verse 26 ends the assent of the false mother. The words spoken with this command correspond as well: the king's order to "give half to one and half to the other" and the false mother's words "it shall be neither mine nor yours" reflect the willingness of both to kill the child in order to divide him "equally."

Finally, Dtr2 focuses the central section of part two, D and D', on the emotions and words of the true mother. The narrator does not often speak directly in this story, preferring instead to speak through his characters. But he intrudes here in order to highlight the motivation of the woman who gives up her right to her son, and to justice itself, so that her son might live.³² She begins with the formal plea, בִּי אֲדֹנִי, "with your permission, my Lord"—perhaps she is now speaking out of order, a dangerous thing to do before a king who has just given an execution order. She then refers to her son with the passive participle of the word for "child" used here, יָלוּד, meaning "the one which has been born," underscoring her deep feeling; at the same time, the impersonal הַיָּלוּד, "*the* child," shifts from בְּנִי, "*my* son," in order to establish the necessary social distance to surrender her son.³³ Thus the true mother's emotions and words of self-sacrifice represent the high point of the story and so take the center of the second part of this narrative.

First Kings 3:16–27—Connecting the Parts

As mentioned earlier in this chapter, the king does not in any way examine the first woman's testimony. He does not address inconsistencies in her story, does not search for possible witnesses or character references, and does not even look to the second woman for a rebuttal.³⁴ If we posit a literary purpose to the detailed story of the first woman, and note that the details are *not* meant to provide a puzzle for the king to unravel (since he does not even attempt to unravel it), then it stands to reason that Dtr2 has some other theological purpose to part 1.

As was mentioned earlier, the king attacks the problem understanding only that there are two women laying claim to a single child, nothing more. Readers often assume that the first woman's words in part 1 are presented by the narrator because they contain pertinent testimony (whether this testimony is wholly true, partially true, or wholly false). But part 2 demonstrates the irrelevance of her testimony *to this story*: the first woman's account does not play any part in the king's actions or words. In fact, if the purpose of this story is to manifest the king's wisdom, then after the introduction of the two women in verse 16, the story proper could just as well begin with verse 22 or 23, with two women arguing before the king about who is the true mother. The king needs nothing from verses 17–21 in order to exhibit his wisdom; the presentation of her

---

32. Trible describes the author as exhibiting "great restraint" prior to verse 26, using only the most minimal narration to this point. Trible, 32–33.

33. Hens-Piazza, *Sociorhetorical,* 149.

34. Lasine, 64, offers a comprehensive list of the King's failings.

testimony at best gives us reason to second-guess the king for his failure to question that testimony.

Why then does the narrator give us the first woman's story? Part of the answer is that it helps to develop the relationship between the two main characters: the true mother, and the king. Many modern commentators conclude that, lacking any clear markers in the story, the identity of the first woman is indeterminate,[35] and several argue that the second woman is the true mother.[36] Yet there are at least two reasons to regard the first woman as the true mother.

First, the narrator gives us several rhetorical clues which link the first woman to the true mother, and distinguish her from her rival. She speaks first each time; this naturally creates sympathy for her.[37] She maintains an air of humility throughout: she begins each speech with the respectful בִּי אֲדֹנִי, "with your permission, my Lord," even when under great duress. This phrase is characteristic of reliable testimony: in each of the other nine times in the Hebrew Bible in which this phrase occurs, the speaker follows with truthful words.[38]

Dtr2 refers to the second woman as הָאִשָּׁה הָאַחֶרֶת, "the other woman." Moshe Garsiel points out that in the two other places in the Hebrew Bible in which this phrase appears (Judg 11:2 and 2 Chr 2:26), it carries the sense of an "outsider" who has borne illegitimate children.[39][40] Furthermore, the second woman/ false mother exhibits not the slightest decorum. In contrast to the first woman, her speeches are bereft of formality, and she never even addresses the court, speaking only to her rival and to the servants of the king. The similarities in the words and manner of speech between the second woman and the false mother mark them as the same person.[41]

Apart from these rhetorical clues, the reader must also consider how the first woman's story relates to the larger context. If the first woman is not the true mother, then she is lying, and her account has no meaning to this story, as the king does not examine her testimony. In this case, then,

---

35. See, for example, van Wolde; Lasine; Reinhartz, *Anonymity*, 109; Sternberg, *Poetics*, 166–69.

36. Rand, "Pronunciation," 246–250; Rendsburg, "Guilty Party," 534–541.

37. Garsiel, 236.

38. Gen 40:20, 44:18; Ex 4:10, 13; Num 12:11; Josh 7:8; Judg 6:13, 15; 1 Sam 1:26.

39. Garsiel, 241.

40. Beuken, "No Wise King," 9.

41. More on this can be found in Brichto, *Grammar*, 52.

from the narrator's point of view, the substance of the lie is immaterial to the story—one lie is as good as another. Why, then, devote nearly five verses to summarizing a false testimony?

Since the first woman's testimony has no real significance *within* the story, we must search for purpose outside of it. If the words are theologically important, then from the narrator's point of view they are likely to be true. Otherwise, her lying words will not advance the theological aims of the story. Therefore the first woman/ true mother is telling the truth.

This story, then, is about a marginal woman trying to reclaim the infant son stolen from her, and a king who finds the means to restore him to her. The second woman, the false mother, is nothing more than a caricature whose presence is required only to vivify the true mother's distress. The second woman offers no testimony, and takes no action; she exists merely to enhance the drama, providing confrontation and vindictiveness.[42] The story is not one of conflict between two women, but rather of a woman who needs justice, and the means used by the king who grants it. Danger comes to the infant because he is in a house shared by both the True Mother and the Other Woman. Here we see the point of the fourfold repetition of בַּבָּיִת, "in the house." This phrase, like the presence of the Other Woman in the house, seems innocuous at first. But the danger becomes palpable precisely because the Other Woman lives in the house with the True Mother.

Dtr2's clearest application of this story to its context renders this as a warning to Solomon. He has brought a foreign woman, the daughter of Pharaoh, into his "house," under questionable circumstances, e.g., in order to become Pharaoh's son-in-law. This creates a latent danger to Solomon, as admission of foreign wives will eventually prove to be the means of his undoing, just as the presence of the "Other Woman" in the house means palpable danger for the living child.

The True Mother: A Woman of Wisdom

In a 1989 article, W. A. M. Beuken argues that the true mother of this story should be numbered among the "wise women" of the Hebrew Bible, particularly given features of her story which she shares with the wise woman of Tekoa. Both use masterful language to sway the king to render

---

42. Long, *1 Kings*, 68–69; Hens-Piazza, 140.

a decision regarded by the people as wise, valuing life over legal dictates.[43] Cogan argues that the parallels are insufficient to label the true mother as a "wise" woman.[44] Yet as I've shown above, the similarities between these accounts go further than the ideas suggested by Beuken.

Both women are anonymous, and they come before anonymous kings (whose identity is clear only from the larger context). Both women are ostensibly trying to save the life of their only remaining son, in the wake of another's death. The law frowns on both: the son of the wise woman of Tekoa has apparently earned the death penalty for killing another, and the "true mother" is trying to get the king to give to her a child who already lives with a mother ("possession is nine-tenths of the law"). Each woman presents her case, yet there is more to their words than each king realizes. And while each king is called wise after rendering his decision, careful readings of each passage suggest that it is the woman who truly has great insight.

The RN thus introduces the concept of a "wise" woman, whose words to an anonymous king have a deeper meaning for him personally. This clues the reader to the technique of using an anonymous woman to educate an anonymous king. As the author of the RN uses the wise woman of Tekoa to speak to David regarding his son Absalom, Dtr2 uses this character type and setting to give Solomon a message as well.

Other Dtr2 Additions

Solomon's Wisdom Discredited

Chapter 1 of this book discusses some of the problems of the Solomon narrative. At times, Solomon appears as an exemplary figure; at other junctures during the height of his reign, the author portrays Solomon as a poor to mediocre ruler. The introduction of the SN into the DH helps to explain this dichotomy.

One of the most compelling issues regarding Solomon is his wisdom. Chapter 2 shows that Dtr2 is not especially interested in Solomon's wisdom for its own sake. Working from his source material, Dtr2 acknowledges Solomon's unsurpassed wisdom, but does not suggest that this wisdom played a role, whether good or bad, in the evaluation of

---

43. Beuken, "No Wise King," 9.
44. Coogan, 197.

Solomon as a king. This tends to follow the overall Deuteronomistic History's disinterest in wisdom.

Disinterest is not sufficient for Dtr2, however. Chapter 2 showed that textual considerations point to Dtr2 work which is critical of Solomon's wisdom. Three passages of 1 Kgs are notable in this light: 3:28, 5:25b–26a, and 10:13. I will briefly discuss 5:25b–26a and 10:13 here, and 3:28 in the second part of this chapter.

First Kings 5:25b–26a: Solomon and Hiram

First Kings 5 describes the conversation between Solomon and Hiram vis-à-vis building materials for the temple. The DH had previously introduced Hiram as a builder in 2 Sam 5:11–12, where Hiram builds a house for David just after David had been acknowledged King over Israel and had conquered Jerusalem for his capital. First Kings 5:24–25a tells us that Hiram, as he had done in 2 Sam 5, provides materials for Solomon's building needs, and in return, Solomon gives Hiram food and oil. The text suggests an equivalent one-time exchange. Hiram frames his specific proposal in 5:22–23, implicitly ratified by Solomon, with the words, אֲנִי אֶעֱשֶׂה אֶת־כָּל־חֶפְצְךָ "I will accomplish all your desires," and וְאַתָּה תַעֲשֶׂה אֶת־חֶפְצִי, "and you will accomplish all my desires"—specifically, wood for Solomon, and foodstuffs for Hiram. Walsh views this language as typical of courteous royal behavior.[45] As demonstrated in chapter 4, Dtr1 designs this exchange to enhance Solomon's stature: while David needed Hiram to promote his kingship (and was thus implicitly the inferior party), Solomon and Hiram interact as equals.

Dtr1 does not reference Solomon's wisdom in his account of the conversation between Hiram and Solomon. But Dtr2's insertion of 5:25b–26a constitutes a negative commentary of Solomon's wisdom. In 11b, Solomon's one-time deal becomes a regular occurrence, which, in light of 4:7, 22, effectively turns Solomon into Hiram's vassal. 5:26a then reports that "Yahweh gave Solomon wisdom, as He promised him (כַּאֲשֶׁר דִּבֶּר־לוֹ)", "according to that which he had spoken to him," alluding to 1 Kgs 3:10–13).[46] This comment must be ironic, since an arrangement

---

45. Walsh, *1 Kings*, 97.

46. 5:26a does not seem aware of the distinction between Elohim and Yahweh in 3:10–13. This further suggests that 5:26a comes from a different author, who was not keen on that distinction.

which effectively turns an Israelite king into the vassal of a foreigner is most certainly *not* indicative of wisdom! Dtr1 is ambivalent about Solomon's wisdom, not connecting its importance to Solomon's activities. Dtr2, however, is willing to bring out a negative dimension to the idea of Solomon's wisdom.

First Kings 10:13—Solomon and the Queen of Sheba

Something similar to the above takes place in 1 Kgs 10:13. Just as he uses Hiram, Dtr1 uses the visit of the Queen of Sheba to demonstrate Solomon's superiority over foreign monarchs. The Queen comes to test, and Solomon's answers so impress her that her breath is taken away. In 10:10, Solomon benefits richly, providing a specific example of the situation of 10:23–25, in which Solomon's wisdom brings visitors bearing material gifts. Solomon effectively provides wisdom and receives riches in return. However, Dtr2 reduces Solomon's stature relative to the Queen of Sheba by turning this episode into an exchange of gifts. Verses 1–10 strongly suggest Solomon's superiority over the Queen of Sheba; this is much less apparent after 10:13.

First Kings 5:29, 31

First Kings 5:29 and 31 prepare the reader for reports of Solomon's fantastic building activity above and beyond the temple. As noted in chapter 2, Solomon's initial levy of thirty thousand men in verses 27–28 to facilitate the logging operation seems designed to ameliorate the idea of forced labor. Solomon drafts conscripts, but requires them to work only one month out of three. The seventy thousand porters and eighty thousand stonecutters are not afforded any similar accommodation. Solomon thus becomes a harsher figure.

First Kings 5:31 uses the adjective, יָקָר "rare, precious," to describe the stones cut by Solomon's workers. This word appears exactly six more times in the Solomon narrative: 7:9, 10, 11, and 10:2, 10, 11. 1 Kings 7:9–11 of course addresses Solomon's building projects beyond the temple, and uses יָקָר for the same purpose as 5:31, namely, to describe building stones. This suggests a connection between 5:31 and the report of Solomon's supplemental building projects in 7:1–12a.[47]

47. Würthwein, 57.

In chapter 3, I attributed 7:1–12a to Dtr1's source materials because I do not see any clear reason to conclude that this section was not part of Dtr1's work (although it does appear to have been moved from its original position). First Kings 5:31, however, is a Dtr2 addition. Therefore, 5:31 was inserted to connect the account of Solomon's acquisition of building materials to Solomon's excessive construction. As De Vries and Walsh point out, the phrase אֲבָנִים גְּדֹלוֹת אֲבָנִים יְקָרוֹת לְיַסֵּד הַבָּיִת אַבְנֵי גָזִית, "great stones, costly stones, dressed stones," in 5:31 stresses the stones' size and the skill needed to acquire and prepare them, further emphasizing the degree to which Solomon is willing to press the Israelites into service.[48] This casts a longer shadow over the report of building projects in 7:1–12a, disturbingly connecting Solomon to the slave labor of Pharaoh prior to the exodus from Egypt.[49]

Re-Positioning 1 Kings 7:1–12a

Gina Hens-Piazza posits that the "illogically sequenced" MT building reports point to Solomon's divided energies. While Solomon is focused on the temple and its furnishings, he also heeds his own position.[50] In the MT, the House of the Forest of Lebanon ("HFL") becomes central to Solomon's activities. First Kings 7:13–50 describes the luxurious gold temple furnishings; 10:14–25 details Solomon's incredible "not intended to be credible"[51] personal wealth stored at the HFL. Some commentators describe the contents of 10:14–25 as a miscellany,[52] but a number of others argue that the repeated references to wealth and its trappings in 10:14, 16, 17, 18, 21, 22, 23, and 25 make wealth the focus of this section.[53] Moreover, the wealth is concentrated about the HFL: this is the

---

48. De Vries, 83; Walsh, *1 Kings*, 100.

49. Brueggemann, *Kings*, 79; Hens-Piazza, 59–60; Laffey, *Kings*, NColl, 30. Laffey connects this passage to 1 Sam 8:11–18, where the prophet Samuel warns the people of potential royal oppression. While both passages speak of a monarch who requires much of the people, there is little else to connect the passages. First Kings 5 speaks only of a large draft to acquire building materials. First Samuel 8 addresses a number of reasons tha the king will press the people into service, but (notably) does not reference construction.

50. Hens-Piazza, 69–70.

51. Knoppers, *Two Nations*, 1:130–31.

52. Montgomery and Gehman, 219; Gray, 262; Jones, *Kings*, 225.

53. Long, 116; Parker, *Wisdom and Law*, 95; Walsh, *1 Kings*, 129–30; Sweeney, 151.

storage area for the ceremonial shields (10:17), the (elaborate) throne, and Solomon's vessels (10:21). By the time of Dtr2, the place where Solomon pronounces judgment (7:7) becomes the focal area of his rule.

The HFL comes at a high price: Solomon institutes slave labor, and effectively becomes a vassal of Hiram of Tyre. Solomon's determination to act in a juridical capacity thus creates difficulties for Israel and becomes a factor in the nation's later division when the people object to their forced labor at the beginning of the reign of Solomon's son Rehoboam in 1 Kgs 12. The placement of this passage in its current position is perhaps designed to disturb the reader by hinting at further disruptions down the road.[54]

First Kings 8:41–53

This passage comprises the final three of Solomon's seven petitions requested in his temple dedication prayer. As I wrote in chapter 2, these petitions do not require a standing temple, and thus hearken to a time when the possibility of Yahwistic religion without a temple is feasible. The three petitions also contain an additional feature in common which distinguishes them from the first four petitions: in each, Solomon calls the temple "the house which I have built (8:43, 44, 48)."[55] Through this means Dtr2 reveals Solomon to be especially interested in his own achievement.

Deuteronomistic Features of Dtr2

Since the body of work of Dtr2 is so much smaller than that of Dtr1, his ideology is more elusive. We nevertheless have enough data to realize an important development in deuteronomistic theology. Dtr2's additions 8:41–53 and 9:6–9 make the temple more relevant for the exiles. Prayer in 8:31–34 must take place in the temple to be effective, but in 44–53 it need be rendered only in the direction of the city designated as temple host. First Kings 8:46–53, which specifically addresses Israelites living in foreign lands, makes this point most emphatically. The house which had hosted the name of Yahweh (8:29) no longer needs to be standing, so that even in the midst of the disaster of 9:6–9, efficacious prayer about a single

---

54 Laffey, 35–36.
55. Noted especially by Walsh, 114.

place is yet feasible.⁵⁶ The concept of the one central location worship endures.

Excursus: Dtr2's Work: A New Structure?

In chapter 2 I surveyed several articles devoted to the structure of the Solomon story. Since we cannot know the extent and ordering of the work of Dtr1, we cannot develop any sure conclusions about its possible overall chiastic structure. But the MT does give us the work of Dtr2, which places the temple construction and dedication more or less at the center of the Solomon story.⁵⁷ The question then, is whether Dtr2 intended to create a "chiastic" Solomon account.

Proponents of a chiastic structure to the Solomon Narrative point to the literary centrality of the temple construction. But their case relies on following Noth in reading 9:10—10:29 as negative toward Solomon.⁵⁸ Most scholars nevertheless reject the view that this section is meant to criticize Solomon, for two reasons.

First, reading 9:10–14 as negative requires one to view Solomon's actions regarding forced labor more positively in 5:27–32 than in 9:14–25. This is problematic, as 5:27–32 discusses Solomon's draft of Israelites, while 9:15–24 clearly references a draft of Canaanites living in Israel. Parker addresses this issue by criticizing Solomon for enslaving Canaanites rather than exterminating them as per Deut 13:12–18, thus fostering syncretism.⁵⁹ But if we criticize Solomon for violating Deut 13 here, then, to be fair, we must carefully examine 1 Kgs 3–8 to be sure that Solomon does not violate some passage of Deuteronomy in those chapters. Furthermore, Parker does not address the apparent distinction between "enslavement" of Canaanites in 1 Kgs 9, versus that of Israelites

---

56. Fretheim, *Kings*, 55–56; Mulder, 441–42.

57. Those who argue that the Solomon narrative was created chiastically include Parker, "Repetition;" Frisch, "Structure;" Brettler, "Structure;" Williams, "Structure;" Walsh, 151–56.

58. Walsh, 153; Römer, *So-Called*, 148; "Ambigu" 108. Römer is a recent proponent of the idea that 1 Kings 3–8 is positive, and 9–11 is negative, although he does not supply arguments for his position. Walsh's conclusions are especially remarkable, as he tends to highlight criticisms of Solomon throughout 1 Kings 1–11. Walsh nevertheless holds that sections before the temple construction and prayer are positive, and sections after the temple are negative.

59. Parker, 91; cf. Weinfeld, *Deuteronomic*, 166–67.

in chapter 5. Enslaving Israelites is certainly as bad or worse behavior than failing to exterminate Canaanites.

The second issue is that the text gives us no direct signal that we are to read 9:10—10:29 as critical of Solomon. The agreement with Hiram in 9:10-14 may reflect negatively on Solomon (although I argue in chapter 3 that this passage merely shows Solomon using superior wisdom to gain wealth from a contemporaneous monarch), and the costs of Solomon's building activity in 9:15-24 may make us uncomfortable, but, unlike the situation in 11:1-13, the author does not directly tell us that Solomon violated some law, or that Yahweh was displeased with Solomon. Parker, Römer, and others must infer these things.[60] Furthermore, matters seem to pick up for Solomon after 9:24, as we no longer see any hint of potential abuse or neglect of his royal duties.[61] This suggests that the major break comes at 11:1 and not earlier, obviating structural readings which look for a change from "good" to "bad" around the temple construction and dedication.

Absent compelling evidence that 9:10—10:29 was intended to criticize Solomon, we are left with only 1 Kgs 11 as negative toward Solomon. We are thus without solid reason to suppose that Dtr2 intended to organize his Solomon story chiastically.

Impact of the SN on 1 Kings 3-11

In chapter 1 I briefly introduced Sweeney's idea that 1 Kgs 3-11 had been originally composed prior to the SN (which, for Sweeney, includes 1 Kgs 1-2), and was then revised in light of the SN. Since 1 Kgs 3-11 makes regular reference to King David, Solomon's father, at some point an editor of 1 Kgs 3-11 apparently expected readers to have the King David narratives in mind as they read about King Solomon. We have reviewed themes of Dtr1's Solomon story, 2 Sam 10-20, and 1 Kgs 1-2, so we are now ready to examine ways in which 2 Sam 10-20 and 1 Kgs 1-2 impact our reading of the Solomon story in 1 Kgs 3-11.

---

60. Brettler, 3. Negatives about 9:10-24 are so difficult to come by that Brettler holds that the break between "good" and "bad" Solomon actually arrives at 9:25. However, Brettler is the only scholar of whom I am aware who reads 9:25—10:29 as more negative toward Solomon than 9:10-24.

61. Jobling, 482, discerns a "downturn" in the portrayal of Solomon in 9:1-24, but the "adulation" of the king in 9:25—10:29, on par with chs. 3-8, cancels this out.

The King as Judge in the RN

Solomon's decision in the story of the two prostitutes is often taken to be an example of his superior wisdom. But when we read the evaluation statement 3:28 in light of the SN, a different picture emerges. Solomon sits in the role of judge in 1 Kgs 3, but the king does not fare well in this role in the SN.

Chapter 5 identifies three passages in the Revolt Narrative which portray the king to be a poor judge: 2 Sam 14:1–20, 15:1–6, and 19:24–30.[62] First Kings 3:16–28 shares several features in common with two of these "king as judge" passages, 2 Sam 14:1–20 and 19:24–30. These three stories all feature an anonymous king (whose identity is clarified by the larger context) who is asked to make a judgment in favor of an aggrieved supplicant. In all three episodes, the king is not quite up to the task. In 2 Sam 14:1–20 David does not realize that the wise woman of Tekoa is engaging in deception to make a point; David renders a poor decision in 2 Sam 19:24–30; and Solomon, instead of following obvious lines of questioning, resorts to a reckless, dangerous test.

Three factors strengthen the idea that Dtr2, following the RN, intends to do more than simply criticize specific performances of David and Solomon. First, as shown in chapter 2, the setting for the Story of Solomon and the Two Prostitutes is a case of imprecation: two women make the same claim, so one must clearly be lying. First Kings 8:31–32 states that in such an instance, each woman should make an oath before Yahweh, so that the truth might be discovered. First Kings 3:16–28 therefore is not merely a story about Solomon's poor execution; rather, this is a case which he should never have taken on in the first place.

Second, these passages involving the judgment of David and Solomon share the feature of an anonymous king: while the identities of David and Solomon are quite clear in each passage, the passages themselves do not name the king involved. This suggests that it is the king,

---

62. Levinson, "Conception," 76, finds this to be rather remarkable, as this idea stands in conflict with the usual ANE practice. ANE monarchs normally judged individual cases in order to enhance their reputations as champions of those who were oppressed and powerless. We see this, for example, in ancient Ugarit texts in which Yatzib objects to his father Kirta's failure to behave like a king by neglecting to hear the cases of widows and orphans, and in the famous claim of Hammurabi of Babylon, that he was appointed "that the strong might not oppress the oppress the weak." Hammurabi thus is endowed by the sun god with special ability to understand principles of justice.

not merely David or Solomon, who is unable to properly perform the adjurative task.[63]

Third, the wider contexts of both the RN and the Solomon narrative reveal a David and a Solomon who do make some good decisions. For example, in 2 Sam 15:14, David immediately discerns on his own that he and his court must flee Jerusalem before he is overwhelmed by Absalom's forces, and in 19:16–23, David wisely spares Shimei in the presence of one thousand of the latter's kinsmen. Similarly, Solomon in 1 Kgs 4 organizes his kingdom so that the people of Israel and Judah become numerous and prosperous. This suggests that the RN and Dtr2 do not set out merely to criticize David and Solomon, but rather are trying to state and reiterate that the king should not act as judge.

Absalom's proposed perversion of justice in 15:1–6 further suggests a dysfunctional system of jurisprudence. Thus the SN accounts of David and Absalom acting as judge, taken together, suggest that Israelite kings do not belong in this role. These negative examples should cause the reader to view 1 Kgs 3 with caution. Solomon asks for and receives wisdom to "judge," then takes on the role of judge in the story of Solomon and the Two Prostitutes, but is his request, along with his further function as judge, proper? Solomon's performance as judge is poor, and Dtr2 clearly links Solomon's performance to his request by use of the particle *za'*, "then," to begin 3:16. (The particle *za'*, "which," when used by a non-perfective verb, indicates that the immediately following action takes place prior to the completion of the immediately preceding account.[64] This indicates that the women came to "the king" while Solomon was still at Gibeon.[65]) Dtr1's presentation of Solomon's request for wisdom to judge may have been questionable, but the history of kings as judges in

---

63. The fact that David is clearly named in 2 Sam 12 does not weaken this argument, since, as per chapter 4, 2 Sam 12 has a different author who is working with a different idea. But even 2 Sam 12 does nothing to promote the idea that kings should exercise a juridical function.

Cartledge, *Samuel*, 514, places this in the category of "juridical parable," which describes "the guilty party's crime in parabolic fashion, so that the targeted hearer will pass judgment on the guilty and thus condemn himself." Cartledge's two other DH examples include that of the wise woman of Tekoa, and the account in 1 Kgs 20:39–40 of King Ahab, another instance in which the juridical king is anonymous.

64. Marvin Sweeney sees this as evidence of a "redaction," but the context does not require this. See Sweeney, *Kings*, 81; Rabinowitz, "*az*," 53–62.

65. Waltke & O'Connor, *Syntax*, 514n.

Solomon in Light of the Succession Narrative

the SN, combined with Solomon's poor performance in 3:16–27, suggests that Dtr2 is quite opposed to this concept.

Poor Judgment of the People

We have observed that kings do not function as capable jurists in the SN. Therefore, a good performance by Solomon in 1 Kgs 3:16–27 would represent the exception, not the rule, especially given that this passage was added to the DH after the inclusion of the SN. But a careful reading of 1 Kgs 3 shows that the author does not necessarily approve of Solomon's decision. 3:28 does not quite say that Solomon's method and decision were good or wise. Instead, the narrator reports that "(all Israel) stood in awe of the king, because they perceived that the wisdom of God was in him, to execute justice."[66] It is not the narrator who approves of Solomon's actions, but it is rather the people of Israel who think well of their king as a result of this episode. Therefore, in order to interpret 3:28, we should consider prior experience with the sentiments of the people of Israel.

At issue is the function of verse 28: was it part of the original story, or was it attached for some special purpose? In his analysis of the structure of this passage, Jerome T. Walsh marks verse 28 as the "narrative conclusion," correlating מִפְּנֵי הַמֶּלֶךְ "from before the king," to וַתַּעֲמֹדְנָה לְפָנָיו "and they stood before him," in 3:16.[67] This seems strained, however, since the subjects and verbs of the two phrases are very different: in verse 16, it is the women who stand before the king, whereas in verse 28, "all Israel" is in awe. As I explained above, a clearer link exists between verses 16 and 22, in which the two women "spoke before the king" (וַתְּדַבֵּרְנָה לִפְנֵי הַמֶּלֶךְ). Bezalel Porten argues that verse 28 thematically connects 3:16–27 to 3:9 and 3:11 through their common linkage of the word שמע to שפט.[68] At the same time, most commentators agree that verse 28 is meant to connect 1 Kgs 3 to what follows.[69]

---

66. Jones, 132–33, argues that the idiom "the wisdom of God" demonstrates Solomon's incomparable, even infallible, judgment. Again, Dtr2 is not saying that this was so, but instead is reporting the perception of the people.

67. Walsh, *Style*, 142.

68. Porten, "Structure and Theme," 99–100.

69. Mulder, *Kings*, 160; Long, 68; Brueggemann, 50; Fritz, *Kings*, 43. These are some of the commentators who explicitly label 3:28 as a linking verse.

Commentators often read 3:28 to say that king Solomon has demonstrated his ability to use divine wisdom to judge correctly.[70] But evidence from the RN discredits this conclusion. Dtr2 does not tell us that the King's juridical method was in any way "wise;" all he says is that the people perceived it to be so, and responded accordingly. Dtr2 undoubtedly understands that many will read this story and be impressed by the king's judgment.[71] It seems quite likely, then, that Dtr2 adopted an existing tale in order to make a point about Solomon's wisdom (not really as good as reputed), and the people's understanding of it (faulty, as usual).

Dtr2 certainly understands that many will be impressed by the king's wisdom in this story. But the lessons of the RN point in a different direction: when the people make a conclusion about the suitable characteristics of the king, it is probably the wrong one. "The people" positively evaluate the king's judgment in 3:28. But since the SN has taken some trouble to disparage the views of the people in terms of their royal evaluations, and since Solomon's actions in 3:16–27 are themselves open to question, we should read 3:28 ironically. The people may perceive God's wisdom in the king, but the reader knows better.

Solomon and Power

Chapter 4 references Tomoo Ishida's suggestion that the author of the SN uses David's administration lists to emphasize Joab's gain of power by the end of 2 Sam 20.[72] It seems apparent that these lists were not created, or necessarily even employed, for specifically *that* purpose; nevertheless, their placement and the absence of David's name at the beginning of the list in 2 Sam 20:23–26 supports the idea that Joab had become the power behind the throne. The lists themselves can hardly be seen to comment negatively on David's reign, but their placement within the narrative casts a negative light.

---

70. Fritz, 43; De Vries, 60, 62; Laffey, 24–25. Brueggemann, 50–55, offers the interesting view that, while this passage demonstrates Solomon's divine wisdom, it is "marked by a kind of crudeness that can damage. Perhaps wisdom that governs must always be a compromised wisdom with coerciveness behind it."

71. Walsh, *1 Kings*, 84–85, notes that while the people conclude that Solomon has demonstrated divine wisdom, the author does not disclose his own feelings on the matter.

72. Ishida, "Political Analysis," 184–85.

The creation of an administration in Dtr1's Solomon story seems to be positive as well. For Dtr1, Solomon appoints officers and district governors (4:1–19), with the result that "Judah and Israel were as numerous as the sand by the sea; they ate and drank and were happy" (1 Kgs 4:20). Yet Dtr1's work does not include the turbulent SN storyline. For Dtr2, whose DH includes an SN bounded by David's officer lists, Solomon's establishment of officers can no longer be taken as a positive development. For Dtr1, officers lead to prosperity and happiness for the nation, but Dtr2's narrative, now with the SN as background, invalidates this connection.

Solomonic Pronouncements

In 1 Kgs 5 and 8, Solomon peppers his speeches with references to the legacy of his father David. In 5:17–19, Solomon links his desire to build a temple to the desire of David to do the same. According to Solomon, David could not build because of extensive external warfare in his day; now Solomon, in a time of peace, can accomplish this task. Solomon does not try to explain his decision to build by appealing to his own relationship with Yahweh, but rather utilizes his father's reputation to justify his intentions. The contrast with respect to temple construction is the result of circumstances, rather than ideological differences.[73] For Dtr1, David has apparently left a positive legacy from which Solomon may draw.

First Kings 2, however, tends to subvert 1 Kgs 5's glowing picture of Solomon. Solomon claims in 5:18 that his kingdom is without פֶּגַע רָע, "evil occurrence." The noun form of פֶּגַע is rare in the MT, occurring only here and in Eccl 9:11. Much more frequent is the verb form, where the idea of "meeting" is often taken to mean "encounter" with hostility—as in 1 Kgs 2:25, 29, 31, 32, 34, and 36.[74] In these verses, Benaiah attacks and kills Adonijah, Joab, and Shimei. The presence of פֶּגַע in 5:18 points to a connection between this verse and 1 Kgs 2. The words פֶּגַע רָע may or may not have been added by Dtr2, but either way it seems clear that Dtr2 intended to connect these two passages. Solomon indeed has rest from enemies, but his "rest" is as much the result of his own questionable actions as it is the fruit of Yahweh's support.[75]

---

73. Walsh, *1 Kings*, 95.
74. *BDB*, 803.
75. Cogan, 232.

Solomon recalls his father David a number of times in 1 Kgs 8 as well. In 8:15–20, Solomon references the covenant with David as he explains the reasoning behind his decision to build a temple in Jerusalem. As in 1 Kgs 5, Solomon again explains that David had desired to construct a temple (8:19). Solomon explains here that it was Yahweh who had told David not to build and instead to permit his son (i.e., Solomon) to do the construction. Solomon then connects his building action to Yahweh's covenant with David, specifically citing the eternal nature of Yahweh's promise to maintain a successor to David on the throne of Israel.

As in 1 Kgs 5, these words seem related to the Davidic covenant of 2 Sam 7 and can be construed as pious by Dtr1. But when we read these words in light of 1 Kgs 2, a different picture emerges. Each time Solomon executes a potential enemy in 1 Kgs 2, he cites his place as David's successor, declaring that David's throne will be established (2:24, 2:33, 2:45). Having seen how Solomon goes about securing David's throne in 1 Kgs 2, we see that his words in 1 Kings are more about human power—what Solomon is willing to do—than about fidelity to Torah.

Dtr2—Summary and Conclusions

Second Sam 11–20 and 1 Kgs 1–2 have a discernable impact on the way we read the Solomon story. The account of Solomon's cabinet in 4:1–6 looks like a positive organizational move when read on its own, but after reading the RN, sandwiched between David's similar lists, Solomon's cabinet becomes much less impressive. Furthermore, the "rest" from enemies cited by Solomon in 1 Kgs 5:18 is now clearly linked to Solomon's dark activity in 1 Kgs 2.

With 2 Sam 11–20 and 1 Kgs 1–2 in place, Dtr2 goes to work on the Solomon story he has inherited from Dtr1. He adapts a popular story of two women who each claim to be the mother of the same child, editing it with the account of the wise woman of Tekoa from 2 Sam 14 in view. Like the wise woman, the "true mother" begins with a parable, ostensibly to save the life of her son, but more importantly transmitting a message to Solomon, that Solomon puts himself in danger by permitting a foreign woman to live with him. Dtr2 renders Solomon anonymous in this account, just as David is anonymous in 2 Sam 14, and Solomon, like David, proves himself to be an inadequate jurist. The people perceive Solomon's judgment to be wise, just as the people have made poor judgments in the

RN, but Dtr2 is careful not to personally credit Solomon with wisdom here.

Dtr2 makes further edits in order to darken Solomon's power with respect to building activity in 1 Kgs 5. He dramatically adds to the number of *corveé* workers, enhances the opulence of Solomon's construction projects, and reminds his readers that, while Solomon was working on the temple, he was also constructing a new palace and other buildings. In addition, Dtr2 cleverly converts stories in which Solomon equals Hiram and exceeds the Queen of Sheba, into accounts where Solomon becomes Hiram's vassal, and the Queen's equal.

Dtr2 thus uses a number of means to make Solomon into a darker, less wise character. He inserts blocks of text and adds verses in strategic places, while expecting that we will keep 2 Sam 11–20 and 1 Kgs 1–2 in mind when we come to the Solomon story. Dtr2's transformation of Solomon is not overwhelming: he is still a king of power, who builds and dedicates the temple, and leads Israel to her height of prosperity. But once Dtr2 is done, we cannot miss Solomon's weaknesses.

8

Conclusions

Tradition has honored the books of Judges, Samuel, Kings and Maccabees as 'religious' or 'biblical' or 'divinely inspired' history. Puzzling indeed.

A question has lingered for centuries. What instruction from Yahweh may be conveyed in these accounts, steeped as they are in mayhem, slaughter, betrayal, intrigue, and bravado; rife as they are with fractious sons and foolish fathers, brothers betraying and killing brothers, women deprived of status and dignity, predatory enmities periodically erupting, and wars breeding wars that breed wars?

'Religious history,' this brimstone brew?[1]

IN HIS COMMENTARY ON Kings, peace activist Daniel Berrigan finds much to disturb him about Yahweh and the rulers of Israel. Examples of virtue are confined almost exclusively to the behavior and words of prophets, with the occasional nod to Berrigan's deuteronomistic author.[2] Berrigan's personal leanings toward the prophetic no doubt influence his reading of 1 Kings, a reading that stresses the sins of the rulers of Israel and Judah, including Solomon. Others have judged Solomon less harshly. But what is Dtr2, the final author of 1 Kgs 1–11, trying to communicate to his readers about Solomon and his reign?

1. Berrigan, *Kings*, 1.
2. Berrigan, 6. "Believers are to act as judges, prophets. Deuteronomists, if you will."

The most direct way to answer this question, of course, is to address exclusively the "final form" of the text.³ We can expect this "final form" to transmit the ideology of the final editor/ author, who we assume was capable of writing a nuanced, sophisticated text containing pros and cons of various ideologies and ideas. Yet we also know that the text transmission process involved edits beyond simple copying.⁴ It appears that scribes were loath to omit parts of an older text, even when older texts seem to teach something which, from the scribe's point of view, may be incorrect. Scribes therefore tended to make "explanatory" additions. The result is a text that often has serious unresolved issues, rendering opaque even the message of the final editor.⁵ At this point synchronic analysis alone may not satisfactorily explain problems of the text. We therefore turn to diachronic analysis in order to determine what each new author/ editor added to the work.

In this book I have adopted the traditional DblR idea of Josianic and exilic Dtrs, which I call Dtr1 and Dtr2. Dtr1 was a scribe who lived in Jerusalem during the reign of King Josiah (c. 641–609 BCE).⁶ He supported the reforms taking place in Judah (described in 2 Kgs 22–23) and so was an enthusiastic supporter of Josiah and of the Davidic monarchy in general. David is the archetypical king, and Josiah is the only one of his successors who "walked in all the ways of his father David" (2 Kgs 22:2). Dtr1 favored cultic centralization and a strong monarchy in general. Dtr1 is quite willing to acknowledge good and bad features of David's successors, and so has no qualms about portraying Solomon as both

---

3. The "final form" itself is elusive, since there are a number of "final" versions of the Hebrew Bible. As explained in chapter 1, I have chosen to work with the Masoretic Text, but even determining the "correct" Masoretic text is an exercise more in theory than in the likelihood that a complete, "correct" text of Kings has ever existed. For more, see Tov, *Criticism*, 161–90.

4. Knoppers, "Theories," 73–76 suggests that Noth was reluctant to consider a diachronic reading of the DH, as in his day European Old Testament studies were influenced by a "back to the Masoretic Text" movement. This movement was overturned as a result of discoveries at Qumran shortly after the publication of ⌧S.

5. Halpern and Lemaire, "Composition," 127–29 offers more on the interpretive problems created by "large tracts" of contradictory texts in the DH.

6. Römer, *So-Called*, 47. Römer theorizes a small group of writers from this era who share similar ideologies and rhetorical and stylistic techniques. But there is no reason to theorize more than one Dtr1.

enormously successful, yet in conflict with dangerous outside elements throughout his reign.[7]

Dtr2 lived during the exile, probably in Babylon. As a scribe, he was an official who worked closely with government institutions of his day. While he was very interested in both the past and the future of Israel, he was not as enamored with the monarchy as his Josianic predecessor. Dtr2 was not necessarily hostile toward the monarchy, but he did not regard it as irreplaceable. In his view, kings of Israel and Judah had been too powerful so that a new monarchy would need restrictions to be effective. He held many of the same views as Dtr1, including the importance of the Mosaic Law and the centralization of the cult in Jerusalem. Dtr1's DH was something that Dtr2 could work with, as it essentially supported Dtr2's ideology. Dtr2 thus brought Dtr1 up to date, while making edits that substantially reduced the value of the monarchy to historical Israel.[8]

Diachronic Layers of 1 Kings 1–11

Chapter 3 contains the "layer" work on 1 Kgs 1–11, breaking the text down according to the DblR. I follow the DblR by positing that Dtr1 selected and organized older materials to form the Josianic version of the DH. Dtr1's additions are most readily identifiable by his stock phrases and ideology, including his preference for the divine name (Yahweh), and his exaltations of the Law of Moses and the Davidic covenant (most apparent in the speeches of various characters). The exilic Dtr2 then revised Dtr1 to bring the work up to date and to reflect his own ideology. I identify work belonging to Dtr2 where the text is seriously at odds ideologically with Dtr1 and where insertions make sense grammatically. I also identify three short passages that seem entirely out of place with the three prior layers (1 Kgs 3:10, 15b; 6:11-14; 8:1-11*) and so were probably added subsequent to the work of Dtr2. (The identification of these last three passages essentially follows prior scholarship).

But there are two important nuances to my work. First, I consider differences in ideology between Dtr1 and his sources (explained below). While scholars tend to agree that Dtr1 chose his source material, our MT suggests that even Dtr1 had to address traditions that perhaps did not fit in well with his DH. Second, I attribute two major blocks of material to

---

7. Cogan, *1 Kings*, 97–99; Römer, 45–49.
8. Cross, *Myth*, 287–88; Cogan, 99–100; Römer, 111–15.

Dtr2 that have in the past generally been attributed to Dtr1. Advocates of the DblR have resisted this idea, instead preferring to allow that Dtr1 used materials that expressed views at odds with his ideology. Yet it seems clear that two passages must be dated subsequent to Dtr1. The material of 1 Kgs 1–2 is clearly based on passages in 2 Sam that portray a King David who cannot be reconciled to the King David of 1 Kgs 3–11. And in the story of Solomon and the Two Prostitutes, Solomon's judgment shows that his "wisdom" is poor, thus in line with other Dtr2 passages criticizing his "wisdom." Also, this account is notably absent from 2 Chr. The trend among DblR theorists of identifying more blocks of text with Dtr2, recently adopted by Campbell and O'Brien, Römer, and others, likely represents the best way to go forward with the DblR.[9]

Dtr1's Solomon

With the text divided into layers, we begin to see what Dtr1 and Dtr2 were trying to accomplish. This is especially clear with respect to the tradition regarding Solomon's wisdom. In 1 Kgs 11:41 Dtr1 informs us that we can find more about Solomon's acts and wisdom in the "Book of the Acts of Solomon." This indicates that Dtr1 was aware that his audience may have been interested in Solomon's wisdom, perhaps subscribing to the idea that wealth and honor flow from wisdom (a tradition to which Dtr1 nods). In his own comments, however, Dtr1 is much more concerned about Solomon's power, linking Solomon's success to fidelity to Yahweh. Neither Solomon's greatest achievement, the construction of the temple, nor his ultimate downfall in 1 Kgs 11 involve wisdom. Dtr1 minimizes the importance of wisdom in his evaluation of Solomon's reign.

Dtr1's selection of materials, along with his edits (principally in the speeches of various characters) stress Solomon's power in a number of areas. Virtually every identifiable Dtr1 section of chapters 3–10 characterizes Solomon as a king in control of the various institutions of his kingdom and as a major player on the international scene. Solomon creates administrative apparatuses to ensure the smooth transfer of taxes and to raise an effective labor force. He acquires quality construction materials, then builds a number of important structures. He takes the leading role in cult worship. Solomon even manages to garner international acclaim, proving himself to be superior to his contemporaries.

---

9. Knoppers, 81; Campbell and O'Brien, *Unfolding*.

And he accomplishes all of these things with only one inconsequential hint of discontent (Hiram's dissatisfaction in 9:13, which quickly comes to naught as we soon see Solomon again working actively and profitably with his favorite trading partner). Finally, at the end of Solomon's story, Dtr1 expresses Solomon's downfall not in terms of wisdom, wealth, or fame, but in terms of Solomon's power, as he begins to lose control of his kingdom due to the rebellious activity of Hadad, Rezon, and Jeroboam.

Dtr1 does hint at danger throughout Solomon's reign, flagging several instances of religious syncretism. Some of these occur at key junctures. Solomon's reign begins ominously, as he seeks to become Pharaoh's son-in-law by marrying Pharaoh's daughter. This woman is a constant distraction, as Solomon regularly needs to consider her appropriate residence in or near Jerusalem. He then offers a spectacular sacrifice at a Canaanite "high place," away from Jerusalem—an act that Dtr1 usually characterizes as taboo. Solomon develops strong ties with Hiram, bringing in a Tyrian metalworker to make temple furniture, and he incorporates a number of Canaanite design features in his construction of the temple and its furnishings. Dtr1 thus makes it clear that it is Solomon's inability to maintain strict separation from foreign influence that leads to his downfall in 1 Kgs 11.

The Revolt Narrative and 2 Samuel 11–12

With Dtr1's description of the reign of Solomon in hand, we move to the account of the reign of Solomon's predecessor, King David, which came into the DH after the exile. The RN offers fascinating points of comparison with the Solomon story, as the two narratives address the reigns of consecutive Davidic kings, and reveal an unusual (for the DH) interest in the topic of wisdom. I identified four major ideas of the RN that impact Dtr2's Solomon story. First, David proves to be ineffective as a ruler, highlighted by his inability to manage women in his charge. Second, the RN portrays wisdom as persuasion, rather than as knowledge of the world or business acumen, as in Dtr1.

Third, the RN presents the notion that kings should not act in a juridical capacity. The most egregious example of this is found in 2 Sam 15, where Absalom commits to the perversion of justice, if it will gain him followers to support his rebellion. But David also proves to be woefully inadequate for the juridical task, as he is deceived by the wise woman of Tekoa in 2 Sam 14 and miscarries justice when judging between Mephibosheth and Ziba in 2 Sam 19. The latter two passages share the interesting feature that David is not referenced by name, suggesting that in these passages the narrator uses David to represent kings in general. Fourth, the RN presents the idea that the people tend to make poor decisions. The people follow the disastrous rebellions of Absalom and Sheba, and in 2 Sam 17, when Absalom's elders seek to follow the counsel of the wise, loyal Ahithophel, it is the people who prefer the advice of the deceiver Hushai.

Consideration of these four idea impacts our reading of the Solomon story that immediately follows in the DH. After the RN was composed, 2 Sam 11–12, containing the infamous account of David and Bathsheba, was added, introducing Bathsheba and telling us more about the prophet Nathan. The RN and the account of David and Bathsheba were not part of Dtr1's DH and so do not figure into Dtr1's interpretation of Solomon's reign. Dtr2, however, expects us to keep the ideas and characters of 2 Sam 11–20 in mind as he presents his revised depiction of Solomon.

Dtr2's Additions

First Kings 1–2 belongs to Dtr2, and was clearly written to connect the RN and 2 Sam 11–12 to the Solomon story. These chapters introduce us to Solomon while closing out the accounts of key 2 Sam figures like Joab, Nathan, and Bathsheba. Besides serving as a literary bridge, these chapters use the figures of Bathsheba, Joab, and Benaiah to illustrate key differences between kings[10] David and Solomon. As had occurred often in the RN, David is easily swayed by the deceptive Bathsheba; Solomon, however, is not. David's general Joab acts independently of his king, repeating this characteristic from 2 Sam. Solomon's general Benaiah, however, is loyal to a fault, entirely willing to carry out questionable executions on the word of his king. Taking these characters together, we see that David is a weak ruler while Solomon takes firm control of his kingdom.

First Kings 1–2 also introduces us to a new dark aspect of Solomon's character. Dtr2 knows where his edited version of the Solomon story is

---

10. It is important to understand that 1 Kgs 1–2 deals with the distinction between these two figures as they reign as rulers of Israel. Modern readers trying to paint a portrait of David usually take into account his life prior to his ascension to the throne. However, 1 Kgs 1–2 demonstrates no interest in David as he was prior to his rule. It is only concerned with David as portrayed in 2 Sam 11–20.

going, so he brings in Nathan in 1 Kgs as a crafty court official. While Dtr2 consistently calls Nathan "the prophet Nathan," Nathan does not engage in any prophetic activity; instead he works the art of intrigue to secure Solomon's succession of David as King. Wisdom is not only used to persuade, as in the RN, but is now also used for darker purposes. David himself recommends this use of wisdom to Solomon in 1 Kgs 2, and Solomon follows his advice, manipulating words and circumstances to effect summary executions of possible future opponents Adonijah, Joab, and Shimei. Wisdom in 1 Kgs 1–2 is certainly effective, but it is not necessarily good.

Dtr2 further adds the famous account of Solomon and the Two Prostitutes to the Solomon story. While the story itself was imported, Dtr2 carefully edits it so that it shares several key features with the story of the wise woman of Tekoa in 2 Sam 14. As David is anonymous in 2 Sam 14, so Solomon is anonymous in 1 Kgs 3:16–28, the only section of 1 Kgs 1–11 in which he is not referenced by name. The "true mother" of 1 Kgs 3 has a hidden message for Solomon in her opening speech (warning the king against the dangers of syncretism), just as the Tekoa woman's case is in fact a parable directed at David. Both kings miss the point, and Solomon further proves to be a poor jurist, opting for an arbitrary, dangerous solution. The end result takes another page from the RN: the people, not the author or Yahweh, decide that Solomon has been wise.

Dtr2 makes several other edits in 1 Kgs 3–10 to denigrate Solomon's character. He adds comments in 1 Kgs 5 and 10 that suddenly reduce Solomon from exceeding his contemporaries Hiram and the Queen of Sheba to becoming merely the Queen's equal and Hiram's vassal. While Dtr1 had Solomon drafting thirty thousand lumberjacks who had to work only one month out of three, Dtr2's Solomon adds one hundred fifty thousand laborers who do not receive the generous leave policies. Dtr2 then moves 1 Kgs 7:1–12a to its current position from (probably) after 1 Kgs 8, further weakening a positive view of Solomon the temple-builder. And as Dtr2 updates Solomon's 1 Kgs 8 prayer to reflect exilic concerns, his Solomon is sure to remind Yahweh that it is he, Solomon, who has built the temple toward which prayers are directed.

Dtr2 on Solomon and the Monarchy

Dtr1's Solomon reflects a positive view of the monarchy, even though the picture of Solomon is not wholly positive toward Solomon himself. For Dtr1, Solomon's control of his kingdom is in itself good, the only worry being Solomon's tendency toward syncretism. Solomon's wisdom leads to wealth and fame, but his wisdom is generally inconsequential for Dtr1. Most important is Solomon's fidelity to Yahweh. Solomon ultimately falls because of his willingness to engage foreign elements. Yet his failure does not necessarily mean that the monarchy is a failure. Solomon is simply one in a line of kings up to Josiah who has ups and downs, never quite reaching the standard set by the greatest of kings, King David.

The exilic Dtr2, however, is not pro-monarchy. He nevertheless has inherited a DH which is probably well-known, and from which he cannot or will not remove elements (such as the repeated references in 1 Kgs to David as the ideal king). But Dtr2 can add to the DH. He inserts the RN and 2 Sam 11–12, which teach David's weakness as a king. The RN also denigrates the idea of a king acting as jurist and presents wisdom merely as the ability to persuade, whether for good or evil. Dtr2 then wrote 1 Kgs 1–2* to connect the RN to the Solomon story. He brings to the fore the idea of David's weakness versus Solomon's strength, and develops the concept of wisdom (especially Solomon's wisdom) as something that can be used for evil purposes. Solomon is certainly wise in 1 Kgs 2, but he does not use his wisdom for good. Dtr2 further denigrates Solomon in these chapters by raising a serious question about his legitimacy, suggesting that Nathan and Bathsheba swayed a senile David into thinking that he had already decided upon Solomon as heir.

Dtr2 inserts and edits the story of Solomon and the Two Prostitutes to strengthen earlier ideas from Dtr1 and the RN: syncretism is dangerous; kings should not act as jurists; the people tend to exhibit poor judgment. He then makes a number of edits to the remainder of the Solomon story in order to denigrate Solomon, making him into a darker figure. Solomon still has his good points, as he retains responsibility for constructing the temple and for delivering the key prayer of 1 Kgs 8. But his questionable actions depreciate the efficacy of the institution of monarchy in Israel—especially coming on the heels of David's dubious reign as rendered in 2 Sam 11–20. Dtr2 certainly is not holding out for democracy—the people cannot be trusted to make wise decisions—but monarchy also may not be the answer, as even the legendary kings David and Solomon, with their vastly different ruling styles, experienced reigns rife with problems.

Dtr2 ends his DH ambiguously, with King Jehoiachin in exile, effectively "playing chess" with the king of Babylon (2 Kgs 25:27–30).[11] Jehoiachin had failed as king, but there is still hope for him: his status remains effectively unresolved.[12] Jehoiachin represents exilic Israel: he is also in exile, also with an uncertain future.

Like Jehoiachin, Dtr2's David and Solomon each represent the nation of Israel in their own way. Israel's legacy as Yahweh's people is questionable in the DH, given Israel's rebellion at Mount Horeb in Deut 9. In a similar vein, David and Solomon both experience questionable rises to the throne. Yet at the beginning of their reigns, each king has real prospects for a good, just reign, just as Israel begins its stay in the Promised Land with realistic expectations for a prosperous future there. Dtr2 denigrates David and Solomon in order to make them more like the nation of Israel. Their reigns are filled with problems brought on by their personal weaknesses, but there is legitimate hope throughout. And like them, Israel goes through many ups and downs through the DH, with both problems (brought on by sin) and hope as companions all the way through. Dtr2's David and Solomon represent Israel herself: promise early on, failures all the way through, but hope to the very end.

Final Conclusions

In this book I have demonstrated the usefulness of a diachronic approach for interpreting problematic passages of 1 Kgs 1–11. By positing two Deuteronomistic author/editors, we can interpret each part of 1 Kgs 1–11 in a consistent manner. I have distributed all of 1 Kings 1–11 into plausible layers, and I have demonstrated ideological features of Dtr1 and Dtr2. This diachronic approach provides plausible solutions to the interpretative problems posed by various rough texts in 1 Kgs 1–11.

---

11 Thanks to my seminary Old Testament professor, Dr. John Worgul, for this wonderful image.

12 Wiseman, Kings, 318; Laffey, Kings, 168; Römer, 177. Römer cites post-exilic texts to argue that 2 Kgs 25:27–30 teaches that "the land of deportation has become a land in which Jews can live, and even manage interesting careers." But Jehoiachin in this passage is not doing anything more than waiting, which seems to reflect one plausible response to the exile. As per Wiseman and Laffey, this passage reflects hope, rather than resolution.

While DblR advocates may well disagree with specific aspects of my layer delineation, the overall idea of two Deuteronomistic Historians, working in the Josianic and exilic eras, satisfactorily help us to interpret effectively the story of King Solomon in the DH.

I have also explained the relationship between the Succession Narrative (particularly the Revolt Narrative) and 1 Kgs 3–11. As per chapter 2, some scholars have suggested that these two sections of the DH may be related, particularly with respect to their interest in the subject of wisdom. Wisdom is certainly an important factor that joins these sections, but it is not the only one. The SN and the Solomon Story constitute the most substantial accounts of Davidic kings in the DH, and their appearance next to each other invites us to compare the reigning kings as well. The RN has recognizable themes that impact our reading of 1 Kgs 3–11. First Kings 1–2 further connects these two sections by cleverly illustrating David's weaknesses and Solomon's strengths as *kings*.

Finally, through use of diachronic analysis, I have laid out the intentions of Dtr2, whose work stands close to our MT. In many ways, Dtr2's evaluation of Solomon is not so far from that of Dtr1. Neither author is a big fan of wisdom, although Dtr2 does deliberately reduce the value of Solomon's wisdom. Dtr2 agrees with Dtr1 that Solomon's power leads to his success and that the main danger to Solomon is his flirtation with syncretism. Dtr2 wants us to read 2 Samuel 11–20 before taking on 1 Kgs 1–11 so that we can ponder issues of David's reign and consider how these issues play out during the reign of Solomon. Dtr2 ends up making Solomon into a darker figure throughout, generally increasing uneasiness about various aspects of Solomon's reign. Like Israel in the DH, Solomon is continually beset with questions of behavior, which can only be solved by strict adherence to the Law of Moses.

Bibliography

Ackerman, James S. "Knowing Good and Evil: A Literary Analysis of the Court History in 2 Samuel 9–20 and 1 Kings 1–2." *JBL* 109 (1990) 41–60.
Ackroyd, Peter R. "The Succession Narrative (So-Called)." *Int* 35 (1986) 383–96.
Ahlström, Gösta W. *Aspects of Syncretism in Israelite Religion*. Translated by Eric J. Sharpe. Horae Soederblomianae 5. Lund: Gleerup, 1963.
———. *The History of Ancient Palestine from the Paleolithic Period to Alexander's Conquest*. JSOTSup 146. Sheffield: Sheffield Academic, 1993.
Alter, Robert. *Ancient Israel: The Former Prophets*. New York: Norton, 2013.
———. *The Art of Biblical Narrative*. New York: Basic, 1981.
———. *The David Story*. New York: Norton, 1999.
Anderson, A. A. *2 Samuel*. Word Biblical Commentary 11. Waco, TX: Word, 1989.
Andersson, Gregor. *Untamable Texts: Literary Studies and Narrative Theory in the Books of Samuel*. LHBOTS 514. London: T. & T. Clark, 2009.
Andreasen, Neils Erik A. "The Role of the Queen Mother in Israelite Society." *CBQ* 45 (1983) 179–94.
Angel, Hayyim. "Cut the Baby in Half: Understanding Solomon's Divinely-Inspired Wisdom." *JBQ* 39 (2011) 189–94.
Aschkenasy, Nehama. *Woman at the Window: Biblical Tales of Oppression and Escape*. Detroit: Wayne State University Press, 1998.
Ash, Paul S. "Solomon's? District? List." *JSOT* 67 (1995) 67–86.
Auld, A. Graeme. *I & II Samuel: A Commentary*. OTL. Louisville: Westminster John Knox, 2011.
———. *Kings without Privilege: David and Moses in the Story of the Bible's Kings*. Edinburgh: T. & T. Clark, 1994.
———. "Solomon and the Deuteronomists." In *Samuel at the Threshold: Selected Works of Graeme Auld*, 119–25. Society for Old Testament Study Monographs Series. Aldershot, UK: Ashgate, 2004.
———. "Solomon at Gibeon: History Glimpsed." In *Samuel at the Threshold: Selected Works of Graeme Auld*, 97–107. Society for Old Testament Study Monograph Series. Aldershot, UK: Ashgate, 2004. Originally published in *Avrham Malamat Volume*, 1–7. Eretz Israel 24. Jerusalem: Israel Exploration Society, 1993.
Avioz, Michael. "The Characterization of Solomon in Solomon's Prayer (1 Kings 8)." *BN* 126 (2005) 19–28.

Avishur, Yitshak, and M. Heltzer. *Studies on the Royal Administration in Ancient Israel in the Light of Epigraphic Sources*. Tel Aviv–Jaffa: Archaeological Center, 2000.

García Bachmann, Mercedes L. *Women at Work in the Deuteronomistic History*. International Voices in Biblical Studies 4. Atlanta: Society of Biblical Literature, 2013.

Balentine, Samuel E. *Prayer in the Hebrew Bible: The Drama of Divine-Human Dialogue*. OBT. Minneapolis: Fortress, 1993.

———. "I Was Ready to Be Sought Out by Those Who Did Not Ask." In *Seeking the Favor of God*. Vol. 1, *The Origins of Penitential Prayer in Second Temple Judaism*, edited by Mark J. Boda et al., 1–20. EJL 21. Atlanta: Society of Biblical Literature, 2006.

Bar-Efrat, Shimon. *Narrative Art in the Bible*. Translated by Dorothea Shefer-Vanson. JSOTSup 70. Bible and Literature Series 17. Sheffield: Almond, 1989.

———. "Rost Revisited: The Stylistic and Formal Features of the Succession Narrative." In *Seitenblicke: Literarische und Historische Studien zu Nebenfiguren im Zweiten Samuelbuch*, edited by Walter Dietrich, 12–23. OBO 249. Fribourg: Academic, 2011.

Barrick, W. Boyd. "Loving too Well: The Negative Portrayal of Solomon and the Composition of the Kings History." *EstBib* 59 (2001) 419–50.

Bautsch, Richard J. *Developments in Genre between Post-Exilic Penitential Prayers and the Psalms of Communal Lament*. Society of Biblical Literature Academia Biblica Series 7. Atlanta: Society of Biblical Literature, 2003.

Bellis, Alice Ogden. "The Queen of Sheba: A Gender-Sensitive Reading." *JRT* 51 (1995) 17–28.

Ben-Barak, Zafrira. "The Status and Right of the Gĕbîrâ." *JBL* 110 (1991) 23–34.

Bergen, Robert D. *1, 2 Samuel*. New American Commentary 7. USA: Broadman and Holman, 1996.

Berlin, Adele. *Poetics and Interpretation of Biblical Narrative*. Winona Lake, IN: Eisenbrauns, 1994.

Berner, Christoph. "The Egyptian Bondage and Solomon's Forced Labor: Literary Connections between Exodus 1–15 and 1 Kings 1–12?" In *Pentateuch, Hexateuch, or Enneateuch? Identifying Literary Works in Genesis through Kings*, edited by Thomas B. Dozeman et al., 211–40. AIL 8. Leiden: Brill, 2012.

Beuken, W. A. M. "No Wise King without a Wise Woman (1 Kings iii 16–28)." In *New Avenues in the Study of the Old Testament*, edited by A. S. van der Woude, 1–10. Oudtestamentische Studiën 25. Leiden: Brill, 1989.

Biddle, Mark. *Deuteronomy*. Smith & Helwys Bible Commentary 4. Macon, GA: Smyth & Helwys, 2003.

Bietenhard, Sophia Katarina. *Des Königs General: die Heerführertraditionen in der vorstaatlichen und frühen staatlichen Zeit und die Joabgestalt in 2 Sam 2–20; 1 Kön 1–2*. OBO 163. Göttingen: Vandenhoeck & Ruprecht, 1998.

Birch, Bruce C. "The First and Second Books of Samuel: Introduction, Commentary, and Reflections." In *The New Interpreter's Bible*, edited by Leander Keck, 2:947–1383. Nashville: Abingdon, 1998.

Bird, Phyllis A. "The Harlot as Heroine: Narrative Art and Social Presupposition in Three Old Testament Texts." *Semeia* 46 (1989) 119–39.

Blenkinsopp, Joseph. "Another Contribution to the Succession Narrative Debate (2 Samuel 11–12; 1 Kings 1–2)." *JSOT* 38 (2013) 35–58.

———. "Theme and Motif in the Succession History (2 Sam Xi 2ff) and the Yahwist Corpus." In *Volume du Congres: Geneve 1965*, 44–57. VTSup 15. Leiden: Brill, 1966.

Bloch-Smith, Elizabeth. "Solomon's Temple: The Politics of Ritual Space." In *Sacred Time, Sacred Place: Archaeology and the Religion of Israel*, edited by Barry M. Gitlen, 83–94. Winona Lake, IN: Eisenbrauns, 2002.

———. "Who Is This King of Glory? Solomon's Temple and Its Symbolism." In *Scripture and Other Artifacts: Essays on the Bible and Archaeology in Honor of Philip J. King*, edited by Michael D. Coogan et al., 18–31. Louisville: Westminster John Knox, 1994.

Boda, Mark J. "Confession as Theological Expression: Ideological Origins of Penitential Prayer." In *Seeking the Favor of God*. Vol. 1, *The Origins of Penitential Prayer in Second Temple Judaism*, edited by Mark J. Boda et al., 21–50. EJL 21. Atlanta: Society of Biblical Literature, 2006.

———. *Praying the Tradition: the Origin and Use of Tradition in Nehemiah 9*. Beihefte zur Zeitschrift für die alttestamentliche Wissenschaft 277. Berlin: de Gruyter, 1999.

Bodner, Keith. *David Observed: A King in the Eyes of His Court*. Hebrew Bible Monographs 5. Sheffield: Sheffield Phoenix, 2005.

Brichto, Herbert C. *Toward a Grammar of Biblical Poetics: Tales of the Prophets*. New York: Oxford University Press, 1992.

Brettler, Marc Zvi. "Interpretation and Prayer: Notes on the Composition of 1 Kings 8:15–53." In *Minhah le-Nahum: Biblical and Other Studies Presented to Nahum M. Sarna in Honour of His 70th Birthday*, edited by Marc Zvi Brettler, 17–35. JSOTSup 154. Sheffield: JSOT Press, 1993.

———. "The Structure of 1 Kings 1–11." *JSOT* 49 (1991) 87–97.

Brown, Francis, S. R. Driver, and Charles A. Briggs. *A Hebrew and English Lexicon of the Old Testament*. 1907. Reprinted, Peabody: Hendrickson, 2004.

Brueggemann, Walter. *1 & 2 Kings*. Smyth and Helwys Bible Commentary. Macon, GA: Smyth & Helwys, 2000.

———. *First and Second Samuel*. Interpretation. Louisville: John Knox, 1990.

———. "On Coping with Curse: A Study of 2 Samuel 16:5–14." *CBQ* 36 (1974) 175–92.

———. "On Trust and Freedom: A Study of Faith in the Succession Narrative." *Int* 26 (1972) 3–19.

———. "The Social Significance of Solomon as a Patron of Wisdom." In *The Sage in Israel and the Ancient near East*, edited by John G. Gammie and Leo G. Perdue, 117–32. Winona Lake, IN: Eisenbrauns, 1990.

———. *Solomon: Israel's Ironic Icon of Human Achievement*. Studies on Personalities of the Old Testament. Columbia, SC: University of South Carolina Press, 2005.

Buis, Pierre. *Le Livre des Rois*. Sources Bibliques. Paris: Gabalda, 1997.

Burney, C.F. *Notes on the Hebrew Text of the Books of Kings*. London/ New York: Clarendon, 1903.

Camp, Claudia. "1 and 2 Kings." In *The Woman's Bible Commentary*, edited by Carol A. Newsome and Sharon Ringer, 96–109. Louisville, Westminster John Knox, 1992.

———. *Wise, Strange and Holy: The Strange Woman and the Making of the Bible*. JSOTSup 320. Gender, Culture, Theory 9. Sheffield: Sheffield Academic, 2000.

———. "The Wise Women of 2 Samuel: A Role Model for Women in Early Israel?" In *Women in the Hebrew Bible: A Reader*, edited by Alice Bach, 195–207. New York: Routledge, 1999.

Campbell, Antony F. *2 Samuel*. Forms of the Old Testament Literature 8. Grand Rapids: Eerdmans, 2005.

———. *Of Prophets and Kings: A Late Ninth-Century Document (1 Samuel 1—2 Kings 10)*. Catholic Biblical Quarterly Monograph Series 17. Washington, DC: Catholic Biblical Association of America, 1986.

Campbell, Antony F., and Mark A. O'Brien. *Unfolding the Deuteronomistic History: Origins, Upgrades, Present Text*. Minneapolis: Fortress, 2000.

Caquot, André, and Philippe de Robert. *Les Livres de Samuel*. Commentaire de L'Ancien Testament 6. Geneva: Labor et Fides, 1994.

Carlson, R. A. *David, the Chosen King: A Traditio-Historical Approach to the Second Book of Samuel*. Translated by Eric J. Sharpe and Stanley Rudman. Stockholm: Almqvist & Wiksell, 1964.

Carr, David M. *From D to Q: A Study of Early Jewish Interpretations of Solomon's Dream at Gibeon*. Society of Biblical Literature Monograph Series 44. Atlanta: Scholars Press, 1991.

———. *Writing on the Tablet of the Heart : Origins of Scripture and Literature*. Oxford: Oxford University Press, 2005.

Cartledge, Tony W. *1 & 2 Samuel*. Smyth & Helwys Bible Commentary 7. Macon, GA: Smyth & Helwys, 2001.

Caspi, Mishael Maswari, and Rachel S. Haverlock. *Women on the Biblical Road: Ruth, Naomi, and the female Journey*. Lanham, MD: University Press of America, 1996.

Cazeaux, Jacques. *Saül, David, Salomon: La Royauté et le Destin d'Israël*. Lectio Divina 193. Paris: Cerf, 2003.

Charpin, Dominique. "Salamon à la lumière des textes syro-mésopotamiens du deuxième millénaire av. J.-C." In *L'image de Salomon, Sources et Postérités: Actes du Colloque organisé par Le Collège de France et La Société Asiatique*, edited by Jean-Louis Bacqué-Grammont and Jean-Marie Durand, 11–21. Cahiers de la Société Asiatique, Nouvelle Série 5. Paris: Peeters, 2007.

Childs, Brevard S. *The Book of Exodus: A Critical, Theological Commentary*. OTL. Westminster: Louisville, 1974.

Clark, W. Malcolm. "Legal Background to the Yahwist's Use of 'Good and Evil' in Genesis 2–3." *JBL* 88 (1969) 266–78.

Clements, Ronald E. "Solomon and the Origins of Wisdom in Israel." *PRSt* 15 (1988) 23–35.

Cogan, Mordechai. *1 Kings*. AB 10. New York: Doubleday, 2001.

Cohn, Robert L. "Characterization in Kings." In *The Books of Kings: Sources, Composition, Historiography, and Reception*, edited by André Lemaire and Baruch Halpern, 89–105. VTSup 129. Leiden: Brill, 2010.

Conroy, Charles. *1–2 Samuel, 1–2 Kings*. Old Testament Message 6. Wilmington, DE: Glazier, 1983.

———. *Absalom Absalom! Narrative and Language in 2 Sam. 13–20*. Analecta Biblica 81. Rome: Biblical Institute Press, 1978.

Cortese, Enzo. *Deuteronomistic Work*. Translated by Silas Musholt. Studium Biblicum Franciscanum 47. Jerusalem: Franciscan Printing, 1999.

Crenshaw, James L. "Method in Determining Wisdom Influence upon 'Historical' Literature." In *Urgent Advice and Probing Questions: Collected Writings on Old Testament Wisdom*, 312–25. Macon, GA: Mercer University Press, 1995.

Cross, Frank Moore. *Canaanite Myth and Hebrew Epic: Essays in the History and Religion of Israel*. Cambridge: Harvard University Press, 1973.

Currid, John S. *Ancient Egypt and the Old Testament*. Grand Rapids: Baker, 1997.

Czövek, Tamás. *Three Seasons of Charismatic Leadership*. Regnum Studies in Mission. Oxford: Paternoster, 2006.

Damrosch, David. *The Narrative Covenant: Transformations of Genre in the Growth of Biblical Literature*. Ithaca, NY: Cornell University, 1987.

Darr, Katheryn Pfisterer. "Asking at Abel: A Wise Woman's Proverb Performance in 2 Samuel 20." In *From the Margins 1: Women of the Hebrew Bible and Their Afterlives*, edited by Peter S. Hawkins and Lesleigh Cushing Stahlberg, 102–21. BMW 18. Sheffield: Sheffield Phoenix, 2009.

Davies, Graham I. " '*Urwot* in I Kings 5:6 (EVV 4:26) and the Assyrian Horse Lists." *JSS* 34 (1989) 25–38.

Davies, John A. "'Discerning between Good and Evil': Solomon as a New Adam in 1 Kings." *WTJ* 73 (2011) 39–57.

Davies, Philip R. *In Search of Ancient 'Israel'*. JSOTSup 148. Sheffield: JSOT Press, 1991.

———. "The Deuteronomistic History and 'Double Redaction.'" In *Raising up a Faithful Exegete: Essays in Honor of Richard D. Nelson*, edited by Kurt L. Noll and Brooks Schramm, 51–59. Winona Lake, IN: Eisenbrauns, 2010.

Day, John. "Gibeon and the Gibeonites in the Old Testament." In *Reflection and Refraction: Studies in Biblical Historiography in Honour of A. Graeme Auld*, edited by Robert Rezetko et al., 113–37. VTSup 113. Leiden: Brill, 2007.

De Vries, Simon J. *1 Kings*. 2nd ed. Word Biblical Commentary 12. Waco, TX: Word, 1985.

Deurloo, K. A. "The King's Wisdom in Judgment: Narration as Example (I Kings iii)." In *New Avenues in the Study of the Old Testament*, edited by A. S. van der Woude, 11–21. Oudtestamentische Studiën 25. Leiden: Brill, 1989.

Dever, William G. "Can Archaeology Serve as a Tool in Textual Criticism of the Hebrew Bible?" In *Sacred History, Sacred Literature: Essays on Ancient Israel, the Bible, and Religion in Honor of R. E. Friedman*, edited by Shawna Dolansky, 225–37. Winona Lake, IN: Eisenbrauns, 2008.

———. *What Did the Biblical Writers Know and When Did They Know It? What Archaeology Can Tell Us about the Reality of Early Israel*. Grand Rapids: Eerdmans, 2001.

Dietrich, Walter. *The Early Monarchy in Israel: The Tenth Century B.C.E.* Translated by Joachim Vette. Biblical Encyclopedia 3. Atlanta: Society of Biblical Literature, 2007.

———. "History and Law: Deuteronomistic Historiography and Deuteronomic Law Exemplified in the Passage from the Period of the Judges to the Monarchical Period." In *Israel Constructs its History: Deuteronomistic Historiography in Recent Research*, edited by Albert de Pury et al., 315–42. JSOTSup 306. Sheffield: Sheffield Academic, 2000.

———. "Martin Noth and the Future of the Deuteronomistic History." Translated by Dwight R. Daniels. In *The History of Israel's Traditions: The Heritage of Martin*

Noth, edited by Steven L. McKenzie and M. Patrick Graham, 153–75. JSOTSup 182. Sheffield: Sheffield Academic, 1994.

———. *Prophetie und Geschichte: Eine redaktionsgeschichtliche Untersuchung zum deuteronomistischen Geschichtswerk*. Forschungen zur Religion und Literatur des Alten und Neuen Testament 108. Göttingen: Vandenhoeck & Ruprecht, 1972.

Dumbrell, William J. *Covenant and Creation: A Theology of the Old Testament Covenants*. Grand Rapids: Baker, 1984.

Durand, Jean-Marie. "Le roi savant en Mésopotamie." In *L'image de Salomon, Sources et Postérités: Actes du Colloque organisé par le Collège de France et la Société Asiatique*, edited by Jean-Louis Bacqué-Grammont and Jean-Marie Durand, 3–10. Cahiers de la Société Asiatique, N.S. 5. Paris: Peeters, 2007.

Edelman, Diana. "Solomon's Adversaries Hadad, Rezon and Jeroboam: A Trio of 'Bad Guy' Characters Illustrating the Theology of Immediate Retribution." In *The Pitcher Is Broken: Memorial Essays for Gösta Ahlström*, edited by Steven W. Holloway and Lowell K. Handy, 166–91. JSOTSup 190. Sheffield: Sheffield Academic, 1995.

Eschelbach, Michael A. *Has Joab Foiled David? A Literary Study of the Importance of Joab's Character in Relation to David*. Studies in Biblical Literature. New York: Lang, 2005.

Eslinger, Lyle. *Into the Hands of the Living God*. JSOTSup 84. Sheffield: Almond, 1989.

Exum, J. Cheryl. "Bathsheba Plotted, Shot, and Painted." *Semeia* 74 (1996) 47–73.

Eynikel, Erik. *The Reform of King Josiah and the Composition of the Deuteronomistic History*. Oudtestamentische Studiën 33. Leiden: Brill, 1996.

Fea, John. *Was America Founded as a Christian Nation? A Historical Introduction*. Louisville: Westminster John Knox, 2011.

Fewell, Dana Nolan, and David M. Gunn. *Gender, Power, and Promise: The Subject of the Bible's First Story*. Nashville: Abingdon, 1993.

Finkelstein, Israel, and Neil Asher Silberman. *David and Solomon: In Search of the Bible's Sacred Kings and the Roots of the Western Tradition*. New York: Free Press, 2006.

Firth, David G. *1 & 2 Samuel*. Apollos Old Testament Commentary 8. Nottingham, UK: Apollos, 2009.

Fischer, A. A. *Von Hebron nach Jerusalem: Eine redaktionsgeschichtliche Studie zur Erzählung von König David in II Sam 1–5*. BZAW 355. Berlin: de Gruyer, 2004.

Flanagan, James W. "Court History or Succession Document? A Study of 2 Samuel 9–20 and 1 Kings 1–2." *JBL* 91 (1972) 172–81.

Fokkelman, J. P. *King David*. Vol. 1 of *Narrative Art and Poetry in the Books of Samuel*. Studia Semitica Neerlandica. Assen: Van Gorcum, 1981.

———. *Throne and City*. Vol. 3 of *Narrative Art and Poetry in the Books of Samuel*. Studia Semitica Neerlandica. Assen: Van Gorcum, 1990.

———. *Vow and Desire*. Vol. 4 of *Narrative Art and Poetry in the Books of Samuel*. Studia Semitica Neerlandica. Assen: Van Gorcum, 1993.

Fontaine, Carole R. "The Bearing of Wisdom on the Shape of II Samuel 11–12 and I Kings 3." *JSOT* 34 (1986) 61–77.

———. "A Response to 'The Bearing of Wisdom.'" In *A Feminist Companion to Samuel and Kings*, edited by Athalya Brenner, 161–69. Feminist Companion to the Bible 5. Sheffield: Sheffield Academic, 1994.

Fox, Nili Sacher. *In the Service of the King: Officialdom in Ancient Israel and Judah*. Monographs of the Hebrew Union College 23. Cincinnati: Hebrew Union College Press, 2000.

Frazier, James George. *Folklore in the Old Testament: Studies in Comparative Religion Legend and Law*, vol. 2:3. London: MacMillan, 1918.
Fretheim, Terence E. *First and Second Kings*. Westminster Bible Companion. Louisville: Westminster John Knox, 1999.
———. "Repentance in the Former Prophets." In *Repentance in Christian Theology*, edited by Mark J. Boda and Gordon T. Smith. Collegeville, MN: Liturgical, 2006.
Friedman, Richard E. *The Exile and Biblical Narrative: The Formation of the Deuteronomistic and Priestly Works*. Harvard Semitic Monographs 22. Chico, CA: Scholars, 1981.
———. "From Egypt to Egypt: Dtr1 and Dtr2." In *Traditions in Transformation: Turning Points in Biblical Faith*, edited by Baruch Halpern and Jon Levenson, 167–92. Winona Lake, IN: Eisenbrauns, 1981.
———. "Solomon and the Great Histories." In *Jerusalem in Bible and Archaeology: The First Temple Period*, edited by Andrew G. Vaughn and Ann E. Killebrew, 171–80. SBLSymSer 18. Atlanta: Society of Biblical Literature, 2003.
Frisch, Amos. "The Exodus Motif in I Kings 1–14." *JSOT* 87 (2000) 3–21.
———. "The Narrative of Solomon's Reign: A Rejoinder." *JSOT* 51 (1991) 22–24.
———. "Structure and its Significance: The Narrative of Solomon's Reign." *JSOT* 51 (1991) 4–14.
Fritz, Volkmar. *1 & 2 Kings*. Translated by Anselm Hagedorn. Continental Commentaries. Minneapolis: Fortress, 2003.
Garsiel, Moshe. "Revealing and Concealing as a Narrative Strategy in Solomon's Judgment." *CBQ* 64 (2002) 229–47.
Gaster, Theodor H. *Myth, Legends, and Customs in the Old Testament*. New York: Harper & Row, 1969.
Geoghegan, Jeffrey C. "The Redaction of Kings and Priestly Authority in Jerusalem." In *Soundings in Kings: Perspectives and Methods in Contemporary Scholarship*, edited by Mark Leuchter and Adam Klaus-Peter, 109–18. Minneapolis: Fortress, 2010.
———. *The Time, Place, and Purpose of the Deuteronomistic History: The Evidence of "Until This Day"*. Brown Judaic Studies 347. Providence: Brown University, 2006.
Gerbrandt, Gerald Eddie. *Kingship According to the Deuteronomistic History*. SBLDS 87. Atlanta: Scholars, 1986.
Geyer, Marcia L. "Stopping the Juggernaut: A Close Reading of 2 Samuel 20:13–22." *USQR* 41 (1986–87) 33–42.
Glatt-Gilad, David A. "The Deuteronomistic Critique of Solomon: A Response to Marvin A Sweeney." *JBL* 116 (1997) 700–703.
Glueck, Nathan. *Hesed in the Bible*. Translated by Alfred Gottschalk, with an introduction by Gerald A. Larue. Cincinnati: Hebrew Union College Press, 1967.
Gnuse, Robert. *No Tolerance for Tyrants: The Biblical Assault on Kings and Kingship*. Collegeville, MN: Liturgical, 2011.
Gordon, Robert P. "A House Divided: Wisdom in Old Testament Narrative Traditions." In *Wisdom in Ancient Israel*, edited by John Day et al., 94–105. Cambridge: Cambridge University Press, 1998.
———. *I & II Samuel: A Commentary*. Library of Biblical Interpretation. Grand Rapids: Zondervan, 1986.
Gray, John. *I & II Kings*. 2nd ed. OTL. London: SCM, 1970.
Gunkel, Hermann. *The Folktale in the Old Testament*. Translated by Michael D. Rutter. Historical Texts and Interpreters in Biblical Scholarship. Sheffield: Almond, 1987.

Gunn, David M. *The Story of King David: Genre and Interpretation.* JSOTSup 6. Sheffield: JSOT Press, 1978.

Gunn, David M., and Dana N. Fewell. *Narrative in the Hebrew Bible.* Oxford Bible Series. Oxford: Oxford University Press, 1993.

Habel, Norman C. *The Land Is Mine: Six Biblical Land Ideologies.* OBT. Minneapolis: Fortress, 1995.

Halpern, Baruch. *David's Secret Demons: Messiah, Murderer, Traitor, King.* The Bible in Its World. Grand Rapids: Eerdmans, 2001.

———. *The First Historians: The Hebrew Bible and History.* San Francisco: Harper & Row, 1988.

———. "Sybil, or the Two Nations? Archaism, Alienation, and the Elite Redefinition of Traditional Culture in Judah in the 8th–7th Centuries BCE." In *The Study of the Ancient Near East in the Twenty-First Century*, edited by Jerrod S. Cooper and Glenn M. Schwartz, 291–338. Winona Lake, IN: Eisenbrauns, 1996.

Halpern, Baruch, and André Lemaire. "The Composition of Kings." In *The Books of Kings: Sources, Composition, Historiography, and Reception*, edited by André Lemaire and Baruch Halpern, 123–53. VTSup 129. Leiden: Brill, 2010.

Halpern, Baruch, and David S. Vanderhooft. "The Edition of Kings in the 7th–6th Century BCE." *HUCA* 62 (1991) 179–244.

Hawk, L. Daniel. "Violent Grace: Tragedy and Transformation in the Oresteia and the Deuteronomistic History." *JSOT* 28 (2003) 73–88.

Hays, Daniel J. "Has the Narrator Come to Praise Solomon or to Bury Him? Narrative Subtlety in 1 Kings 1–11." *JSOT* 28 (2003) 149–74.

Heaton, E.W. *Solomon's New Men: The Emergence of Ancient Israel as a National State.* New York: Pica, 1974.

Hens-Piazza, Gina. *1–2 Kings.* Abingdon Old Testament Commentaries. Nashville: Abingdon, 2006.

———. *Of Methods, Monarchs, and Meanings: A Sociorhetorical Approach to Exegesis.* Studies in Old Testament Interpretation 3. Macon, GA: Mercer University Press, 1996.

Herrmann, Siegfried. "Die Königsnovelle in Ägypten und Israel." *Wissenschaftliche Zeitschrift der Karl Marx-Universität Leipzig* 3 (1953–54) 51–62.

Hertzberg, Hans Wilhelm. *I & II Samuel: A Commentary.* Translated by John S. Bowden. OTL. Philadelphia: Westminster, 1976.

Hess, Richard S. "David and Abishag: The Purpose of 1 Kings 1:1–4." In *Homeland and Exile: Biblical and Ancient near Eastern Studies in Honor of Bustenay Oded*, edited by Gershon Galil et al., 427–38. VTSup 130. Leiden: Brill, 2009.

———. "The Form and Structure of the Solomonic District List in 1 Kings 4:7–19." In *Crossing Boundaries and Linking Horizons*, edited by Gordon D. Young et al., 279–92. Bethesda, MD: CDL, 1997.

Heym, Stefan. *The King David Report: A Novel.* New York: Putnam, 1973.

Hoffmann, Hans-Detlef. *Reform und Reformen: Untersuchungen zu einem Grundthema der deuteronomistischen Geschichtsschreibung.* Abhandlungen zur Theologies des Alten und Neuen Testaments 66. Zurich: Theologischer Verlag, 1980.

Hoffman, Yair. "Patterns of Religious Response to National Crisis in the Hebrew Bible, and Some Methodological Reflections." In *Religious Responses to Political Crisis*, edited by Henning Graf Reventlow and Yair Hoffman, 18–35. LHBOTS. London: T. & T. Clark, 2008.

Hollenback, George M. "The Dimensions and Capacity of the 'Molten Sea' in 1 Kings 7,23.26." *Bib* 81 (2000) 391–92.
Hoppe, Leslie. J. "The Afterlife of a Text: The Case of Solomon's Prayer in 1 Kings 8." *LASBF* 51 (2001) 9–30.
House, Paul R. *1, 2 Kings*. New American Commentary 8. Nashville: Broadman & Holman, 1995.
Hurowitz, Victor. *I Have Built You an Exalted House: Temple Building in the Bible in the Light of Mesopotamian and North-West Semitic Writings*. JSOTSup 115. Sheffield: Sheffield Academic, 1992.
———. "'Solomon Built the Temple and Completed It': Building the First Temple according to the Book of Kings." In *From the Foundation to the Crenellations: Essays on Temple Building in the Ancient Near East and Hebrew Bible*, edited by Mark J. Boda and Jamie Novotny, 281–302. Alter Orient und Altes Testament 366. Münster: Ugarit-Verlag, 2010.
———. "Solomon's Golden Vessels (1 Kings 7:48–50) and the Cult of the First Temple." In *Pomegranates and Golden Bells: Studies in Biblical, Jewish, and Near Eastern Ritual, Law, and Literature in Honor of Jacob Milgrom*, edited by David P. Wright et al., 151–64. Winona Lake, IN: Eisenbrauns, 1995.
———. "YHWH's Exalted House: Aspects of the Design and Symbolism of Solomon's Temple." In *Temple and Worship in Biblical Israel*, edited by John Day, 63–110. JSOTSup 422. London: T. & T. Clark, 2005.
Husser, Jean-Marie. *Dreams and Dream Narratives in the Biblical World*. Translated by Jill M. Munro. BibSem 63. Sheffield: Sheffield Academic, 1999.
Ikeda, Yutaka. "King Solomon and His Red Sea Trade." In *Near Eastern Studies Dedicated to H. I. H. Prince Takahito Mikasa on the Occasion of His Seventy-Fifth Birthday*, 113–32. Wiesbaden: Harrassowitz, 1991.
Ipsen, Avaren E. "Solomon and the Two Prostitutes." In *Marxist Feminist Criticism of the Bible*, edited by Roland Boer and Jorunn Okland, 134–50. BMW 14. Sheffield: Sheffield Phoenix, 2008.
Ishida, Tomoo. "Solomon's Succession to the Throne of David: A Political Analysis." In *Studies in the Period of David and Solomon, and Other Essays*, edited by Tomoo Ishida, 175–88. Winona Lake, IN: Eisenbrauns, 1982.
Jacobs, Mignon R. "Mothering a Leader: Bathsheba's Relational and Functional Identities." In *Mother Goose, Mother Jones, Mommie Dearest: Biblical Mothers and Their Children*, edited by Cheryl A. Kirk-Duggan and Tina Pippin, 67–84. Semeia Studies 61. Atlanta: Society of Biblical Literature, 2009.
Janzen, David. *The Violent Gift: Trauma's Subversion of the Deuteronomistic History's Narrative*. LHBOTS 561. London: T. & T. Clark, 2012.
Jensen, Hans J. L. "Desire, Rivalry, and Collective Violence in the 'Succession Narrative.'" In *The Historical Books: A Sheffield Reader*, edited by J. Cheryl Exum, 184–203. BibSem 40. Sheffield: Sheffield Academic, 1997.
Jeon, Yong Ho. "The Retroactive Re-Evaluation Technique with Pharaoh's Daughter and the Nature of Solomon's Corruption in 1 Kings 1–12." *TynBul* 62 (2011) 15–40.
Jepsen, Alfred. *Die Quellen des Königsbuches*. Halle/Salle: Niemeyer, 1953.
Jobling, David. *1 Samuel*. Berit Olam. Collegeville, MN: Liturgical, 1998.
———. "'Forced Labor': Solomon's Golden Age and the Question of Literary Representation." *Semeia* 54 (1991) 57–76.

———. "The Value of Solomon's Age for the Biblical Reader." In *The Age of Solomon*, edited by Lowell K. Handy, 470–92. SHCANE 11. Leiden: Brill, 1997.

Jones, Gwilym H. *1 and 2 Kings*. Vol. 1, *1 Kings 1–16:34*. New Century Bible Commentary. Grand Rapids: Eerdmans, 1984.

———. *The Nathan Narratives*. JSOTSup 80. Sheffield: JSOT Press, 1990.

Joüon, Paul, and T. Maruoka. *A Grammar of Biblical Hebrew*. 2 vols. Subsidia biblica 14. Rome: Editrice Pontificio Istituto Biblico, 2003.

Kaiser, Otto. "Das Verhältnis Der Erzählung Vom König David zum Sogenannten Deuteronomistischen Geschichtswerk: Am Beispiel von 1 Kön 1–2 Untersucht." In *Sogenannte Thronfolgegeschichte Davids: Neue Einsichten und Anfragen*, edited by Albert de Pury and Thomas Römer, 94–122. OBO 176. Göttingen: Vandenhoeck & Ruprecht, 2000.

Kalimi, Isaac. "The Rise of Solomon in the Ancient Israelite Historiography." In *The Figure of Solomon in Jewish, Christian, and Islamic Tradition*, edited by Joseph Verheyden, 7–44. Themes in Biblical Narrative 16. Leiden: Brill, 2013.

Kalugila, Leonidas. *The Wise King: Studies in Royal Wisdom as Divine Revelation in the Old Testament and Its Environment*. Coniectanea biblica: Old Testament Series 15. Stockholm: Gleerup, 1980.

Kang, Jung Ju. *The Persuasive Portrayal of Solomon in 1 Kings 1–11*. European University Studies Series 23: Theology 760. Bern: Lang, 2003.

Kenik, Helen. *Design for Kingship: The Deuteronomistic Narrative Technique in I Kings 3:4–15*. SBLDS 69. Chico, CA: Scholars, 1983.

Keulen, Percy S. F. van. *Two Versions of the Solomon Narrative: An Inquiry into the Relationship between MT 1 Kgs. 2–11 and LXX 3 Reg. 2–11*. VTSup 104. Leiden: Brill, 2005.

Keys, Gilliam. *The Wages of Sin: A Reappraisal of the 'Succession Narrative'*. JSOTSup 221. Sheffield: Sheffield Academic, 1996.

Kitchen, Kenneth A. "Egypt and Israel during the First Millenium BC." In *Congress Volume: Jerusalem 1986*, edited by J. A. Emerton, 107–23. VTSup 40. Leiden: Brill, 1988.

———. *The Third Intermediate Period in Egypt (1100–650 BC)*. 2nd ed. with Supplement. Warminster, UK: Aris & Phillips, 1986.

Klein, Lilian R. "Bathsheba Revealed." In *Samuel and Kings: A Feminist Companion to the Bible*, edited by Athalya Brenner, 47–64. Feminist Companion to the Bible 2. Sheffield: Sheffield Academic, 2000.

———. *From Deborah to Esther: Sexual Politics in the Hebrew Bible*. Minneapolis: Fortress, 2003.

Klein, Ralph W. *1 Chronicles: A Commentary*. Hermeneia. Minneapolis: Fortress, 1986.

Knauf, Ernst Axel. "Does 'Deuteronomistic Historiography' (DtrH) Exist?" In *Israel Constructs Its History: Deuteronomistic Historiography in Recent Research*, edited by Albert de Pury et al., 388–98. JSOTSup 306. Sheffield: Sheffield Academic, 2000.

———. "King Solomon's Copper Supply." In *Phoenicia and the Bible: Proceedings of the Conference Held at the University of Leuven on the 15th and 16th of March 1990*, edited by E. Lipinski, 167–86. Studia Phoenicia XI. Orientalia Lovaniensia Analecta 44. Leuven: Peeters, 1991.

Knoppers, Gary A. "The Deuteronomist and the Deuteronomistic Law of the King." *ZAW* 108 (1996) 329–46.

———. "Prayer and Propaganda: Solomon's Dedication of the Temple and the Deuteronomist's Program." *CBQ* 57 (1995) 229–54.
———. "Solomon's Fall and Deuteronomy." In *The Age of Solomon*, edited by Lowell K. Handy, 392–410. SHCANE 11. Leiden: Brill, 1997.
———. "Theories of the Redaction(s) of Kings." In *The Books of Kings: Sources, Composition, Historiography, and Reception*, edited by André Lemaire and Baruch Halpern, 69–88. VTSup 129. Leiden: Brill, 2010.
———. "'There was none like him': Incomparability in the Books of Kings." *CBQ* 54 (1992) 411–31.
———. *Two Nations under God: The Deuteronomistic History of Solomon and the Dual Monarchies*. 2 vols. Harvard Semitic Monographs 52, 53. Atlanta: Scholars, 1993.
———. "YHWH's Rejection of the House Built for His Name: On the Significance of Anti-Temple Rhetoric in the Deuteronomistic History." In *Essays on Ancient Israel in Its Near Eastern Context*, edited by Yaira Amit et al., 221–38. Winona Lake, IN: Eisenbrauns, 2006.
Koenig, Sara M. *Isn't This Bathsheba? A Study in Characterization*. Princeton Theological Monograph Series 177. Eugene, OR: Pickwick Publications, 2011.
Koopmans, W. T. "The Testament of David in 1 Kings 2:1–10." *VT* 41 (1991) 429–49.
Koulagna, Jean. "L'image de Salomon dans L'historiographie Deuteronomiste: A Propos de la Place de 1 Rois 1–2." *RHPR* 87 (2007) 287–300.
Kratz, Reinhard G. *The Composition of the Narrative Books of the Old Testament*. Translated by John Bowden. London: T. & T. Clark, 2005.
Kuan, Jeffrey K. "Third Kingdoms 5.1 and Israelite–Tyrian Relations during the Reign of Solomon." *JSOT* 46 (1990) 31–46.
Kunz-Lübke, Andreas. *Salomo: Von der Weisheit eines Frauenliebhabers*. Biblische Gestalten 8. Leipzig: Evangelische Verlagsanstalt, 2004.
Laato, Antti. "Second Samuel 7 and Ancient Near Eastern Royal Ideology." *CBQ* 59 (1997) 244–269.
Laffey, Alice L. *First and Second Kings*. New Collegeville Bible Commentary. Collegeville, MN: Liturgical, 2011.
Lasine, Stuart A. "Jehoram and the Cannibal Mothers (2 Kings 6.24–33): Solomon's Judgment in an Inverted World." *JSOT* 50 (1991) 27–53.
———. "The King of Desire: Indeterminancy, Audience, and the Solomon Narrative." *Semeia* 71 (1985) 85–118.
———. "The Riddle of Solomon's Judgment and the Riddle of Human Nature in the Hebrew Bible." *JSOT* 45 (1989) 61–86.
———. "The Ups and Downs of Monarchical Justice: Solomon and Jehoram in an Intertextual World." *JSOT* 59 (1993) 37–53.
Law, T. M., "How Not to Use 3 Reigns: A Plea to Scholars of the Books of Kings." *VT* 61 (2011) 280–97.
Leibowitz, E. and G. "Solomon's Judgment." *BethM* 35 (1989) 242–44.
Leithart, Peter. *1 and 2 Kings*. Brazos Theological Commentary on the Bible. Grand Rapids: Brazos, 2006.
Lemaire, André. "Salomon dans l'Histoire." In *L'image de Salomon, Sources et Postérités: Actes du Colloque Organisé par le Collège de France et la Société Asiatique*, edited by Jean-Louis Bacqué-Grammont and Jean-Marie Durand, 23–35. Cahiers de la Société Asiatique, Nouvelle Série 5. Leuven: Peeters, 2007.

———. "Toward a Redactional History of the Book of Kings." Translated by Samuel W. Heldenbrand. Translation of "Vers l'Histoire de la Redaction des Livres des Rois." *ZAW* 98 (1986) 221–36. In *Reconsidering Israel and Judah: Recent Studies on the Deuteronomistic History*, edited by Gary N. Knoppers and J. Gordon McConville, 446–61. SBTS 8. Winona Lake, IN: Eisenbrauns, 2000.

———. "Wisdom in Solomonic Historiography." In *Wisdom in Ancient Israel: Essays in Honour of J. A. Emerton*, edited by John Day et al., 106–18. Cambridge: Cambridge University Press, 1998.

Lemche, Niels Peter. "The Deuteronomistic History: Historical Reconsiderations." In *Raising up a Faithful Exegete: Essays in Honor of Richard D. Nelson*, edited by Kurt L. Noll and Brooks Schramm, 41–50. Winona Lake, IN: Eisenbrauns, 2010.

Leuchter, Mark. "The Sociolinguistic and Rhetorical Implications of the Source Citations in Kings." In *Soundings in Kings: Perspectives and Methods in Contemporary Scholarship*, edited by Mark Leuchter and Klaus-Peter Adam, 119–34. Minneapolis: Fortress, 2010.

Levenson, Jon D. "From Temple to Synagogue: 1 Kings 8." In *Traditions in Transformation: Turning Points in Biblical Faith*, edited by Baruch Halpern and Jon Levenson, 142–66. Winona Lake, IN: Eisenbrauns, 1981.

Levinson, Bernard M. "Deuteronomy's Conception of Law as an 'Ideal Type': A Missing Chapter in the History of Constitutional Law. In *"The Right Chorale": Studies in Biblical Law and Interpretation*, 52–86. Forschungen zum Alten Testament 54. Tübingen: Mohr/Siebeck, 2008.

———. "The Right Chorale: From the Poetics to the Hermeneutics of the Hebrew Bible." In *"Not in Heaven": Coherence and Complexity in Biblical Narrative*, edited by Jason P. Rosenblatt and Joseph C. Sitterson, 129–53. Indiana Studies in Biblical Literature. Bloomington: Indiana University Press, 1991.

———. "The Reconceptualization of Kingship in Deuteronomy and the Deuteronomistic History's Transformation of Torah." *VT* 51 (2001) 511–34.

Lingen, Anton van der. "*bw'- ys*' ('To Go Out and To Come In') as a Military Term." *VT* 42 (1992) 59–66.

Linville, James R. *Israel in the Book of Kings: The Past as a Product of Social Identity*. JSOTSup 272. Sheffield: Sheffield Academic, 1998.

Lipiński, Edward. "Hiram of Tyre and Sidon." In *The Books of Kings: Sources, Composition, Historiography, and Reception*, edited by André Lemaire and Baruch Halpern, 251–72. VTSup 129. Leiden: Brill, 2010.

Liver, Jacob. "Book of the Acts of Solomon." *Bib* 48 (1967) 75–101.

Lohfink, Norbert. "Distribution of the Functions of Power: The Laws Concerning Public Offices in Deuteronomy 16:18—18:22." In *A Song of Power and the Power of Song: Essays on the Book of Deuteronomy*, edited by Duane L. Christensen. SBTS 3. Winona Lake, IN: Eisenbrauns, 1993.

Long, Burke O. *I Kings, With an Introduction to Historical Literature*. Forms of the Old Testament Literature 9. Grand Rapids: Eerdmans, 1984.

———. "The 'New' Biblical Poetics of Alter and Sternberg." *JSOT* 51 (1991) 71–84.

Lopez, Marcena Mena, and Paul Burns. "Wise Women in 1 Kings 3–11." In *The Many Voices of the Bible*, edited by Sean Freyne and Ellen van Wolde, 24–32. Concilium 2002/1 London: SCM, 2002.

Lyke, Larry L. *King David with the Wise Woman of Tekoa: The Resonance of Tradition in Parabolic Narrative*. JSOTSup 255. Sheffield: Sheffield Academic, 1997.

Malamat, Abraham. "Aspects of the Foreign Policies of David and Solomon." *JNES* 22 (1963) 1–17.

———. "A Political Look at the Kingdom of David and Solomon and Its Relations with Egypt." In *Studies in the Period of David and Solomon, and Other Essays*, edited by Tomoo Ishida, 189–204. Winona Lake, IN: Eisenbrauns, 1982.

Mann, Thomas W. *The Book of the Former Prophets*. Eugene, OR: Cascade Books, 2011.

Marsman, Hennie J. *Women in Ugarit and Israel: Their Social and Religious Position in the Context of the Ancient near East*. Oudtestamentische Studiën 49. Leiden: Brill, 2003.

Master, Daniel M. "Institutions of Trade in 1 and 2 Kings." In *The Books of Kings: Sources, Composition, Historiography, and Reception,* edited by André Lemaire and Baruch Halpern, 501–16. VTSup 129. Leiden: Brill, 2010.

Matthews, Victor H., and Don C. Benjamin. *Social World of Ancient Israel 1250–587 BCE*. Peabody, MA: Hendrickson, 1993.

Mayes, A. D. H. *The Story of Israel between Settlement and Exile*. London: SCM, 1983.

McCarter, P. Kyle Jr. *I Samuel*. AB 8. Garden City, NY: Doubleday, 1980.

———. *II Samuel*. AB 9. Garden City, NY: Doubleday, 1984.

———. "Plots, True or False: The Succession Narrative as Court Apologetic." *Int* 35 (1981) 355–67.

McCormick, Clifford M. *Palace and Temple: A Study of Architectural and Verbal Icons*. BZAW 313. Berlin: de Gruyter, 2002.

McConville, J. Gordon. *Deuteronomy*. Apollos Old Testament Commentary 5. Downers Grove, IL: InterVarsity, 2002.

———. *God and Earthly Power: An Old Testament Political Theology: Genesis–Kings*. LHBOTS 454. London: T. & T. Clark, 2006.

———. *Grace in the End: A Study in Deuteronomic Theology*. Grand Rapids: Zondervan, 1993.

———. "King and Messiah in Deuteronomy and the Deuteronomistic History." In *King and Messiah in Israel and in the Ancient Near East,* edited by John Day, 271–85. JSOTSup 270. Sheffield: Sheffield Academic, 1998.

———. "Narrative and Meaning in the Books of Kings." *Bib* 70 (1989) 31–49.

McKenzie, Steven L. *King David: A Biography*. Oxford: Oxford University Press, 2000.

———. "*Ledavid* (for David!)! 'Except in the Matter of Uriah the Hittite.'" In *For and Against David: Story and History in the Books of Samuel*, edited by A. G. Auld and E. Eynikel, 307–13. Bibliothetheca Ephemeridum Theologicarum Lovaniensium 232. Leuven: Peeters, 2010.

———. "A Sample Study into the Texts of Kings used by the Chronicler and Translated by the Old Greek: 1 Kings 8." *BIOSCS* 19 (1986) 15–34.

———. "The So-Called Succession Narrative in the Deuteronomistic History." In *Die sogenannte Thronfolgegeschichte Davids,* edited by Albert de Pury and Thomas Römer, 123–35. OBO 176. Göttingen: Vandenhoeck & Ruprecht, 2000.

———. *The Trouble with Kings: The Composition of the Book of Kings in the Deuteronomistic History*. VTSup 42. Leiden: Brill, 1991.

———. "The Trouble with Kingship." In *Israel Constructs Its History: Deuteronomistic Historiography in Recent Research*, edited by Albert de Pury et al., 286–314. JSOTSup 306. Sheffield: Sheffield Academic, 2000.

———. "Why Did David Stay Home? An Exegetical Study of 2 Samuel 11:1." In *Raising up a Faithful Exegete: Essays in Honor of Richard D. Nelson*, edited by K. L. Noll and Brooks Schramm, 149–58. Winona Lake, IN: Eisenbrauns, 2010.
Mendenhall, George E. "The Shady Side of Wisdom: The Date and Purpose of Genesis 3." In *A Light unto My Path: Old Testament Studies in Honor of Jacob M. Myers*, edited by Howard N. Bream et al., 319–34. Philadelphia: Temple University Press, 1974.
Meyers, Carol. "David as Temple Builder." In *Ancient Israelite Religion: Essays in Honor of Frank Moore Cross*, edited by Patrick D. Miller Jr. et al., 357–76. Philadelphia: Fortress, 1987.
Miles, Johnny E. *Wise King—Royal Fool: Semiotics, Satire, and Proverbs 1–9*. JSOTSup 399. London: T. & T. Clark, 2004.
Miller, Robert D. "Solomon the Trickster." *BibInt* 19 (2011) 496–504.
Moberly, R. W. L. "Solomon and Job: Divine Wisdom in Human Life." In *Where Shall Wisdom Be Found: Wisdom in the Bible, the Church, and the Contemporary World*, edited by Stephen C. Barton, 3–17. Edinburgh: T. & T. Clark, 1999.
Mobley, Gregory. *The Empty Men: The Heroic Tradition of Ancient Israel*. Anchor Bible Reference Library. New York: Doubleday, 2005.
Monson, John M. "The Temple of Solomon: Heart of Jerusalem." In *Zion, City of Our God*, edited by Richard S. Hess and Gordon J. Wenham, 1–22. Grand Rapids: Eerdmans, 1999.
Montgomery, James A., and Henry Snyder Gehman. *The Books of Kings*. International Critical Commentary. Edinburgh: T. & T. Clark, 1951.
Moore, Michael S. "Bathsheba's Silence (1 Kings 1:11–31)." In *Inspired Speech: Prophecy in the Ancient Near East*, edited by John Kaltner and Louis Stulman, 336–46. JSOTSup 378. London: T. & T. Clark, 2004.
———. *Faith under Pressure: A Study of Biblical Leadership in Conflict*. Siloam Springs, AZ: Leafwood, 2003.
Moran, William L. *The Amarna Letters*. Baltimore: Johns Hopkins University Press, 1992.
Mowinckel, Sigmund. "Israelite Historiography." *ASTI* 2 (1963) 4–26.
Mulder, Martin J. *1 Kings*. Vol. 1, *1 Kings 1–11*. Translated by John Vriend. Historical Commentary on the Old Testament. Leuven: Peeters, 1998.
———. "Solomon's Temple and YHWH's Exclusivity." In *New Avenues in the Study of the Old Testament*, edited by A. S. van der Woude, 49–62. Oudtestamentische Studiën 25. Leiden: Brill, 1989.
Mullen, E. Theodore, Jr. *Narrative History and Ethnic Boundaries*. SBL Semeia Studies. Atlanta: Society of Biblical Literature, 1993.
Na'aman, Nadav. "Sources and Composition in the History of David." In *The Origins of the Ancient Israelite States*, edited by Volkmar Fritz and Philip K. Davies, 170–86. JSOTSup 228. Sheffield: Sheffield Academic, 1996.
———. "Sources and Composition in the History of Solomon." In *The Age of Solomon: Scholarship at the Turn of the Millennium*, edited by Lowell K. Handy, 57–80. SHCANE 11. Leiden: Brill, 1997.
———. "The Temple Library of Jerusalem and the Composition of the Book of Kings." In *Congress Volume: Leiden 2004*, edited by André Lemaire, 129–52. VTSup 109. Leiden: Brill, 2006.

———. "When and How Did Jerusalem Become a Great City? The Rise of Jerusalem as Judah's Premier City in the Eighth–Seventh Centuries BCE." *BASOR* 347 (2007) 21–56.
Nam, Roger S. *Portrayals of Economic Exchange in the Book of Kings*. Biblical Interpretation Series 112. Leiden: Brill, 2012.
Nelson, Richard D. *The Double Redaction of the Deuteronomistic History*. JSOTSup 18. Sheffield: JSOT Press, 1981.
———. "The Double Redaction of the Deuteronomistic History: The Case is Still Compelling." *JSOT* 29 (2005) 319–37.
———. *First and Second Kings*. Interpretation. Atlanta: John Knox, 1987.
———. "The Role of the Priesthood in the Deuteronomistic History." In *Reconsidering Israel and Judah: Recent Studies on the Deuteronomistic History*, edited by Gary N. Knoppers and J. Gordon McConville, 179–93. SBTS 8. Winona Lake, IN: Eisenbrauns, 2000.
Newman, Judith H. *Praying by the Book: The Scripturalization of Prayer in Second Temple Judaism*. EJL 14. Atlanta: Scholars, 1999.
Niditch, Susan. *Oral World and Written Word*. Library of Ancient Israel. Louisville: Westminster John Knox, 1996.
Noll, K. L. "The Deuteronomistic History and 'Double Redaction.'" In *Raising up a Faithful Exegete: Essays in Honor of Richard D. Nelson*, edited by K. L. Noll and Brooks Schramm, 51–59. Winona Lake, IN: Eisenbrauns, 2010.
Noth, Martin. *The Deuteronomistic History*. Translated by Jane Doull and John Barton. JSOTSup 15. Sheffield: Sheffield Academic, 1991.
———. *Könige 1*. Biblischer Kommentar Altes Testament 9/1. Neukirchen-Vluyn: Neukirchener, 1968.
O'Brien, Mark A. *The Deuteronomistic History Hypothesis: A Reassessment*. Orbus Biblicus et Orientalis 92. Freiburg: Freiburg Universitätsverlag, 1989.
Olley, John W. "Pharaoh's Daughter, Solomon's Palace, and the Temple: Another Look at the Structure of I Kings 1–11." *JSOT* 27 (2003) 355–69.
Omanson, Roger L., and John E. Ellington. *A Handbook on 1–2 Kings*. Vol. 1. United Bible Societies Handbook Series. New York: United Bible Societies, 2008.
Oswald, Wolfgang. "Nathan." In *Seitenblicke: Literarische und Historische Studien zu Nebenfiguren im Zweiten Samuelbuch*, edited by Walter Dietrich, 209–18. Orbus biblicus et orientalis 249. Fribourg: Academic Press, 2011.
Pakkala, Juha. *Intolerant Monolatry in the Deuteronomistic History*. Publications of the Finnish Exegetical Society 76. Göttingen: Vandenhoeck & Ruprecht, 1999.
Parker, Kim Ian. "The Limits to Solomon's Reign: A Response to Amos Frisch." *JSOT* 51 (1991) 15–21.
———. "Repetition as a Structuring Device." *JSOT* 42 (1988) 19–27.
———. *Wisdom and Law in the Reign of Solomon*. Lewiston, NY: Mellen, 1992.
Perdue, Leo G. "'Is There Anyone Left in the House of Saul . . .?' Ambiguity and the Characterization of David in the Succession Narrative." In *The Historical Books: A Sheffield Reader*, edited by J. Cheryl Exum, 167–83. BibSem 40. Sheffield: Sheffield Academic, 1997.
Person, Raymond F. Jr. *The Deuteronomic History and the Book of Chronicles: Scribal Works in an Oral World*. AIL 6. Atlanta: Society of Biblical Literature, 2010.
———. *The Deuteronomic School: History, Social Setting, and Literature*. Studies in Biblical Literature 2. Atlanta: Society of Biblical Literature, 2002.

Polak, Frank H. "The Septuagint Account of Solomon's Reign: Revision and Ancient Recension." In *X Congress of the International Organization for Septuagint and Cognate Studies, Oslo, 1998*, edited by Bernard A. Taylor, 139–64. Society of Biblical Literature Septuagint and Cognate Studies Series 51. Atlanta: Society of Biblical Literature, 2001.

Polzin, Robert. *David and the Deuteronomist: A Literary Study of the Deuteronomic History*. Vol. 3, 2 Samuel. ISBL. Bloomington: Indiana University Press, 1993.

———. *Samuel and the Deuteronomist: A Literary Study of the Deuteronomic History*. Vol. 2, 1 Samuel. ISBL. Bloomington: Indiana University Press, 1993.

Porten, Bezalel. "The Structure and Theme of the Solomon Narrative (1 Kings 3–11)." *HUCA* 38 (1967) 93–128.

Power, Bruce A. "'All the King's Horses...' Narrative Subversion in the Story of Solomon's Golden Age." In *From Babel to Babylon: Essays on Biblical History and Literature in Honour of Brian Peckham*, edited by Joyce Rilett Wood et al., 111–23. LHBOTS. London: T. & T. Clark, 2006.

Provan, Iain W. *Hezekiah and the Book of Kings: A Contribution to the Debate about the Composition of the Deuteronomistic History*. BZAW 172. Berlin: de Gruyter, 1988.

———. "On 'Seeing' the Trees While Missing the Forest: The Wisdom of Characters and Readers in 2 Samuel and 1 Kings." In *In Search of True Wisdom: Essays in Old Testament Interpretation in Honor of Ronald E. Clements*, edited by Edward Ball, 153–73. JSOTSup 300. Sheffield: Sheffield Academic, 1999.

———. "Why Barzillai of Gilead (1 Kings 2:7)? Narrative Art and the Hermeneutics of Suspicion in 1 Kings 1–2." *TynBul* 46 (1995) 103–16.

Pyper, Hugh S. *David as Reader: 2 Samuel 12:1–15 and the Poetics of Fatherhood*. Biblical Interpretation Series 23. Leiden: Brill, 1996).

———. "Judging the Wisdom of Solomon: The Two-Way Effect of Intertextuality." *JSOT* 59 (1993) 25–36.

Rabinowitz, I. "*āz* Followed by Imperfect Verb Forms in Preterite Contexts: A Redactional Device in Biblical Hebrew." *VT* 34 (1984) 53–62.

Rad, Gerhard von. "The Beginnings of Historical Writing in Ancient Israel." In *The Problem of the Hexateuch and Other Essays*, edited by Gerhard von Rad, translated by E. W. Trueman Dicken, 166–204. Oliver and Boyd, 1966.

Rand, Herbert. "Pronunciation: A Key to Meaning in 1 Kings 3:16–28." *JBQ* 25 (1997) 246–50.

Redford, Donald B. *Egypt, Canaan, and Israel in Ancient Times*. Princeton: Princeton University Press, 1992.

Reich, Ronny, and Eli Shukron. "The Urban Development of Jerusalem in the Late Eighth Century B.C.E." In *Jerusalem in Bible and Archaeology: The First Temple Period*, edited by Andrew G. Vaughn and Ann E. Killebrew, 209–18. SBLSymSer 18. Atlanta: Society of Biblical Literature, 2003.

Reis, Pamela Tamarkin. "Cupidity and Stupidity: Women's Agency and the 'Rape' of Tamar." In *Reading the Lines: A Fresh Look at the Hebrew Bible*, 169–95. Peabody, MA: Hendrickson, 2002.

———. "Unspeakable Names: Solomon's Tax Collectors." *ZAW* 120 (2008) 261–66.

Reinhartz, Adele. "Anonymous Women and the Collapse of the Monarchy: A Study in Narrative Technique." In *The Feminist Companion to the Bible: Samuel and Kings*, edited by Athalya Brenner, 43–65. Feminist Companion to the Bible 5. Sheffield: Sheffield Academic, 1994.

———. *Why Ask My Name? Anonymity and Identity in Biblical Narrative.* New York: Oxford University Press, 1998.
Rendsburg, Gary A. "The Guilty Party in 1 Kings 3:16–28." *VT* 48 (1998) 534–41.
Richter, Sandra L. *The Deuteronomistic History and the Name Theology: lesakken semô sam in the Bible and the Ancient Near East.* BZAW 318. Berlin: de Gruyter, 2002.
———. "Elders or Youngsters? Critical Remarks on 1 Kings 12." In *One God—One Cult—One Nation: Archaeological and Biblical Perspectives,* edited by Reinhard G. Kratz and Hermann Spieckermann, 79–86. BZAW 405. Berlin: de Gruyter, 2010.
Robinson, J. *The First Book of Kings.* Cambridge Bible Commentary. London: Cambridge University Press, 1972.
Rofé, Alexander. "The Organization of the Judiciary in Deuteronomy." In *Deuteronomy: Issues and Interpretation,* edited by David J. Reimer, 103–20. Old Testament Studies. Edinburgh: T. & T. Clark, 2002.
Rogers, Jeffrey S. "Narrative Stock and Deuteronomistic Elaboration in 1 Kings 2." *CBQ* 50 (1988) 398–413.
Römer, Thomas A. "'Redaction Criticism': 1 Kings 8 and the Deuteronomists." In *Method Matters: Essays on the Interpretation of the Hebrew Bible in Honor of David L. Petersen,* edited by Joel M. LeMon and Kent Harold Richards, 63–76. Resources for Biblical Study 56. Atlanta: Society of Biblical Literature, 2009.
———. *The So-Called Deuteronomistic History.* London: T. & T. Clark, 2005.
———. "Salomon d'Après les Deutéronomistes: un Roi Ambigu." In *Le Roi Salomon: un Heritage en Question,* edited by Claude Lichtert and Dany Nocquet, 98–130. Le Livre et le Rouleau 33. Bruxelles: Lessius, 2008.
Römer, Thomas, and Albert de Pury. "Deuteronomistic Historiography (DH): History of Research and Debated Issues." In *Israel Constructs Its History: Deuteronomistic Historiography in Recent Research,* edited by Albert de Pury et al., 24–143. JSOTSup 306. Sheffield: Sheffield Academic, 2000.
Rösel, Martin. "Salomo und die Sonne: Zur Rekonstruktion des Tempelweihspruchs I Reg 8,12f." *ZAW* 121 (2009) 402–17.
Rosenberg, Joel. *King and Kin: Political Allegory in the Hebrew Bible.* ISBL. Bloomington: Indiana University Press, 1986.
Rost, Leonhard. *The Succession to the Throne of David.* Translated by Michael D. Rutter and David M. Gunn. Historical Texts and Interpreters in Biblical Scholarship. Sheffield: Almond, 1982.
Rudnig, Thilo A. *Davids Thron: Redaktionskriticshe Studien zur Geschichte von der Thronnachfolge Davids.* BZAW 358. Berlin: de Gruyter, 2006.
Ruppert, L. "*ya'as*⌷." In *Theological Dictionary of the Old Testament,* edited by G. Johannes Botterweck et al., 6:151. Grand Rapids: Eerdmans, 1990.
Rupprecht, Konrad. *Der Tempel von Jerusalem: Gründung Salomos oder jebusitisches Erbe?* BZAW 144. Berlin: de Gruyter, 1977.
Russell, Stephen C. *Images of Egypt in Early Biblical Literature: Cisjordan-Israelite, Transjordan-Israelite, and Judahite Portrayals.* BZAW 403. Berlin: de Gruyter, 2009.
Sackenfeld, Katherine Doob. *Just Wives? Stories of Power and Survival in the Old Testament and Today.* Louisville: Westminster John Knox, 1996.
Särkiö, Pekka. *Die Weisheit und Macht Salomos in der Israelitischen Historiographie.* Schriften der Finnischen Exegetischen Gesellschaft 60. Helsinki: Finnische Exegetische Gesellschaft, 1994.

Sarna, Nahum M. *Exodus*. JPS Torah Commentary. Philadelphia: Jewish Publication Society, 1991.

Savran, George. "1 and 2 Kings." In *The Literary Guide to the Bible*, edited by Robert Alter and Frank Kermode, 146–64. Cambridge, MA: Belknap, 1987.

———. *Telling and Retelling: Quotation in Biblical Narrative*. ISBL. Bloomington: Indiana University Press, 1988.

Schenker, Adrian. "Jeroboam and the Division of the Kingdom in the Ancient Septuagint: LXX 3 Kingdoms 12.24 a-z, MT 1 Kings 11–12; 14 and the Deuteronomistic History." In *Israel Constructs its History: Deuteronomistic Historiography in Recent Research*, edited by Albert de Pury et al., 214–57. JSOTSup 306. Sheffield: Sheffield Academic, 2000.

———. *Septante et texte massorétique dans l'histoire la plus ancienne du texte de 1 Rois 2–14*. Cahiers de la revue biblique 48. Paris: Gabalda, 2000.

Schipper, Jeremy. *Disability Studies and the Hebrew Bible: Figuring Mephibosheth in the David Story*. LHBOTS 441. Sheffield: Sheffield Academic, 1997.

Schley, D. G. "1 Kings 10:26–29: A Reconsideration." *JBL* 106 (1987) 595–601.

Schniedewind, William M. *How the Bible Became a Book: The Textualization of Ancient Israel*. Cambridge: Cambridge University Press, 2004.

———. "Jerusalem, the Late Judahite Monarchy, and the Composition of the Biblical Texts." In *Jerusalem in Bible and Archaeology: The First Temple Period*, edited by Andrew G. Vaughn and Ann E. Killebrew, 375–93. SBLSymSer 18. Atlanta: Society of Biblical Literature, 2003.

Schulman, Alan R. "Diplomatic Marriage in the Egyptian New Kingdom." *JNES* 38 (1979) 177–93.

Scott, R.B.Y. "The Pillars of Jachin and Boaz." *JBL* 58 (1939) 143–49.

———. "Solomon and the Beginnings of Wisdom in Israel." In *Wisdom in Israel and the Ancient Near East*, edited by M. Noth and D. Winton Thomas, 262–79. VTSup 3. Leiden: Brill, 1955.

Seibert, Eric A. *Subversive Scribes and the Solomonic Narrative: A Rereading of 1 Kings 1–11*. Library of Hebrew Bible/ Old Testament Series (Journal for the Study of the Old Testament) 436. New York: T. & T. Clark, 2006.

Seiler, Stefan. *Die Geschichte von der Throngefolge Davids (2 Sam 9–20; 1 Kön 1–2): Untersuchungen zur Literarkritik und Tendenz*. BZAW 267. Berlin: de Gruyter, 1998.

Seow, Choon-Leong. "1 and 2 Kings." In *New Interpreter's Bible*, edited by Leander E. Keck, vol. 3, 1–295. Nashville: Abingdon, 1999.

———. "The Syro-Palestinian Context of Solomon's Dream." *HTR* 77 (1984) 141–52.

Shupak, Nili. *Where Can Wisdom Be Found? The Sage's Language in the Bible and in Ancient Egyptian Literature*. Orbus biblicus et orientalis 130. Friborg, Switzerland: University Press, 1993.

Smend, Rudolph. "The Law and the Nations: A Contribution to Deuteronomistic Tradition History." Translated by Peter T. Daniels. In *Reconsidering Israel and Judah: Recent Studies on the Deuteronomistic History*, edited by Gary N. Knoppers and J. Gordon McConville, 95–110. SBTS 8. Winona Lake, IN: Eisenbrauns, 2000.

Smith, Brendan Powell. *The Brick Bible: A New Spin on the Old Testament*. New York: Skyhorse, 2011.

Smith, Mark S. *The Memoirs of God: History, Memory, and the Experience of the Divine in Ancient Israel*. Minneapolis: Fortress, 2004.

Soggin, J. A. "King Solomon." In *Birkat Shalom: Studies in the Bible, Ancient Near Eastern Literature, and Postbiblical Judaism Presented to Shalom M. Paul on the Occasion of His Seventieth Birthday*, edited by Chaim Cohen et al., 1:169–74. Winona Lake, IN: Eisenbrauns, 2008.

Sonsino, Rifat. *Motive Clauses in Hebrew Law: Biblical Forms and Near Eastern Parallels*. SBLDS 45. Missoula, MT: Scholars, 1980.

Spina, Frank A. "In but not of the World: The Confluence of Wisdom and Torah in the Solomon Story (1 Kings 1–11)." *ATJ* 56 (2001) 17–30.

Stahlberg, Lesleigh Cushing. "From Biblical Blanket to Post-Biblical Blank Slate: The Lives and Times of Abishag the Shunammite." In *From the Margins 1: Women of the Hebrew Bible and Their Afterlives*, edited by Peter S. Hawkins and Lesleigh Cushing Stahlberg, 122–40. BMW 18. Sheffield: Sheffield Phoenix, 2009.

Sternberg, Meir. *The Poetics of Biblical Narrative: Ideological Literature and the Drama of Reading*. ISBL. Bloomington: Indiana University Press, 1987.

Steussy, Marti J. *David: Biblical Portraits of Power*. Studies on Personalities of the Old Testament. Columbia: University of South Carolina Press, 1999.

Stevens, Marty. *Temple, Tithes, and Taxes: The Temple and the Economic Life of Ancient Israel*. Peabody, MA: Hendrickson, 2006.

Stone, Ken. *Sex, Honor, and Power in the Deuteronomistic History*. JSOTSup 234. Sheffield: Sheffield Academic, 1996.

Stott, Katherine M. *Why Did They Write This Way? Reflections on References to Written Documents in the Hebrew Bible and Ancient Literature*. LHBOTS 492. New York: T. & T. Clark, 2008.

Sweeney, Marvin A. "The Critique of Solomon in the Josianic Edition of the Deuteronomistic History." *JBL* 114 (1995) 607–22.

———. *I and II Kings: A Commentary*. OTL. Louisville: Westminster John Knox, 2007.

———. *King Josiah of Judah: The Lost Messiah of Israel*. Oxford: Oxford University Press, 2001.

———. "Synchronic and Diachronic Considerations in the DtrH Portrayal of the Demise of Solomon's Kingdom." In *Birkat Shalom: Studies in the Bible, Ancient Near Eastern Literature, and Postbiblical Judaism Presented to Shalom M. Paul on the Occasion of His Seventieth Birthday*, edited by Chaim Cohen et al., 1:175–89. Winona Lake, IN: Eisenbrauns, 2008.

Talshir, Zipora. *The Alternative Story of the Division of the Kingdom: 3 Kingdoms 12:24a-z*. Jerusalem Biblical Studies 6. Jerusalem: Simor, 1993.

———. "Literary Design: A Criterion for Originality? A Case Study: 3 Kingdoms 12:24a-z; I K 11–14." In *La double transmission du texte biblique: Etudes d'histoire du texte offertes en hommage a Adrian Schenker*, edited by Yohanan Goldman and Christoph Uehlinger, 41–57. Fribourg: Göttingen, 2001.

———. "The Reign of Solomon in the Making: Pseudo-Connections Between 3 Kingdoms and Chronicles." *VT* 50 (2000) 233–49.

———. Review of *Two Versions of the Solomon Narrative: An Inquiry into the Relationship between MT 1 Kgs. 2–11 and LXX 3 Reg. 2–11*, by Percy S. F. van Keulen. *RBL* (online) 12/29/07.

Talstra, E. *Solomon's Prayer: Synchrony and Diachrony in the Composition of 1 Kings 8, 14–61*. Contributions to Biblical Exegesis and Theology 3. Kampen: Kok Pharos, 1993.

Tessitori, L. P. "Two Jaina Versions of the Story of Solomon's Judgment." *TIA* 43 (1913) 148–52.

Tigay, Jeffrey H. *Deuteronomy*. JPS Torah Commentary. Philadelphia: Jewish Publication Society, 1996.

Tomes, Roger. "'Our Holy and Beautiful House': When and Why Was 1 Kings 6–8 Written?" *JSOT* 70 (1996) 33–50.

Toorn, Karel van der. *Scribal Culture and the Making of the Hebrew Bible*. Cambridge: Harvard University Press, 2007.

Tov, Emanuel. *Textual Criticism of the Hebrew Bible*. 3rd ed. Minneapolis: Fortress, 2012.

Trebolle Barrera, Julio. "Kings (MT/LXX) and Chronicles: The Double and Triple Textual Tradition." In *Reflection and Refraction: Studies in Biblical Historiography in Honour of A. Graeme Auld*, edited by Robert Rezetko et al., 483–502. VTSup 113. Leiden: Brill, 2007.

———. "Redaction, Recension, and Midrash." *BIOSCS* 15 (1982) 25–28.

———. *Salomon y Jereboan: Historia de la recension y redaccion de 1 Reyes 2–12, 14*. Bibliotheca Salmanticensis. Dissertationes 3. Salamanca: Valencia, 1980.

———. "The Text-Critical Use of the Septuagint in the Books of Kings." In *VII Congress of the International Organization for Septuagint and Cognate Studies, Leuven, 1989*, edited by Claude E. Cox, 285–99. Septuagint and Cognate Studies Series 31. Atlanta: Scholars, 1991.

Trible, Phyllis. *God and the Rhetoric of Sexuality*. OBT. Philadelphia: Fortress, 1978.

———. *Texts of Terror: Literary-Feminist Readings of Biblical Narratives*. OBT. Philadelphia: Fortress, 1994.

Tsumura, David Toshio. *The First Book of Samuel*. New International Commentary on the Old Testament. Grand Rapids: Eerdmans, 2007.

Turkanik, Andrzej S. *Of Kings and Reigns: A Study of Translation Technique in the gamma/gamma Section of 3 Reigns (1 Kings)*. Forschungen zum Alten Testament 2/30. Tübingen: Mohr/Siebeck, 2008.

Van Seters, John. *The Biblical Saga of King David*. Winona Lake, IN: Eisenbrauns, 2009.

———. "The Court History and DtrH: Conflicting Perspectives on the House of David." In *Die sogenannte Thronfolgegeschichte Davids*, edited by Albert de Pury and Thomas Römer, 70–93. OBO 176. Göttingen: Vandenhoeck & Ruprecht, 2000.

———. *In Search of History: History in the Ancient World and the Origins of Biblical History*. New Haven: Yale University Press, 1983.

———. Review of *The Deuteronomistic History and the Name Theology: lesakken semô sam in the Bible and the Ancient Near East*, by Sandra L Richter. *JAOS* 123 (2003) 871–72.

———. "The 'Shared Text' of Samuel-Kings and Chronicles Re-examined." In *Reflection and Refraction: Studies in Biblical Historiography in Honour of A. Graeme Auld*, edited by Robert Rezetko et al., 502–15. VTSup 113. Leiden: Brill, 2007.

———. "Solomon's Temple: Fact and Ideology in Biblical and Near Eastern Historiography." *CBQ* 59 (1997) 45–57.

Veijola, Timo. *Die ewige Dynastie: David und die Entstehung seiner Dynastie nach der deuteronomistischen Darstellung*. Annales Academiæ Scientiarum Fennicæ, Ser. B, 193. Helsinki: Suomalainen Tiedeakatemia, 1975.

———. *Das Königtum in der Beurteilung der deuteronomistischen Historiographie: eine redaktionsgeschichtliche Untersuchung*. Annales Academiæ Scientiarum Fennicæ, Ser. B, 198. Helsinki: Suomalainen Tiedeakatemia, 1977.
Viviano, Pauline A. "Glory Lost: The Reign of Solomon in the Deuteronomistic History." In *The Age of Solomon*, edited by Lowell K. Handy, 336-47. SHCANE 11. Leiden: Brill, 1997.
Vogt, Peter T. *Deuteronomic Theology and the Significance of Torah: A Reappraisal*. Winona Lake, IN: Eisenbrauns, 2006.
Wälchli, Stefan. *Der weise König Salomo*. Beiträge zur Wissenschaft vom Alten und Neuen Testament 8/141. Stuttgart: Kohlhammer, 1999.
Walsh, Jerome T. *1 Kings*. Berit Olam. Collegeville, MN: Liturgical, 1996.
———. "The Characterization of Solomon in First Kings 1-5." *CBQ* 57 (1995) 471-93.
———. *Style and Structure in Biblical Hebrew Narrative*. Collegeville, MN: Liturgical, 2001.
———. "Symmetry and the Sin of Solomon." *SHOFAR* 12 (1993) 11-27.
Waltke, Bruce, and Mark O'Connor. *An Introduction to Biblical Hebrew Syntax*. Winona Lake, IN: Eisenbrauns, 1990.
Watts, John D. W. *Isaiah 34-66*. Word Biblical Commentary 25. Waco, TX: Word, 1987.
Weeks, Stuart. *Early Israelite Wisdom*. Oxford Theological Monographs. Oxford: Oxford University Press, 1994.
Weinfeld, Moshe. *Deuteronomy 1-11*. AB 5. New Haven: Yale University Press, 1991.
———. *Deuteronomy and the Deuteronomic School*. Oxford: Oxford University Press, 1972.
———. "Judge and Officer in Ancient Israel and the Ancient Near East." *Israel Oriental Studies* 7 (1977) 65-88.
Weippert, Helga. "Die 'deuteronomistischen' Beurteilungen der Könige von Israel und Juda und das Problem der Redaktion der Königsbücher." *Bib* 53 (1972) 301-39.
Weitzman, Steven. *Solomon: The Lure of Wisdom*. Jewish Lives. New Haven: Yale University Press, 2011.
Wellhausen, Julius. *Prolegomena to the History of Israel*. Scholars Press Reprints and Translations Series. Atlanta: Scholars, 1994.
Werline, Rodney Alan. *Penitential Prayer in Second Temple Judaism: The Development of a Religious Institution*. EJL 13. Atlanta: Scholars, 1998.
Westermann, Claus. *Elements of Old Testament Theology*. Translated by Douglas W. Stott. Atlanta: John Knox, 1982.
Weyde, Karl William. "The Narrative of King Solomon and the Law of the King: On the Relationship between 1 Kings 3-11 and Deut 17:14-20." In *Enigmas and Images: Studies in Honor of Tryggve N. D. Mettinger*, edited by Göran Eidevall and Blaženka Scheuer, 75-91. Coniectanea biblica: Old Testament Series 58. Winona Lake, IN: Eisenbrauns, 2011.
White, Marsha C. "The Elijah Legends and Jehu's Coup: An Examination of a Biblical Accession Text." PhD diss., Harvard University, 1994.
Whybray, R. N. *The Intellectual Tradition in the Old Testament*. BZAW 135. Berlin: de Gruyter, 1974.
———. "The Sage in the Israelite Royal Court." In *The Sage in Israel and the Ancient Near East*, edited by John G. Gammie and Leo G. Perdue, 133-39. Winona Lake, IN: Eisenbrauns, 1990.

———. *The Succession Narrative: A Study of II Samuel 9–20; 1 Kings 1 and 2*. Studies in Biblical Theology 2/9. London: SCM, 1968.
Wijk-Bos, Johanna W. H. van. *Reading Samuel: A Literary and Theological Commentary*. Reading the Old Testament. Macon, GA: Smyth & Helwys, 2011.
Willis, Joyce, Andrew Pleffer, and Stephen Llewelyn. "Conversation in the Succession Narrative of Solomon." *VT* 61 (2011) 133–47.
Wills, Garry. *Certain Trumpets: The Call of Leaders*. New York: Simon & Schuster, 1994.
Williams, David S. "Once Again: The Structure of the Narrative of Solomon's Reign." *JSOT* 86 (1999) 49–66.
Wiseman, Donald J. *1 and 2 Kings: An Introduction and Commentary*. Tyndale Old Testament Commentaries 9. Downers Grove, IL: InterVarsity, 1993.
Wissmann, Felipe Blanco. "'He Did What Was Right': Criteria of Judgment and Deuteronomism in the Books of Kings." In *Pentateuch, Hexateuch, or Enneateuch? Identifying Literary Works in Genesis through Kings*, edited by Thomas B. Dozeman et al., 241–59. AIL 8. Leiden: Brill, 2012.
Wolde, Ellen van. "Who Guides Whom? Embeddedness and Perspective in Biblical Hebrew and in I Kings 3:16–28." *JBL* 114 (1995) 623–42.
Wolff, Hans Walter. "The Kerygma of the Deuteronomic Historical Work." In *The Vitality of Old Testament Traditions*, by Walter Brueggemann and Hans Walter Wolff, 83–100. 2nd ed. Atlanta: John Knox, 1982.
Wolpe, David. *David: the Divided Heart*. New Haven: Yale University Press, 2014.
Würthwein, Ernst. *Die Bücher der Könige: Das erste Buch der Könige Kaptiel 1–16*. Das Alte Testamente Deutsch 11/1. Göttingen: Vandenhoeck & Ruprecht, 1977.
———. "Erwagingen zum sog. Deuteronomistischen Geschichtswerk: Eine Skizze." In *Studien zum deuteronomistischen Geschichtswerk*, edited by Ernst Würthwein, 1–11. BZAW 227. Berlin: de Gruyter, 1994.
Younger, K. Lawson Jr. "The Figurative Aspect and the Contextual Method in the Evaluation of the Solomonic Empire (1 Kings 1–11)." In *the Bible in Three Dimensions: Essays in Celebration of Forty Years of Biblical Studies in the University of Sheffield*, edited by David J. A. Clines et al., 157–76. JSOTSup 87. Sheffield: Sheffield Academic, 1990.
Zwickel, Wolfgang. *Der Salomonische Tempel*. Kulturgeschichte der antiken Welt 83. Mainz: von Zabern, 1999.

Scripture Index

Genesis
18:19 — 126
27 — 153

Exodus
1:11 — 24, 63
1:20 — 24
5 — 104n
18:13–23 — 96
21:12–14 — 170, 171

Leviticus
9:22–23 — 106
21:23 — 106

Numbers
11:11–17 — 96

Deuteronomy
1:3 — 52
1:9–18 — 32, 96
1:9–12 — 58
1:9 — 96n
1:13 — 96
1:15 — 96
1:16 — 143
5:1—26:15 — 97n
7:1–6 — 82, 92
7:1–4 — 39
7:1–2 — 92
7:3 — 111
7:9–10 — 39
12:11 — 38
13:12–18 — 195
14:23 — 38
16:2 — 38
16:6 — 38
16:11 — 38
16:16–17 — 106
16:18—18:21 — 97
17:8–9 — 143
17:14–20 — 12, 29n, 88
17:15 — 74, 75n, 101
17:17 — 97
20:10–11 — 76
23:8 — 92
26:2 — 38
28 — 70n
28:30 — 132n

Joshua
16:10 — 76
23:6–13 — 92
23:11–13 — 39
23:12 — 92

Judges
1:30–35 — 76
2 — 111
5:29 — 5
14:12 — 102

1 Samuel

8–12	85
8	23n, 97, 193n
10:1–13	161
12	111
12:14	97
12:20–25	109
16:18	117
17:37	117
18	125
18:12	117
18:14	117
18:28	117
20	125
20:13	117
20:14–16	127
25:23–34	158
29:4	108
29:9	142

2 Samuel

3:3	135
5:10	117
5:11–12	101, 105, 191
5:14	160n
6:17–18	93
6:18	106
7	14, 60, 88, 109n, 162
7:1–2	174
7:2	100, 105, 109n, 161
7:4–16	4, 161
7:11–16	14
7:11–12	23
7:14–15	19, 111
7:16	51
7:18–29	14
7:19	109
8–10	82
8	125
8:13	126
8:15	125–26, 127
8:16–18	126
9	127
9:1	125, 127
9:1—11:1	127
9:7	163
10:1—11:1	58, 127
10:1–5	127
10:2	163
11–12	8, 32, 123–24, 117n, 123–131, 146–47, 151, 156, 181
11	123
11:21	129–130
12:1–4	139
12:7–12	161
12:25	123, 124, 161
12:26–31	58, 127, 146n
13–20	8, 120, 128-45, 147
13	116, 135–36, 139, 143, 162
13:3	133, 134
13:7	132
13:19–20	146
13:21	132n, 134n
13:30–36	161–62
14:1–20	5, 59, 136, 141–43, 152, 153, 156, 180, 197
14:2	133
14:6	144
14:11	165–66
14:14	138
14:20	133
15–17	117n, 133–34
15:1–6	116, 141, 143, 197, 198
15:16	132
15:31–37	140
16:1–4	124, 125, 144
16:15–23	140
16:17	161
16:21–22	119, 132
16:21	140
16:23	118, 130n, 140, 145, 161
17	209
17:1–14	140–41, 144–45
17:5–14	118
18:5	116, 168
18:9–13	171
18:14	175
19:1–7	168
19:13	168
19:23	108, 166, 167n
19:24–30	141, 143–44, 156, 197
19:24	127
19:27	142
19:28	130n
19:31–38	144n, 163

20	125	2:13–25	154–59
20:3	132	2:24	173
20:5–10	171	2:25	170
20:6	122	2:28	170, 173
20:8–23	117	2:30	30
20:10	168	2:31	171
20:16–22	136–38, 143n, 154	2:33	173
20:16	133	2:35	171
20:22	133	2:36–45	166–67
20:23–26	200	2:45	173
21:10–12	158	2:46	52, 53, 89–93, 121, 173–74
22:8–16	107	3:1–15	25–26, 27, 28n, 32–33, 113
23:1–7	51, 93n	3:1–3	25, 52–55, 89–93
23:20–22	168	3:1	98, 133
24	99n	3:3	16, 89–93
24:9	104	3:4–15	27, 32–33, 55–58, 63, 83, 84, 87, 93–98, 109, 111, 113–114
24:18–25	93	3:6	116
24:25	106	3:9	96, 142
		3:11–12	112

1 Kings

1–2	6, 8, 15, 18, 19, 20n, 21, 29–31, 41–42, 49–52, 84, 85, 122–24, 130–131, 148, 149–176	3:12–13	80, 84n
		3:13	75, 133
		3:14	54, 56, 73, 93n, 97, 113
1:1–51	123	3:16–28	5, 8, 27–28, 32, 33–34, 58–59, 138, 142, 154, 156, 177–190, 197, 199, 210
1:1–4	30, 175–176		
1:7–10	168–69	3:16	182, 198
1:11–38	159–62	3:17–18	108
1:17–21	152–53	3:28	191, 197, 199–200
1:20	124	4–5	34–35, 59–64, 84, 112
1:30	120	4:1—5:14	84
1:32	170	4:1–19	112, 201
1:35–37	12, 170	4:1–6	150
1:39	171	4:5	133n
1:42	165	4:6	76
1:50–53	165–66, 170	4:7–19	35n, 59, 61, 98–99, 172
1:52	171	4:11	131, 133n
2:1–9	51	4:15	131, 133n
2:1–4	18, 51	4:20—5:14	60
2:3–4	12, 61	4:20	133, 172
2:4	14, 73	4:30	101
2:5	30	5–8	36
2:7	162n	5–7	62
2:5–11	50	5	84
2:5–9	28n, 31n, 162–65	5:1	101n
2:9	166	5:2–3	61
2:10–12	51–52, 89–93	5:3–4	100
2:12–46	52	5:9–14	103, 111
2:12	109, 119n, 173		

1 Kings (cont.)

5:9	112
5:15—9:25	35
5:15–32	60
5:15–23	101
5:15	84
5:17–21	62–63
5:17–19	60, 100, 201
5:18	109, 201
5:19	173
5:23	112
5:24–26	62, 79–80, 84–85, 191–192
5:27–32	19, 63–64, 77, 103–4, 195–96
5:27	76–77
5:28	104
5:29	192–93
5:30	99
5:31	192–93
6:1—9:9	25
6–7	27, 35–36, 39, 64–65
6:1	11
6:11–14	17, 65, 206
6:11–13	14
6:12	39
6:36	66
7:1–12	65–67, 80, 84, 104, 112, 192–94
7:7	105, 194
7:8	77, 101
7:9–12a	105, 192
7:9	133
7:13–51	65, 66, 107, 193
7:14	107
7:15–22	107
7:23–26	107
7:25	65
7:44	65
7:52	84
8	2, 37–38, 67–72, 86, 106, 109–13, 121
8:1	84
8:1–11	67–68, 106, 109, 206
8:3–6	21
8:4–13	39
8:5	109
8:12–13	68–69
8:14–53	11
8:14–21	68, 69, 74
8:14–19	60
8:15–20	202
8:16	38
8:17–20	174
8:20–27	112
8:21	109
8:22–63	11
8:23	18
8:25	14
8:25–26	73
8:27–30	71n, 110
8:29	38, 194
8:31–53	37, 69–70, 74
8:31–40	59, 110
8:31–32	59, 197
8:41–53	84, 194
8:41–43	110n
8:44–51	15
8:46–53	14, 37n, 194
8:52	174
8:53	38, 55
8:57–58	18
8:59	174
8:60	13
8:61	18
8:62–66	67, 68
8:62–63	106
8:63–64	106n, 109
9–11	75
9–10	38, 84, 101
9:1–9	16n, 56, 73–74
9:3	38
9:4–9	13, 14. 23
9:4	51, 73, 116
9:6–9	15, 17, 18, 73, 86, 194
9:10–25	77
9:10–14	19, 74–76, 84, 101, 111, 195, 196
9:13	208
9:14	78, 108
9:15–25	13n, 76–77, 104, 105, 195–96
9:15	77, 90n, 103
9:16	101
9:21	76–22
9:23	99
9:24–25	25, 54–55

9:24	66, 101, 131, 133	15:5	115n
9:25	2n, 77, 106, 109		
9:26–28	78, 84	## 3 Kingdoms	
9:27	84	1–11	42–46
9:28	75, 108	4:34	52
10:1–13	27–28, 78–79, 84, 111	10:14–22	80
10:1–5	102		
10:1	78, 111	## 2 Kings	
10:8	172	4:34	175
10:9	78, 111, 126	5:18	110–11
10:11–12	79, 108	6:26–31	33, 156
10:13	79–80, 84–85, 192	16:12–15	106
10:14–29	108	16:17	65
10:14–25	193–94	17:1	14
10:14–22	80	17:17	14
10:14–15	84	21:8–15	17
10:17	108	21:24	88
10:21	108	22–23	206
10:23–29	38, 97	22:1	88
10:23–25	79n, 80, 111	22:2	4, 14, 93n
10:23–24	103	23:15	14
10:24	112	23:4–19	88
10:26–29	80	23:25	4, 18, 88, 115n
10:29	84	23:26–25:30	14, 17
11	39, 113	25:13–17	64
11:1–40	5	25:27–30	9, 212
11:1	101, 108		
11:1–13	18, 25, 39, 81–82, 196	## Isaiah	
11:1–10	92	11:1–5	32
11:2–10	12	55:5	71n
11:3	28	56:6–8	70n
11:5	18	56:7	110n
11:6	116		
11:8	18	## Jeremiah	
11:9–13	18	18:18	139
11:11	109	22:3	126
11:14–40	39, 82–83, 108–9	22:15	126
11:14	108	23:5	126
11:23	108	33:15	126
11:25	108		
11:37–38	109	## Psalms	
11:41–43	81	21	32
11:41	11, 16, 26, 39, 81, 82, 111, 114, 207	29	107
12	75n, 140	45:10	154
12:1–20	118	46	68
12:14	25	48	68
12:32	106		
12:33	106n		

Psalms *(cont.)*

72	32
72:1	142
76	69
110:1	154
132:13–14	68

Proverbs

1–9	27

Ruth

1:2	135n

Esther

7	156n

Ezra

9	69–70

Nehemiah

9	69–70

1 Chronicles

28:5–6	50

2 Chronicles

1:1–13	67
1:10	57n
1:13	56
1:16	38
2:7n	79
6	110
8:3–12	44
8:8	76
8:11	43n
9:1	78
9:10n	79n
9:28	38

Sirach

47:13–21	1

www.ingramcontent.com/pod-product-compliance
Lightning Source LLC
Chambersburg PA
CBHW050439240426
43661CB00055B/2440